THE
CONCISE
ENCYCLOPEDIA OF
GARDENING

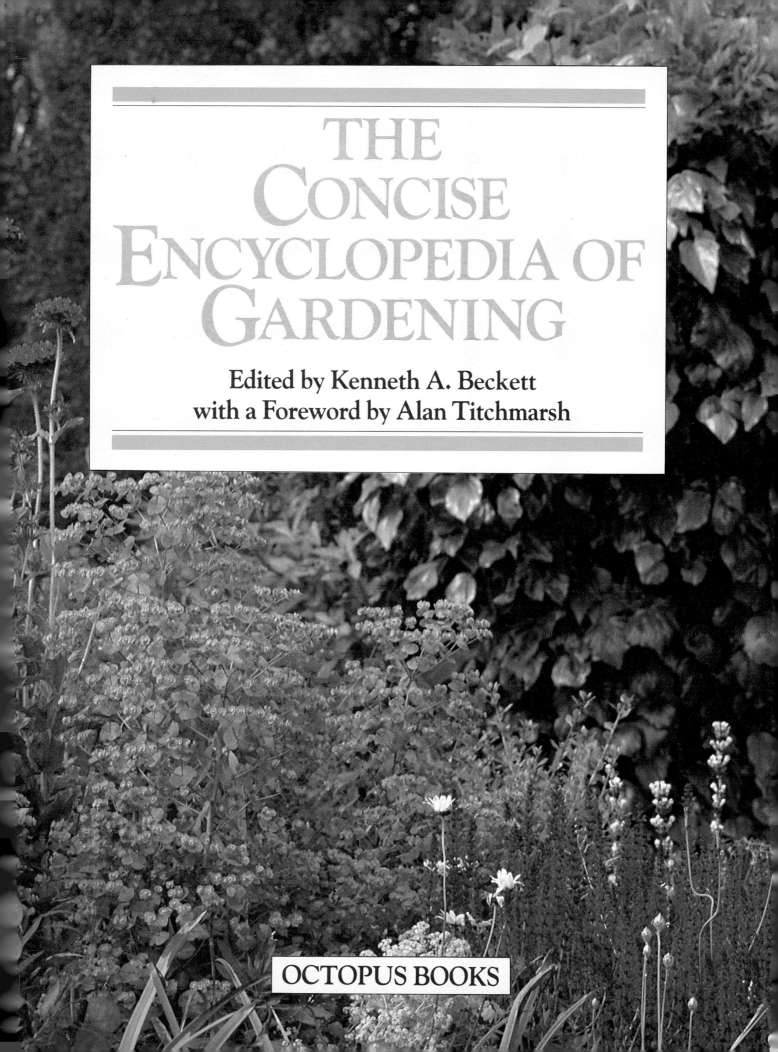

THE
CONCISE
ENCYCLOPEDIA OF
GARDENING

Edited by Kenneth A. Beckett
with a Foreword by Alan Titchmarsh

OCTOPUS BOOKS

First published in 1987 by
Octopus Books Limited
59 Grosvenor Street
London W1

ISBN 0–7064–2854–4

Designer: David Allen
Art editor: Jeremy Bratt
Editor: Tessa Rose
Indexer: Richard Bird
Production controller: Shane Lask

Typeset by J & L Composition Ltd,
Filey, North Yorkshire, England
Printed in Great Britain by
Blantyre Printing and Binding Co.
Ltd, Glasgow

CONTENTS

FOREWORD

Gardening is a funny thing. Some folk like it and some folk don't, but sooner or later the bug bites nearly everybody simply because there's nothing nicer than sitting out in the sun, surrounded by flowers and fruits and vegetables that are home-grown.

I started early, being crazy about gardening at the age of 12 when I'd sow packets of seeds straight into the soil of our Yorkshire garden. Sometimes they'd grow, and the thrill of seeing flowers that I'd never set eyes on before is one that's never faded. In a corner of the tiny garden I built a polythene greenhouse just 3ft by 6ft and packed it with potted plants. When other lads were playing football, I was pricking out petunias.

At last I got a job in the local nursery. That first day, when the foreman ushered me into a cathedral-like greenhouse and told me it was mine, was one of the happiest days of my life. I stood in the doorway gazing down the 75ft pathway with banks of flowering pot plants on either side. All was silent, except for the gentle dripping of water from the benches into the underground water tanks. Red and yellow plumes of celosia sprouted up among coleus and silk-barked oaks; primulas rubbed shoulders with geraniums and asparagus ferns. All I had to do was keep them alive! From that day onward, growing plants has been an obsession.

There's an endless list of things to try, whether you've a patio or stately acres, a doorstep or a windowbox, a windowsill or a bottle garden. But one thing that gardening shouldn't be is boring. If it strikes you that a garden is simply something that must be kept tidy so that the neighbours don't complain, then you're missing out. It's not something to fit in between washing the car and doing the shopping on a Saturday morning; get the other jobs out of the way so that you can *enjoy* the gardening and take a bit of time over it.

The fact that things don't happen instantaneously in the garden is a positive advantage in a jet-set age. Mind you, the weeds can come through with jet-set speed even if your seedlings don't! And that's another point to remember, for even the most experienced gardeners have their failures. There are those who try once and then give up if they don't succeed. But they are the types who would never have scaled Everest, or broken the World Land Speed Record or crossed the Atlantic in record time. Oh yes, gardening can be exciting stuff!

It's often very difficult to persuade new gardeners that there's more commonsense to be found in this craft than there is muck and mystery. There is much to learn and many mistakes to be made. But with a book like *The Concise Encyclopedia Of Gardening* on your shelf, you'll always have somewhere to turn for the answers. Treat your plants as individuals and observe them and you'll soon notice when they are not happy. The book will help you to pinpoint the cause of the problem and put it right, but your plants will still need a bit of tender loving care on your part.

Be original. Many gardeners are stick-in-the-mud when it comes to devising a garden scheme and plant groupings. I don't believe it's for lack of imagination but because fear prevents them from trying anything different. A long time ago, one gardener decided to plant up a summer bedding scheme with those pretty annual flowers. He liked the look of lobelia and alyssum along the front edge of the border to make a blue and yellow line. Behind these he put orange French marigolds, and behind the marigolds he planted scarlet salvias. To break the monotony he put 'dot plants' of grey-leaved cinerarias every yard or so. It made a bright scheme, but for some reason or other thousands of gardeners now copy this design as though there were no other. Where annuals are concerned, it's much more fun to think up a new colour scheme for a bed or border each year, and to 'decorate' that border as though you were decorating a room. Use shades of pink and pale blue, or oranges and yellows. Your garden will be far more varied as a result.

Don't be afraid of failure. Sometimes a group of plants that you thought would look tremendous looks just plain

silly. But every now and again you'll strike lucky and the result will look stunning

There are a few rules in gardening that it's as well not to break, but hundreds of others that are crying out to be bent. What you must do above all is to make a garden that fits your needs. *You* are the person who must tend it. *You* are the person who must enjoy it. So, to hell with what the neighbours say – just get out there and have fun!

What about the plants that just won't grow? The chances are that it's your fault. You've probably put them in the wrong spot, or not given them the kind of treatment they need to do well. Generally speaking, most plants will thrive in well-drained soil that's been laced with manure or garden compost and where the light is good. Most gardeners, though, are faced with a plot that has rotten soil,

more than its fair share of shade and otherwise far from ideal growing conditions. Don't worry. This fat book contains plenty of plants that are adapted to thrive in such inhospitable spots. Choose the right plant for the right place and your problems will become a thing of the past. Unless they are caused by pests and diseases, that is. Bugs, beasts and blights cause more worry in the garden than anything else. The tables on pp. 166–70 will help you become a dab hand at recognizing the most common ailments that are likely to assail your plants.

Have I made gardening sound like a minefield? It isn't really. It's quite simply one of the most rewarding, frustrating, fulfilling and irritating pursuits on earth – and it's much safer than trying to break the World Land Speed Record!

BACK TO BASICS

With little or no gardening experience at all, a new garden can be a daunting prospect, especially if it is wildly overgrown, littered with builders' debris or completely stripped of its topsoil during building operations. Whatever the state of your plot however, and whatever you would like to make of it, it is a great advantage to acquire some basic knowledge of local climate, soil and situation before setting to work.

Climate

The British Isles lies in the northern temperate zone, but because of its island status and the influence of the Gulf Stream it has milder winters than northern Europe to the south. For the same reason, temperature gradients run roughly from the west to the east rather than south to north. The prevailing westerly winds ensure that the west side of the country has a moderate to heavy rainfall, usually around 150cm (60in) or more per annum and seldom less than 100cm (40in). In the east, by contrast, there are areas which get little more than 50cm (20in). From a temperature point of view the west has milder winters and cooler summers than the east. On the other hand, the farther one gets from the influence of the sea, the colder the winters can be. The coldest winter area in England is around Shropshire in the lee of the Welsh mountains. In fact, in areas of increasing altitude, which are found mainly in Scotland, the mean air temperature drops by 0.6°C (1°F) per 100m (325ft), but few people live there.

In conjunction with soil types (see below), temperature and rainfall conditions greatly affect what we can grow. For example, if there is a desire to grow half-hardy shrubs and perennials there is not much point living in the east or Shropshire. Then again, if you are bitten by the rhododendron bug, not only must the soil be right but an annual rainfall of at least 75cm (30in) is required and preferably double this or more if they are to thrive to perfection.

Within the broader zones of climate there are pockets of difference. Large towns generate appreciable atmospheric warmth both from the sun's heat trapped in brick and stonework and, especially in winter, from the countless fires and heating units. For this reason town gardens experience less winter cold and more summer warmth than those in the surrounding countryside. Areas sheltered from the north and east, perhaps by a range of hills or a forest, can also expect a less severe winter, particularly if they are on a slope. Cold air flows downhill and only where it builds up to any depth — against a thick hedge or wall or in the valley below — does frost become intense. South-facing slopes receive the sun's rays more or less at right angles during the late autumn to early spring period, and are therefore warmer than slopes facing other directions.

Soil

A fertile soil is the key to good plant growth, so it is worthwhile finding out what sort you have.

Soil is composed of inorganic matter (minute rock particles), and organic matter (from decayed plants and animals), bacteria and other microorganisms, water and air. It is the proportions of these ingredients that create the various soil types.

The final breakdown of organic matter results in the colloid known as humus. This coats all the rock particles and, being of a jelly-like nature, holds moisture and dissolved minerals, which are essential plant foods.

Soils composed largely of very fine particles (clay and silt) are heavy and have very small air spaces. They hang wet and are poorly aerated. On the other hand, such soils also have a high mineral content and are rich in plant food. For most plants, however, soils need breaking up with a fork and the addition of organic matter and/or coarse mineral particles, such as sand, to make them better drained. Soils with a high clay content can be readily hand-moulded into balls and other shapes when moist, and this is the easiest identification test to apply.

Soils composed of larger particles (sand) are the opposite of clay, being very loose, free-draining and aerated but have very poor supplies of plant food.

Loam is a name given to a blend of clay and sand. It is a very variable soil, depending on the amounts of clay and sand present. The best loams have more clay than sand, plus a good organic matter content.

Soils composed largely of organic matter are those known as peat or mull. Peat is formed in bogs or fens and is composed mostly of dead plant remains in a state of arrested decay owing to lack of oxygen in waterlogged conditions. Bog or moss peat is largely formed of sphagnum moss; sedge or fen peat of the roots and leaves of sedges. They are low in plant food but are excellent humus providers and conditioners to add to clay and sandy soils. Mixed with mineral plant foods they form the basis of modern potting mixes. Mull is the top layer of partially decayed soil in woodland and is better known as leaf mould. It is best used in the same way as peat.

Acidity and alkalinity

In addition to all other factors, soil is either acid, alkaline (limy) or neutral

in reaction. All plants need lime for healthy growth, but usually in small quantities. Most plants do best under neutral conditions; ie halfway between acid and alkaline. Some plants thrive best where there is plenty of lime, eg members of the cabbage family, while others must have acid conditions, eg rhododendrons and their allies. For these reasons it is worthwhile assaying your soil for its lime content. There are several very simple testing kits on the market which use the chemical pH scale; this is a numbered scale from 0–14, 0 being the quintessence of acidity, 14 the height of alkalinity, 7 neutral. The kits use an indicator chart: red = acid, blue = alkaline, green = neutral.

Soil minerals

For satisfactory growth, plants need certain basic minerals. These fall into two groups, the major nutrient elements and the minor or trace elements. The first group contains nitrogen, phosphorus, potassium, magnesium and sulphur, all of which are needed in relatively large amounts. Trace elements are needed in minute amounts (but their deficiency can cause serious disorders to certain plants); they are calcium, iron, manganese, copper, zinc, boron, molybdenum and chlorine. Some of these occur as impurities in the major elements, and it is seldom that they need to be purposefully added. All the best general fertilizers now contain the most important of them.

Major elements

These are essential for all plants and each one fufils a need in the plant tissue.
Nitrogen is essential for the formation of proteins which, in turn, are constituents of protoplasm, the life-stuff of all plants. It is in short supply in most soils, especially in the vegetable garden where crops are continually being harvested. It can easily be added by dressing the soil with a nitrogenous fertilizer; eg sulphate of ammonia, nitrate of lime, urea.
Phosphorus enters into the complex process of photosynthesis and is a constituent of protoplasm. It can be added to the soil by dressing with fertilizers known as phosphates; eg superphosphate, steamed bone flour.
Potassium is an essential constituent of the plant cell nucleus. It is also needed for the functioning of several enzymes which result in the formation of starches, sugars and fibrous tissue. It is added as a potash fertilizer; eg sulphate of potash. (Contrary to popular belief there is very little in pure wood ash.)

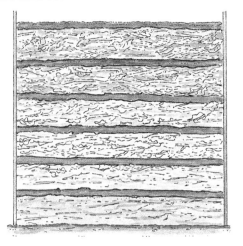

Compost is built up in layers of soil, vegetable matter and an activator. Proprietary containers are available or you can make your own.

Magnesium is essential for certain enzymes involved in the movement of phosphates within the plant and is a constituent of chlorophyll. It is added as magnesium sulphate (Epsom Salts) at 30g (1¼oz) per sq m (yd) in spring.
Sulphur, an essential constituent of proteins, also enters into the make-up of protoplasm, the life-stuff of plants. In the soil it is usually combined with other minerals as a sulphate and is applied as a fertilizer in this form; eg sulphate of potash.

Preparation

Before one can improve the soil and make it ready for planting, the site must be cleared. This may mean removing builders' rubble, clearing overgrown shrubs, or areas seriously infested with deep seated perennial weeds. There is now a range of substances called herbicides (weedkillers), stocked by every garden centre, which can be used to kill woody and deep-rooted perennial weeds. Used according to instructions, these can be a boon to the gardener. Once the site is cleared, work on improving the soil can commence.

On average, most of the soils found in the British Isles are adequate to grow the plants we wish to try, but few do not benefit from improvement.

Drainage

Soils that quickly become waterlogged after rain require the most improvement. Few plants thrive in soil that is wet for most of the year, and some sort of drainage system should be installed. The most efficient method is to lay land drainage pipes, which involves a herring-bone pattern of trenches leading to an outlet ditch. This needs professional advice and is seldom practical in the small garden. An alternative is to create raised beds, either by digging out paths and placing the soil on the bed

sites or buying in well-drained top soil. Although often expensive, the latter alternative is to be recommended. Indeed, it is the only really effective alternative if the garden site has been denuded of its topsoil during building operations. Subsoil can be rendered fertile with organic matter, but this is likely to be at least as expensive as soil.

If the soil is of a clay type and only lies wet after heavy rain, there are several less drastic measures one can take. Acid clays benefit from an application of hydrated lime. This has the effect of clumping the tiny clay particles into larger ones, creating air spaces between them and allowing freer passage of water. Both acid and limy clays benefit greatly from doses of organic matter (humus) provided by such substances as rotted farmyard manure, garden compost, spent hops (hop manure) or peat. Humus, by coating the clay particles, opens them up. Another method of opening up a clay soil is to add generous quantities of coarse sand or grit.

Making compost

Well-made compost is an invaluable component that helps the soil maintain its fertility. Any refuse which will rot is suitable but it is sensible to exclude diseased material and weeds that have gone to seed. Too many grass cuttings should not be put into the heap at one time as they will turn into a soggy mess.

Put a 13–15cm (5–6in) layer of vegetable matter directly onto the soil base. Add a sprinkling of garden soil and then another layer of vegetable matter. Top with a sprinkling of garden lime or suitable proprietary activator. Repeat these layers until the container is full. Cover the full container with plastic sheeting which has ventilation holes and top with an insulating layer of soil.

The quality of the compost will be improved and decomposition hastened if the less rotted sides of the heap are turned in to the middle after 2–3 weeks. The compost will generally be ready for use after about 6 months but may take longer.

Digging

Forking and turning the top layer of soil over is necessary for the working in of humus and sand. Digging by itself also opens up the soil and provides temporary drainage channels. An additional benefit is gained if the soil is dug in autumn and the surface left in a very rough or irregular state. This allows frost to penetrate, expanding the held water and separating the particles. All soils benefit from an initial digging and the working in of organic matter — especially if they are sandy, chalky or otherwise very free-draining — in addition to clays, as we have already seen above. In the past soils were deeply dug often twice or three times the depth of a spade or fork. Nobody wants to do that sort of thing nowadays and, happily, it is not essential. One fork's depth (one spit as it is called) or even a bit less is enough: 15–23cm (6–9in) deep.

No digging
There is a school of thought which says, not without justification, that it is unnecessary and wrong to dig and invert the upper soil layers. Non-diggers apply organic matter as a top dressing (layer) to allow worms and other soil organisms to work it in naturally. This system works well if the soil has no persistent perennial weeds and there is a plentiful supply of organic matter (it must be applied annually on the vegetable plot) and the site is not waterlogged.

The no-digging approach has much to commend it if one is creating a perennials, shrub or mixed bed or border, or is planting trees. A hormone weedkiller is used to remove weeds, or grass if the site was a field or lawn. Holes are dug at the tree or shrub sites and organic matter incorporated as each plant is set in position. For a perennials bed or border, organic matter is spread in a layer not less than 5–7.5cm (2–3in) deep and is worked in around the roots.

If you favour a digging system, incorporate the organic matter before planting. Weedkillers can still be used initially, or perennial weed roots must be picked out during the digging operation.

Tools
A wide range of tools is available from garden centres, horticultural sundriesmen, supermarkets etc. Some are basic and essential, others have a very limited use or are downright gimmicky. For the beginner gardener, the following tools will prove indispensable:
Spade for digging and taking out trenches and planting holes. A full-sized one is best, but smaller so-called ladies' spades are also available for those who are not used to manual toil.
Fork of the same size as the spade but with five tines instead of the blade, for digging, loosening the soil surface and using as a rake for rough levelling. Smaller versions are available.

Trowel for planting and lifting young plants and bulbs. A model which has the blade on an L-shaped shaft so that it sits below the level of the handle is best.
Handfork as a companion to the trowel preferably with at least four tines twisted into a vertical plane. It is ideal for weeding, loosening compacted surface soil around young plants, lifting and separating larger plants.
Hoe for weeding and loosening the soil surface, also for taking out seed drills. There are two main types: Dutch and draw. Also known as a push or thrust hoe, the Dutch sort has a forwards pointing blade which is pushed through the soil surface as the operator moves backwards. The draw or swan-necked hoe has the blade on a down-curving shaft so that it is almost at right angles to the handle. It is used with a smooth yet chopping action when walking forwards. It is the best hoe for drawing out drills, one point being steadied against a garden line.
Rake for levelling the soil, especially

prior to drawing out drills and sowing grass seed.
Secateurs and a **garden line** are well worth acquiring with the basic tools just discussed. A garden line is essential for drawing out straight seed drills and for marking out beds and borders. Secateurs are necessary for pruning trees and shrubs and even for removing light scrub from an overgrown garden.

With all tools, go for the best. Choose a reputable maker who uses quality steel. It is also essential to handle each tool you think of buying to see if it feels comfortable to use. Good tools of this sort should last for many years if you look after them. Although it may seem a chore, always clean tools after use and, ideally, wipe them over with an oily rag.

The sections which follow are planned to give you ideas of what to grow in your garden, plus some basic information on how to do it. The A–Z plant lists contain only well tried plants which are guaranteed to thrive and give pleasure.

*Digging with the correct weight spade (**top**) and preparing the seed bed with a rake.*

*Using a long-handled cultivator (**top**) and weeding with a dutch hoe.*

THE LAWN

Despite the chore of mowing, there is no doubt that a lawn can add an air of peace and maturity to a garden and provide a splendid foil for the flowers. At the other extreme, a lawn can be an important recreation area for children's and adults' games and barbecues. In general, the larger the lawn the more effective and useful it is, provided there are flower and/or shrub beds of sufficient depth and substance to enclose it. Not enough thought is given to the shape of a lawn. It is usually thought of as a square or oblong carpet when an irregular curving shape would be more effective. To be both useful and aesthetically pleasing, a lawn must not be too small. The very small lawn, say anything less than 3 × 3m (10 × 10ft), usually looks rather paltry and is really not worth the cost of a mower. In such a situation a paved area would be more sensible, especially with a few tough but pleasing rock plants erupting from the crevices.

Preparing the site

As the lawn is likely to occupy more than half of your flower garden, it is seldom possible to choose a site which is best for the grasses that will compose it. Ideally, the best site is open to the sky with no large trees nearby. At least it should not be shaded for more than half the day in summer. Grass does of course grow in shade and there are some special mixtures for under trees, but they form a loose sward which does not stand up to hard wear. The soil should be reasonably well drained; waterlogged land is no good for a lawn and must be drained first. Laying tile drains (earthenware pipes) is the usual solution. A herringbone pattern of trenches at least 30cm (1ft) deep are dug across the lawn area with the bottom of

the main (central) trench at the lowest point. The tile drains, 5–7.5cm (2–3in) in diameter, are laid, butted end to end and just covered with gravel. The trenches are then filled and firmed. For the less wet site, stones or coarse gravel alone can be used about 13–15cm (5–6in) deep. At the lowest point there must be a ditch or soak-away to take surplus water. Horizontal lawns are the norm, but sloping ones can be very effective. Whichever you choose to create, the surface must be level enough for a mower to negotiate easily. This is the primary consideration when preparing the site. If the site is a new one, remove any builders' rubbish, making sure there are no half-buried lumps of concrete or bricks. At this point, if the soil is thin, chalky or sandy, apply a dressing (at least 5cm (2in) thick) of peat, garden compost or decayed manure. Afterwards, fork over at least the top 23cm (9in) or use a mechanical rotovator. Level any bumps and hollows, and tread the surface to finish. Rake thoroughly down the plot then across, removing all the larger stones. Ideally, allow the soil to settle for at least a month, preferably twice as long. Any weeds which appear during this period must be hoed off or treated with a short-term herbicide weedkiller such as Tumbleweed.

Sowing

Grass seed can be sown at almost any time of the year except winter, but the best periods are late summer to early autumn, and spring. (For those who prefer to use turf to start their lawn, see Turfing, p. 13.) There are several seed mixtures to choose from and they fall into three groups: fine-leaved, hard-wearing and shade tolerant. Unless you want an impeccably fine lawn, go for a

hard-wearing mixture; looked after and mown regularly, this can look almost as good. The basic grass used is perennial rye-grass, a tough and strong-growing species. With it are mixed variable quantities of chewings fescue and crested dog's-tail.

Grass seed is light and not easily sown evenly by hand, so if possible borrow or hire a seed-sowing machine. If you do sow by hand, mark out the lawn area in 1m (1yd) wide strips with string and pegs or canes (see illustration overleaf). If the soil is very fertile and has been weeded once or twice beforehand, allow 15g (½oz) of seed per sq m (yd). If the soil is less rich and has not been weeded before sowing, double this quantity. As much as 60g (2oz) per sq m (yd) is sometimes recommended, but this is very wasteful of seed and can lead to such troubles as damping-off disease. Mark off a sq m (yd), weigh out the appropriate amount of seed and do a trial sowing to see what the density looks like. Thereafter, it should be possible to continue at that rate along each strip. When the entire lawn has been sown, gently rake the surface with long, steady strokes first down and then across to cover as much of the seed as possible. Cover the area with netting or black cotton raised up on short sticks if birds are troublesome. (It is important to use cotton rather than nylon, which can trap birds by their legs.) Nothing need be done until the seedlings are well grown if the soil was moist. If the surface dries out before germination, use a fine spray or lawn sprinkler.

Maintenance: When the seedling grasses are about 2.5cm (1in) high, give them a light rolling. This helps to firm the little plants and encourages tillering (branching from the base). A week later, carry out the first mowing, setting the

ABOVE: Mark out the ground in 1m/yd strips to ensure even sowing or (**right**) the even application of fertilizer or weedkiller.

Turf should be laid in staggered rows (top), working from one corner. If you need to cut a turf, use a half-moon edger, and not a spade, which would have a scalloped edge. A turf-beater (above) can be used for firming instead of a spade.

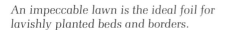
An impeccable lawn is the ideal foil for lavishly planted beds and borders.

cutting blade at 2–2.5cm (¾–1in). About two months after germination or the spring following an autumn sowing, a light top dressing of sandy soil can be applied to advantage, though it is not essential. Use a dressing of compost or 50–50 garden soil and sand, making it about 12mm (½in) deep. Alternatively, apply a lawn fertilizer according to makers' instructions, or use Growmore at 60g (2oz) per sq m (yd). Water regularly during dry spells and remove any broad-leaved weeds by hand. Thereafter, feed at least annually in spring and, ideally, in early autumn also. Apply weed and moss killers as required, always to makers' instructions. It is advisable to apply a top dressing of fine compost or soil or sand and peat at least each other year. Prior to this, work over the grass with a wire-tined rake to remove dead grass and moss. If the soil surface becomes compacted, go over it with a spiked roller or a hand fork to let in the air. Fallen leaves should be raked off regularly in autumn to prevent the grass yellowing and even browning.

Turfing

Starting a lawn from turf is more expensive than seed, especially if you buy a good quality product. Most turf comes from old meadows and building sites and invariably contains coarse grasses and weeds. The advantages are that a turf lawn can be used and looks good within a few months of a spring laying.

Prepare the site as for seed; early autumn and spring are the best times for laying. Turves are usually obtained cut 90cm (3ft) long by 30cm (1ft) wide and should be of uniform thickness. Apply a lawn fertilizer before laying and rake it in. Stand to one side of the lawn site and lay a row along one edge, butting them end to end. Now place a plank across the laid turves and put down the next row, staggering them like rows of bricks in a wall. Move the plank over and lay the next row and so on until the job is complete. If the lawn has curving edges, bend the turves accordingly, here and there removing small wedge-shaped pieces from the ends to make them fit. Don't worry about odd points or edges of turf protruding over the lawn outline as these can be trimmed with an edging iron when the laying is completed. Walking along the plank will firm the turves as they are laid. Any that miss the plank should be tapped down with the back of a spade. A light rolling can be carried out but should not be necessary. If there are any cracks between the turves, fill them with fine soil and sand, which should be worked in with the back edge of a rake.

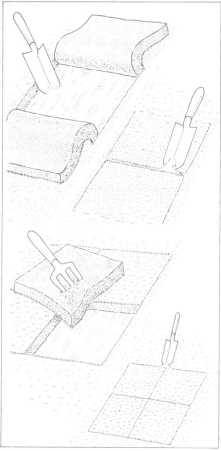

TOP: *To remedy bumps or hollows, make an H-shaped cut in the turf, roll back the flaps and remove the surplus soil or fill in with fresh compost.*

ABOVE: *Damaged patches of lawn can be re-seeded or lifted and replaced with new turf. Firm well. Keep the area well watered for 2–3 weeks to help the edges knit together.*

Maintenance: Autumn-laid turf will not need mowing until the following spring. Spring-laid turf will need a first cut about 3–4 weeks later. Make the first cut a high one, about 2.5cm (1in), but thereafter mow as required. The procedures for feeding, watering and weeding are the same as for a seeded lawn.

Neglected lawns

Moving into an older property with an established garden, one might be faced with a lawn which has been neglected and looks unkempt and weedy. It will be quite easy to renovate if you carry out the following procedure. First, mow it, setting the blade of the mower as high as is necessary so as not to get fouled by over-thick grass. A rotary mower is best and for very long thick grass an auto-scythe may be needed. After mowing, work the lawn over with a wire-tined rake to remove dead grass bases and moss; choose mild spells if this is done in winter. Apply a proprietary lawn fertilizer in late winter and water in if need be. Dig out the worst broad-leaved weeds, if any, and apply a lawn weed-killer such as verdone. If the lawn is taken over in the spring to early autumn period, apply the fertilizers and weed-killer immediately after raking. If there are bare areas after weeding and using the weedkiller, loosen any compacted soil, rake smooth and sow seed or insert a plug of turf. From now on, follow the lawn maintenance as outlined in Sowing. A neglected lawn that receives treatment should be virtually back to normal again after one growing season.

Tools

There are certain basic tools needed to maintain a good lawn. Essentials are a lawn mower, digging fork, shovel, a standard rake and a wire-tined lawn rake, edging shears and a birch broom. A roller is not essential, especially if a cylinder mower with a roller attached is used. A fertilizer spreader and a leaf sweeper are very useful for a large lawn. If your lawn is on heavy soil which gets compacted and needs regular aerating, then a hollow-tined spiker or a spiked roller is well worthwhile. A power-driven edger is definitely a luxury item but nevertheless nice to have.

The many lawn mowers today can be classified into two groups according to the cutting design. Cylinder machines have a ring of blades which curve round a central spindle which revolves when the machine is used bringing each blade in turn across a fixed plate. A scissor-like action is created as each blade crosses the plate and grass trapped between the two is cut cleanly. Whether motor-powered or hand-operated, cylinder machines give the neatest finish, providing the lawn surface is level and the grass dry. Rotary mowers are always motor-operated. They have propeller-like blades set horizontally which cut the grass as much by their high speed as by their sharpness. They are best suited to the hard-wearing lawn or shallow rough banks where they will also deal effectively with grass allowed to grow overlong.

Rotary machines can be on wheels or operate on the hovercraft principle (Flymo-type). If the lawn surface is undulating or the rough banks are steep, a Flymo is the only mower to do an efficient job. It can also be used when the grass is wet.

Whichever machine you use it must be maintained in good order. Hand-operated machines must be regularly cleaned and oiled and the blades sharpened. Motor mowers must be regularly serviced, ideally once a year. If your mower is not working efficiently, do not expect to have a lawn worthy of admiration.

Pests and diseases

Among pests, the grubs of chafer beetles and crane flies or 'flying daddy-long-legs' (leatherjackets) eat grass roots, and worms leave unsightly casts. Grass which is in poor condition may suffer from various fungal diseases, notably dollar spot, snow mould and red thread. Fairy rings do no lasting damage but they do spoil the overall appearance of a lawn.

GARDEN FLOWERS

I t would be an odd sort of garden without any of the annuals, perennials and bulbs which make up the bulk of cultivated flowering plants. Very varied in their height, mode of growth, flower size, shape and colour, they can be used in every garden and all situations. Their primary limitation is lack of winter interest, but there is a surprising number of plants, mostly bulbs, which even perform in that 'dead' season during mild spells.

Annuals and biennials

These grow from seed, flower and die. Annuals do this within one growing season; biennials make leafy growth one year and flower the next. Few biennials are grown in these days, the most popular being Canterbury bells and foxgloves. Some perennials are grown as biennials, eg double daises (bellis) and wallflowers (cheiranthus). A wide variety of annuals is available. They are indispensable for a quick display in a new garden and to fill in gaps among other plants; for example where spring bulbs have died down. There are two groups of annuals: hardy and half-hardy. The latter must be raised in warmth and the young plants set out when threat of frost has passed. Hardy annuals tolerate low temperatures and can be sown in situ in spring or even the previous autumn in mild areas for an extra early flowering. Both sorts can also be used in their own right to fill beds and borders, creating a spectacular display in high summer. The only disadvantage of this sort of gardening is its fairly brief season: summer and early autumn. However, with the aid of biennials, notably forget-me-not (myosotis), cheiranthus and bellis plus bulbs such as tulips, a spring display can easily be created. It gives you a colourful garden, but this spring and summer bedding approach to gardening requires planning and is fairly labour intensive, what with the raising of young plants, firstly for the spring then the summer displays, the clearing out between, the planting and weeding. Much depends on the size of your garden and the time you have to spare.

Perennials

These are more versatile and are basically long-lived plants which annually grow up from a perennial root, bloom, and die back to ground level for the winter. The true herbaceous perennial dies away completely in autumn, but others retain their basal leaves and are essentially evergreen. Bergenia is a fine example of an evergreen perennial with handsome winter leaves. Beds and borders composed entirely of hardy perennials have long been popular, having something to offer the whole year, though there will be very little in winter. Perennial borders do have maintenance chores. Cutting down dead stems, staking tall species, feeding and weeding and lifting and dividing every 3–5 years are essential for a lively and healthy display. Nowadays, mixed borders are gaining in popularity. Shrubs are used as the backbone of a bed or border and in-filled with perennials, annuals and bulbs. A nicely chosen ensemble of plants can create a very satisfying feature.

Bulbs

Our third category of garden flowers can be looked upon as full grown plants in a capsular form. Within each one is a flower spike and embryo leaves just waiting for sufficient warmth and moisture to pump them up to full size, hence the speed at which most bulbs perform when given the right conditions. Where would the spring garden be without its snowdrops, crocus, hyacinths, narcissi and tulips? They are, in fact, perfect plants for providing winter and spring colour in either the mixed, perennial or shrub borders, bedded out alone, or with a few biennials to provide the major display.

Cultivation

None of these garden flowers demands anything more than a reasonably well drained ordinary garden soil. However, within reason, the better the soil the better the floral display. The lighter sandy or chalky soils in particular will benefit from organic matter. Rotted manure, garden compost, peat or composted bark at one 9lt (2gal) bucketful per sq m (yard) will condition the soil and greatly improve the plants' performance. Make sure that all perennial weeds are removed during soil preparation. Failure to do so could result in perennial plants being invaded by the weed roots, spoiling their performance.

Planting

Hardy perennials can be purchased in containers or bare root direct from the nursery soil. The planting procedure is the same for both. Dig a hole with trowel or spade about half as large again as the root ball. Set the plant in the hole so that its crown (the point at which the annual stems arise) is about 2.5cm (1in) below the surrounding soil surface. Fill in around the roots and firm with fists or feet, depending on the size of the plant. If a no-digging approach is being followed, make the hole a little larger and add organic matter as the hole is filled in. Bulbs (including corms and tubers) are bought in a dormant state and are

more easily dealt with. Dig out a hole three times the length of the bulb, eg place a 5cm (2in) long narcissus bulb in the bottom of a hole 15cm (6in) deep, fill in with soil and firm well. Some corms, notably crocus and gladiolus, are disc-shaped; plant these at a depth equal to three or four times their diameter. Half-hardy annual plants raised under glass for setting out in late spring or early summer, though generally smaller, are dealt with as described above under hardy perennials.

The distance apart at which to space individual plants and bulbs is often found in books, on garden centre information labels and seed packets, but there is no immutable measurement laid down for each species. As a quick and easy guide, set plants at a distance apart equal to one half (for bulbs, one third) of their mature height.

Supporting

Although many sturdy wind-firm annuals are available and quite a number of perennials, there are still many desirable species liable to damage from a strong blow, especially if accompanied by rain. Annuals and perennials that are known to exceed 60cm (2ft) in height are best given some means of support. This should be as inconspicuous as possible so as not to detract from the floral effect. A time-honoured method is to surround each plant with several short pea sticks. Push these in firmly so that the tops are about half the full grown height of the plants (see illustration). Do this while the growth is still young and short. Ultimately the stems will grow up through and overtop the sticks and be perfectly supported. Really tall plants, like delphiniums, will need tying to canes. There are also custom-made supports available at garden centres based upon squares or circles of strong galvanized wire, usually with a grid of cross wires. These are placed over individual plants in the spring so that the stems can grow through and be supported. They are ideal for peonies and other heavy-

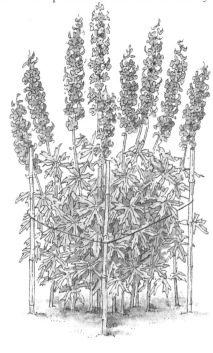

LEFT: *Dianthus, an easy rock garden plant.*
ABOVE: *Support a clump of tall plants by means of pea sticks and twine*

LEFT: *Garden flowers can look as good in containers as in a formal flower bed.*
BELOW: *Outdoor cultivation – sow seed in shallow drills (top) and thin out to leave the strongest plants (bottom).*
BOTTOM: *Indoor cultivation – sow seed in an electric propagator or in a seed tray (top). Thin out to leave about 28 seedlings (bottom left). The plants can be hardened off in a cold frame (bottom right).*

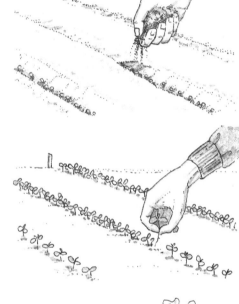

headed perennials. Bulbous species are mainly self-supporting, but large-bloomed gladioli and lilies can suffer in a summer gale and are best secured to slim canes or stabilized with some of the grids mentioned above.

Aftercare and maintenance
Weeding must be attended to early in the season or throughout the first year in a perennials border or bed. Once the plants are established and growing well they knit together and suppress all summer weeds. Annuals also need weeding when young but should soon meet and prevent all but the odd extra vigorous weed. Ideally, apply a mulch but, unless the soil is very thin and poor, each other year is enough. In addition, on all but the richer soils give a dressing of general fertilizer annually in spring; eg Growmore at 90g (3oz) per sq m (yd).

Propagation
The majority of the perennials, annuals and bulbs described below are easily multiplied by one or several of the following techniques.
Seed: True annuals can only be propagated by seed and many perennials can easily be raised by this means. Bulbs, too, are raised from seed by enthusiasts but, though easily done, one must expect to wait several years before the young plants reach flowering size. Half-hardy annuals are sown in warmth from

late winter to mid spring. As comparatively small numbers of plants are needed for the average garden, fill 7.5–10cm (3–4in) pots or 13cm (5in) pans with a standard seed mix. Lightly firm and sow the seed thinly. Large seeds are best sown individually (space sown); eg sweet peas can go in at 2.5cm (1in) apart. Cover the seed shallowly with the same

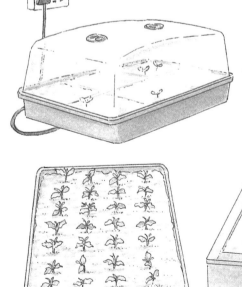

Plan to have colour throughout the year.

soil at a depth no more than twice the diameter of the seeds. Water and place in a propagating case, in a plastic bag or cover with a sheet of glass and keep out of direct sunlight. Most half-hardy annuals need a minimum temperature of 16°C (60°F) to germinate, and respond even more positively to 18–21°C (65–70°F). Hardy annuals and bulbs are generally happy with lower values, around 13–16°C (55–60°F) though some appreciate more. When the seedlings appear, remove the glass or plastic and acclimatize them to bright light. As soon as the seed leaves are fully expanded and one or two true leaves show, prick off into larger containers. This involves carefully separating the tiny plants and spacing them out into larger containers, using a dibber or widger. Hardy perennials can be pricked off into a cold frame, but seedling bulbs are best kept in pots in a cool or cold greenhouse. Most bulb seedlings, eg tulip, narcissus and hyacinth, make one leaf only in the first year and form a tiny bulb which is best grown on for a further year in containers before planting outside. In

late spring half-hardy annuals must be hardened off prior to planting out when the threat of frost has passed. Place the containers of young plants in a cold frame, or turn off the heat in the greenhouse. Ventilate on all sunny days for the first 5 days, then take off the frame lid (light) each day and close at night; finally, leave the frames open all the time. Hardening-off takes 10–14 days. Hardy perennials raised in warmth should also have a hardening-off period to planting out. They can also be sown in cold frames or outside in mid to late spring, which is standard for biennials from late spring to early summer.

Division: Among garden flowers this method is restricted to hardy perennials. Established clumps are lifted in late winter or early spring and prised apart. The easiest way is to thrust two forks back-to-back into the centre of the clump then pull the handles apart. This can be repeated on the halves to make four nice plants. Some vigorous perennials, notably aster (Michaelmas daisy) are best reduced to small pieces with one to three shoots. Some woody-

crowned perennials, eg peony and thick fleshy ones such as anchusa are best divided with the hands and judicious cuts with an old bread knife. Divisions are planted immediately where they are to bloom. Congested clumps of daffodil and snowdrop bulbs etc, can also be divided either when dormant or just after flowering.

Cuttings: These are of two kinds, leafy shoots and pieces of root. For both kinds a cold frame or propagating case is required; even one or two closed cloches are suitable. Make sure the soil is sandy and sharply drained, or prepare a bed or box of 50–50 moss peat and coarse sand. Basal shoots with 4–6 leaves are chosen and these are ready from mid-spring to early summer depending on the species of plant. Cut off the shoots as near to ground level as possible, trim off the lowest leaf or two, dip in a rooting powder and insert the lower one third in the rooting mixture. Space the cuttings about 2–5cm (1½–2in) apart each way. When well rooted and started to grow, lift the young plants and grow on in nursery rows until autumn.

Root cuttings: Certain perennials, eg Anchusa, *Anemone × hybrida*, dicentra, phlox, can produce shoots directly from their roots, either naturally or when damaged. For propagation purposes, in late winter either lift a plant or carefully fork away the soil to one side to expose roots. Fibrous rooted plants such as the *Anemone × hybrida* and phlox are easily dealt with in this latter way. Choose the thickest roots and cut them into 5–7.5cm (2–3in) long pieces. Bury these horizontally about 1cm (⅖in) deep in containers of sandy soil or insert directly into a prepared soil bed of a cold frame. The deeply-delving fleshy roots of anchusa are dealt with differently. Choose pieces of pencil thickness and cut into 4–5cm (1½–2in) lengths. Cut the tops (the end nearest the plant) straight and make a sloping cut at the bottom so that you know which way up to plant. Insert these vertically with the tops just covered with soil. When the shoots are well developed, transfer them to a nursery bed and grow on until autumn.

Layering: Another propagation method, especially suitable for carnations and pinks, is layering. A non-flowering shoot is covered with soil and pinned down by a stone or piece of tile (see illustration). The layered shoot is left attached to the parent plant until well rooted. It is then cut off and planted.

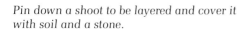

Pin down a shoot to be layered and cover it with soil and a stone.

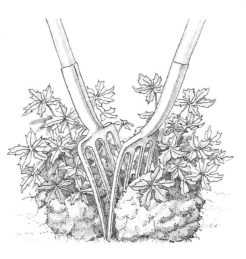

Divide hardy perennials by using two forks placed back to back in the plant.

A-Z
GARDEN FLOWERS

ACANTHUS
The best hardy member of Acanthus or bear's breech is indispensable as a specimen plant in the flower garden. *A. spinosus* forms bold clumps of arching, deeply dissected dark glossy green leaves and erect 1.2m (4ft) tall spikes of mauve-purple bracts sheltering hooded white flowers in summer.
General care: A sunny sheltered site and a fertile soil give the best results.
Propagation: Divide in spring or take root cuttings in late winter.
Pests and diseases: Generally trouble-free.

ACHILLEA
All the yarrows have aromatic fern-like foliage and flattish clusters of small closely packed flowers.
The following are good varieties for the herbaceous border: 'Coronation Gold', which flowers in July/August, bearing golden-yellow heads on slender stems clothed with silver grey foliage and grows 90cm (3ft) tall; 'Gold Plate', a taller variety that can grow up to 1.2m (4ft) tall and flowers from July through to September, bearing large golden yellow flower-heads on stiff stems clothed in grey-green foliage; and 'Moonshine' a dwarf variety growing only 60cm (2ft) high which is useful for the front of the border.

Achillea

This is a new pale yellow hybrid with silver foliage and is a good variety.
General care: These hardy perennials do best in well-drained sunny situations and they should be divided and replanted in the spring. If they are left for several seasons the flowers deteriorate.
Propagation: Divide in autumn or early spring.
Pests and diseases: Generally trouble-free.

ACROCLINIUM
See under Helipterum

AGAPANTHUS
Although of South African origin the selected hybrids of agapanthus or African lily are fully hardy and add a touch of the exotic to the summer garden. They make dense clumps of narrowly strap-shaped leaves above which are carried globular heads of lily-like flowers in shades of blue, purple and white on stems to 90cm (3ft) tall. Make sure to obtain the Headbourne Hybrids.
General care: A sunny, reasonably sheltered site and ordinary but not dry soil is all they require.
Propagation: Divide or seed under glass in spring.
Pests and diseases: Generally trouble-free.

AGERATUM
Soft cushion-like flower-heads are the feature of this edging or bedding annual.

Ageratum 'Blue Mink'

The height of the different varieties varies from 15–45cm (6–18in). The taller varieties provide a useful cut flower. The colours also vary from a clear blue of 'Blue Mink' to bluish-mauve of 'Blue Blazer' and lavender blue of 'Blue Bouquet'.

General care: Given a moisture-retentive soil and a sunny position it will flower from early summer until the first frosts. Water it if there is any danger of the ground getting dry and dead-head when the flowers die.

Propagation: Sow in February/March under glass and keep at a temperature of 10–15°C (50–60°F) to germinate.

Pests and diseases: Generally trouble-free.

ALCHEMILLA

This well-loved hardy perennial, *A. mollis*, popularly known as lady's mantle, produces its clouds of tiny lime-green flowers in June. However, it is its pale green foliage that makes it so lovely.

General care: Any soil that is not waterlogged is suitable, in sun or deep shade.

Propagation: It is easily grown from seed, sown outside in spring, or by division from autumn to spring, and will seed itself freely.

Pests and diseases: Generally trouble-free.

ALLIUM

There are many different types of ornamental onion, some tall enough for the back of the border, others sufficiently small to make them suitable for the rock garden. Planted among low-growing shrubs, the taller alliums make effective and unusual displays.

Allium aflatunense grows to 75cm (2½ft) tall, and with its large purple-lilac heads is exceptionally ornamental. It flowers in late May. *A. caeruleum* grows to 45cm (1½ft) high and is widely available. It is a graceful plant with cornflower blue flowerheads carried on strong wiry stems, and flowers in June. *A. moly* grows to only 30cm (1ft) high and is an old garden favourite. It has umbels of golden yellow flowers which appear in June.

General care: All appreciate well-drained soil and as much sunshine as possible. Early autumn is the best time to plant all varieties. Once planted, leave them to multiply until the clumps become overcrowded, at which point the bulbs should be lifted and then replanted separately.

Propagation: Sow seed outside in a seed bed immediately after it has ripened or, if you buy it, try to make sure it is as fresh as possible. Leave it for a season before pricking the seedlings out into a bed. Divide clumps in autumn or spring.

Pests and diseases: Generally trouble-free.

ALSTROEMERIA

The Peruvian lily produces erect stems clad with narrow upside-down leaves and broad clusters of beautifully coloured funnel-shaped blooms in summer.

One of the hardiest species is *A. Aurantiaca* which grows to 90cm (3ft); its 4cm (1½in) orange flowers are streaked red. The 'Ligtu' hybrids, which grow 60cm (2ft) tall, and are well known for their pale pink, pale lilac or whitish trumpet-shaped flowers are also a good choice. Both flower from June to August and will provide excellent cut flower material.

Alchemilla mollis

Alyssum saxatile and Aubrieta

General care and propagation: Peruvian lilies vary considerably in hardiness, so to be on the safe side, plant the fleshy roots at least 15cm (6in) deep. It is a good plan to raise your own plants from seed which should be very fresh or foil-packed. Sow very thinly in trays or pots in spring, and put these in a cool greenhouse. Germination time will vary greatly in relation to the freshness of the seed; it can be from 1–6 months. When the seedlings are large enough to handle, put them individually into 8cm (3½in) pots, trying to disturb the roots as little as possible. When they are well established, plant them outside about 30cm (12in) apart in the warmest sheltered position possible, again with the minimum of root disturbance. They are happiest when the soil is deep, on the dry side with some sand in it, and drains well.

Pests and diseases: Young shoots are prone to attack by slugs and snails, so apply proprietary slug pellets as soon as growth commences.

ALTHAEA

The tall statuesque spires of hollyhocks are everyone's favourites and nowadays there are many kinds to choose from. Both the double and the single varieties come true to colour from seed. If you enjoy watching bees at work, grow Sutton's 'Single Brilliant-Mixture'; the bees simply love the wide open flowers. For double flowers, Chater's 'Double Mixed' is an excellent selection. 'Summer Carnival' also produces a good mixture of fully double flowers, which grow low down the stems.

While hollyhocks can be grown as annuals or perennials, it is more usual nowadays to treat them as biennials. By doing so it is possible to minimize the risk of hollyhock rust, a disease

which becomes a scourge on old plants, especially in the warmer and dryer parts of the country.

General care: All well-drained soils are suitable in a sunny site and with shelter from strong winds.

Propagation: Sow the seed outdoors in May or June in a well-prepared seed bed. Space out the strongest seedlings so as to get robust plants for planting out in late summer.

Pests and diseases: Rust disease may spoil the foliage.

ALYSSUM

The commonly grown perennial rock plant, *A. saxatile* or gold dust has grey foliage and yellow clusters of flowers that appear in profusion in the spring. It grows to a height of about 30cm (12in).

General care: All well-drained soils are acceptable, the poorer the better, plus full sun.

Propagation: Very easily propagated from cuttings of non-flowering shoots taken after flowering.

Pests and diseases: Generally trouble-free.

SWEET ALYSSUM
See under Lobularia

AMARANTHUS

The red version of *Amaranthus caudatus* is commonly known as Love Lies Bleeding. It is tall enough to grow in the centre of an annual bed or border. The flowers occur in long graceful tassels from July to October, and are ideal for cutting as they last well in water. The green variety 'Viridis' in particular is prized by flower arrangers. *A. tricolor* (syn. *A. gangeticus*) is known as prince's feather and is grown entirely for its brightly coloured leaves. Amaranthus grow to 75–90cm (2½–3ft) and is happiest in a sunny position.

General care: An ordinary soil is adequate, but more impressive growth will result from planting in a deep, rich soil.

Propagation: Sow under glass in March and keep at 15°C (60°F) or in March/May outside.

Pests and diseases: Generally trouble-free.

ANCHUSA

This genus is famed for its trusses of gentian blue flowers. *A. azurea* is an erect, robust perennial which has given rise to several superior cultivars. 'Loddon Royalist' is a splendid, relatively new variety. Although it grows 90cm (3ft) tall, it tends to be bushy and should not require staking to keep its large royal blue flowers off the ground. 'Morning Glory', which grows to 1.2m (4ft), has super gentian-blue flowers on tall stems which will need support. 'Royal Blue' also has pure gentian-blue flowers which, like other varieties, appear in June. It grows 90–120cm (3–4ft) high and needs staking, otherwise the plants will be untidy and you will lose much of their beauty. Even taller, growing to 1.2–1.5m (4ft), is 'Azurea Dropmore', which has rich, deep blue flowers that appear just a little bit later on in the summer. *A. capensis* is a biennial from which a strain has been developed for use as an annual. A good blue in the flower garden can be scarce at midsummer, but from July to October, anchusa can fill the gap with its large forget-me-not flower-heads. A good cultivar is 'Blue Angel'.

General care: Ordinary but not dry soils are needed, ideally enriched with garden compost, well rotted manure or peat and a general fertilizer. Choose a sunny, sheltered site.

Propagation: Sow seeds of A. *capensis* in March/May in open ground and transplant groups to the border. Growing to a height of 23cm (9in) it is also ideal to grow in a container. Divide in spring or take root cuttings of A. *azurea*.

Pests and diseases: Generally trouble-free.

ANEMONE

The wind flowers are a varied and highly decorative group of plants with many uses in the garden. Most widely grown are the so-called Japanese anemones (A. × *hybrida* syn. A. *japonica* of gardens). These form wide clumps or colonies in time, producing coarsely dissected foliage and wiry erect stems, 60cm (2ft) or more tall, bearing several bowl-shaped blooms in shades of pink and white. Go for the large 'White Queen', the soft pink 'September Charm' or the rosy-red, semi-double 'Bressingham Glow'. Some of the most garden-worthy anemones are tuberous rooted and can be used in the same way as bulbs. A. *coronaria* is the best of these, and is usually sold under the following names: 'De Caen', the single flowered sort, is usually offered as a mixture of brilliant colours but named varieties are available in separate colours. 'St Brigid' has semi-double flowers and is not quite so free flowering. Seed of both can be purchased for sowing any time, January–June, in a greenhouse or cold frame.

Among the small flowered varieties for rockery and wild gardens is the easy-to-grow A. *blanda* which

reaches a height of 10–15cm (4–6in) and has blue flowers that bloom in March/April. It is delightful and is even successful when planted in semi-shade. A. *blanda atro-caerulea* is another small one with lovely blue flowers. It increases rapidly after planting. Separate colours are available such as 'Charmer', pale pink, 'Radar', bright carmine and 'Splendour', white. You can also buy these as a mixture.

General care: Any moisture-retentive but well-drained soil is suitable. Japanese anemones thrive in sun or shade, the others are best in sun. Plant the tubers of A. *coronaria* at intervals from autumn to spring to get a long succession of flowers.

Propagation: Divide Japanese anemones in spring and divide or separate the tubers

of the others when they are dormant. All may be raised from seed when ripe or in spring, but 2 or more years will elapse before seedlings bloom.

Pests and diseases: Generally trouble-free.

AQUILEGIA

There are many varieties of aquilegia, or columbine, to choose from. The hardy perennial *Aquilegia vulgaris*, so charmingly known as Granny's Bonnet, has mainly blue or purple flowers with short spurs and is indeed inferior to some of the hybrids now available.

The long-spurred hybrids are most attractive with their many combinations of colours, from crimson through to the delicate shades of pink, yellow and

white. The 'McKana Giant Hybrids' which grow 75–90cm (2½–3ft) tall are outstanding, and can be grown from seed sown outside or from plants purchased in the spring.

A. *formosa* has dainty brick-red flowers produced on slender stems. Growing to 90cm (3ft), it is so graceful and as a bonus it will come true from seed.

General care: Virtually any soil is suitable, even those which stay wettish for long periods. Partial shade is best but full sun is tolerated.

Propagation: Sow seed when ripe or in spring outside, thinning and transplanting as necessary.

Pests and diseases: Generally trouble-free, though aphids (greenfly) can be a nuisance. Spray with malathion.

ARABIS ALBIDA

Rock cress forms low cushions or mats that grow no more than 15cm (6in) high and are especially suitable for rockeries and walls. Flowering commences early in spring and is a beautiful sight. This hardy perennial is easily grown, needing only plenty of sun and tidying up after flowering.

Seed in the separate colours (white, pink or rose-purple) is catalogued, as well as mixtures of the colours. All will give you mass displays of their tiny flowers.

General care: Any well-drained soil is suitable.

Propagation: Grow from seed sown either in a cold frame in March/April or outside in May/June. Alternatively, take cuttings of non-flowering shoots in summer.

Pests and diseases: Generally trouble-free.

ARCTOTIS

This grey-green leaved annual, also known as African daisy, has large daisy-like flowers which come in a

Aquilegia

Arabis

ARTEMISIA

Most members of this genus, which is also known as wormwood, are grown for their silver or grey, often dissected leaves which contrast so well with the more brightly-coloured flowering plants. They are clump-forming with unbranched stems which may or may not terminate in sprays of small greyish flowers. *A. absinthium* is woody based producing stems 90–120cm (3–4ft) in height clad in filigree foliage. *A. a.* 'Lambrook Silver' is bright grey, while 'Powys Castle' has a silver sheen. *A. lactiflora* is the odd man out, being grown for its astilbe-like, creamy-white floral plumes in late summer.
General care: Sun or light shade and ordinary soil are acceptable.
Propagation: Divide this perennial in early spring or take basal cuttings in late spring.
Pests and diseases: Generally trouble-free.

ASTER

Michaelmas daisies, with their easy-going nature and wealth of colourful daisy flowers in autumn, are everybody's favourites. *Aster novi-belgii* is the best known species but most of the many cultivars are of hybrid origin.

There are many good named varieties with heights ranging from 60–120cm (2–4ft) in colours from crimson-red through to light pink and blue. A few well known ones are: 'Ada Ballard', which has lavender-blue flowers and grows 90cm (3ft) tall; 'Crimson Brocade', which has semi-double, rose crimson flowers and grows 90cm (3ft) tall; 'Ernest Ballard', which has very large semi-double rose crimson flowers and grows 90cm (3ft) tall, and 'Pride of Colwall', which has double violet-blue flowers and grows 75cm (2½ft) tall. 'Jenny' (double red), 'Little Pink Beauty' (semi-double pink), 'Professor Kippenburg' (single blue) and 'Snowsprite' (single white) are all under 30–40cm (12–16in) in height and are more useful than the tall sorts.
General care: Any ordinary soil which does not dry out is suitable. A sunny site is best but partial shade is tolerated. In exposed areas a support of twiggy sticks will be needed for the tall growers.
Propagation: Divide in spring, breaking each clump into small pieces with one to three shoots.
Pests and diseases: Mildew is the main nuisance. Spray with dinocap or benomyl.

wide range of both pale and bright colours from late June until the first frosts. Some flowers have zones of contrasting colour towards the centre, making them particularly striking. They grow to a height of 30–75cm (1–2½ft), and the taller varieties may need some twigs for support. Arctotis makes an attractive if short-lived cut flower.
General care: Fertile, well-drained soil and a sunny, sheltered site are needed. After planting out, pinch out the growing tips at about 15cm (6in) to encourage branching and cut or dead-head after the blooms have died to encourage further flowering.
Propagation: Sow in February/March under glass and keep at a temperature of 10–15°C (50–60°F).
Pests and diseases: Reasonably trouble-free.

ARMERIA

Thrift or sea pink is a familiar plant of wild sea coasts around the British Isles and has produced several desirable garden varieties. *A. maritima*, the wild species, is pink; 'Alba' is white, while 'Dusseldorf Pride' is richest pink and 'Ruby Glow' almost ruby-red.
General care: Any well-drained soil is suitable provided the site is a sunny one. Remove spent flowering stems promptly.
Propagation: Cuttings of single shoots or small branchlets can be inserted *in situ* in early spring or autumn. Sow seed in spring in pots in a cold frame.
Pests and diseases: Generally trouble-free.

Armeria maritima

ASTILBE

The ferny foliage and shapely, feathery plumes of astilbe place it among the most desirable of perennials where the ground is moist enough. Hybrids are the most popular, being available in colours from white through pinks and lilacs to deepest red. Good varieties include 'Bressingham Beauty', rich pink; 'Deutschland', intense white; and 'Fanal', deep red.

General care: Moisture-retentive to wet soil is essential for success unless one is prepared to water heavily in dry spells.

Propagation: Divide in spring just as the plants start into growth. Regular division every 3-4 years will keep them floriferous.

Pests and diseases: Generally trouble-free.

AUBRIETA DELTOIDEA

This low-growing hardy perennial is well known for its mass displays early in the spring. Ideal for pockets in a dry wall, it will soon spread itself out into large mat-like plants. Do not be tempted to despise it because it is common; if you plant named varieties or grow your plants from seed, you can have a considerable range of colours.

Of the named varieties, the following are recommended: 'Barker's Double', deep rosy purple; 'Bressingham Pink'; 'Dr. Mules', violet purple; and 'Riverslea', mauve pink. Do not be afraid to cut aubrietas back immediately after flowering; they will benefit.

General care: Well-drained soil and full sun are essential to prolific blooming.

Propagation: Sow seeds in March in trays and place in the greenhouse. When the seedlings are large enough to handle, prick them out into pots. They will be ready for planting in their final positions in October.

Pests and diseases: Generally trouble-free.

Aubrieta

BEGONIA

The 900 species plus many hybrids and cultivars in this very garden-worthy genus are mainly tropical in origin and best known as pot plants for the greenhouse and home. Two different sorts are, however, grown both under glass and as summer bedding subjects outside. *B. × herbeo-hybrida* is tuberous rooted. The best known sorts produce robust erect stems, large ear-shaped leaves and massive double blooms rather like roses. More recent is the Pendula strain, having slimmer, lax stems and smaller, less stiffly double flowers. Both have a wide colour range. Long familiar as bedding plants are the fibrous-rooted *B. semperflorens*, low bushy plants with glistening rounded leaves and a profusion of small blooms composed of two large and two small petals. Try the delicate pink 'Pink Avalanche', the rose-pink 'Danica Rose' with bronze leaves and the brick-red 'Danica Red', also with bronze leaves. Alternatively, choose one of the mixtures which also includes white, eg 'Organdy' or 'Stara'; the latter with a cascading habit.

General care: Moisture-retentive, humus-rich soil gives the best results. Full sun and partial shade are acceptable. Plant out both sorts of begonia in late spring/early summer after the threat of frost has passed. Start tubers in warmth in boxes of compost two months before planting out, potting singly as growth starts. Lift in autumn, clean the tubers and store in dry peat at around 13°C (55°F).

Propagation: Cut tubers into two or more pieces, each with at least one shoot, just prior to potting, or take the shoots as cuttings. Sow seed in late winter. *Semperflorens*, though perennials, are raised annually from seed sown in warmth in late winter.

Pests and diseases: Generally trouble-free, but aphids can be a nuisance and sometimes virus appears. The latter shows as stunted, mottled shoots and plants must be destroyed.

BELLIS

The common species, *Bellis perennis*, is the well-known, un-loved lawn weed, daisy, but there are various large-flowered and double miniature varieties well worth a space in the flower garden. For example *Bellis perennis* 'Monstrosa', with its double flowers that reach 5cm (2in) or more across, has a colour range from white through pink to scarlet red and makes an excellent bedding plant. It is at its best in May/June, and is sometimes catalogued as 'Goliath Mixed'. Among the miniature varieties is 'Pomponette', which has tightly quilled double daisies in shades of red, rose and white.

General care: Any soil is suitable, but humus-rich ones give the best results. Choose a sunny site.

Propagation: Sow seeds outside in June in shallow drills in a seed bed. Transplant them to their permanent quarters in September.

Pests and diseases: Generally trouble-free except for aphids (greenfly), which are easily controlled with derris or malathion.

BERGENIA

Boldly handsome, paddle-shaped, evergreen ground-hugging leaves and clusters of pink to rose-purple flowers in early spring or earlier are the hallmarks of this desirable genus of perennials. They can be used as ground cover, specimen clumps or in the front of a shrub or perennials border. *B. cordifolia* and *crassifolia* are the common ones often seen in old gardens. Modern cultivars give better garden value. Try 'Admiral' with red flowers and glossy rich green

leaves; 'Bressingham White' (pure white) and 'Sunningdale', a deep pink sort with leaves which take on dark bronze-red tints in winter.
General care: Almost any soil which is not waterlogged, though light, sandy and chalky soils should be enriched with garden compost or peat. Sunny or shady sites are equally acceptable.
Propagation: Divide in autumn or spring, separating single-rooted shoots. Plant 5cm (2in) sections of leafless stems shallowly in a cold frame to produce plants.
Pests and diseases: Generally trouble-free, though leaf spot disease may disfigure the foliage. Remove the worst affected leaves and spray with captan or zineb, though neither is fully effective.

BRACHYCOME
Brachycome iberidifolia, the Swan River daisy, produces fragrant cineraria-like flowers of blue, pink, purple and white shades from June to September. Growing to a height of 23cm (9in), it is useful for group planting at the front of the border.
General care: Any well-drained soil is suitable provided it is in a sunny site.
Propagation: Sow seeds in early spring under glass or in situ outside in late spring when frosts are less likely.
Pests and diseases: Generally trouble-free.

CALENDULA OFFICINALIS
Common or pot marigold rewards the sower with a glorious summer show of orange and yellow shades for almost no effort. The large double daisy-type flowers look colourful and last well in water. Growing to 30–60cm (1–2ft) high, recommended varieties are 'Radio', deep orange; 'Lemon Queen', yellow; and 'Fiesta Gitana', a colourful mixture.
General care: Any soil that is not waterlogged is satisfactory. A sunny site is best, but partial shade is tolerated.

Remove all faded blooms promptly or self-sown seedlings will create weeds.
Propagation: Sow seed in situ in spring, or in early autumn for a much earlier display. Seedlings need to be cloched in cold winters.
Pests and diseases: Trouble-free, except for occasional attacks of aphids (greenfly) and caterpillars; use derris or malathion.

CALLISTEPHUS
The big single and double daisy flowers of China aster have long been favourite half-hardy annuals. The original species Callistephus chinensis is single and comes in a variety of colours. More popular are the varied double sorts, especially the elegant 'Ostrich Plume' with large flower-heads on plants to 45cm (1½ft). Other recommended varieties are 'Milady', dwarf selections in colours of rose, blue, white and mixed; 'Lilliput', miniature pompom; and 'Super sinensis', single. All are excellent for bedding out. There are several forms, ranging from the tall, feathery-headed ostrich plume type to the chrysanthemum flowered ones, including those with incurving petals. There are also those with miniature pom-pom flowers.
General care: Moisture-retentive, but well-drained, fertile soil and a sunny site are essential for success. Light sandy and chalky soils must be liberally enriched with garden compost, decayed manure or peat and general fertilizer.
Propagation: Sow under glass in March/April and keep at 15–20°C (60–68°F) to germinate. Plant out in well-drained soil in a sunny position.
Pests and diseases: Aphids (greenfly) may curl and stunt young shoots. Spray with derris or malathion. Virus also stunts and mottles the leaves yellow. Destroy as soon as the trouble is recognized. Wilt disease causes

wilting, yellowing, withering and death. Destroy plants and grow only wilt-resistant varieties.

CAMPANULA
The bellflowers form a large and varied genus of great garden value, ranging from dwarf alpines to large herbaceous plants. It is impossible to list more than a few, all of which make excellent subjects for the herbaceous border and which flower in June/July. They are: C. glomerata dahurica, which has violet-purple flowers and grows 45cm (18in) tall; C. lactiflora 'Loddon Anna', which has lilac-pink flowers and grows 75cm (2½ft) tall; C. lactiflora 'Pritchard's Variety', which has violet-blue flowers and grows 90cm (3ft) tall; and C. latifolia, which has foxglove-like spikes of amethyst-violet flowers and grows 105cm (3½ft) tall. At the other end of the scale, there is C. lactiflora 'Pouffe', which at 23cm (9in) is a real dwarf. It has lavender-blue star-like flowers, and is well worth considering. One of the most popular is the biennial C. medium, better known as Canterbury bell. Best is the cup and saucer type C. M. calycanthema, which grows up to 75–90cm (2½–3ft) high and has softly coloured flowers in white, rose and various shades of blue. Dwarf bedding mixture and 'Bells of Holland' seed is available for plants that only grow 45cm (18in) high, but the flowers, although produced in a similar colour range, have single blooms without 'saucers'.
General care: Ordinary soil, provided it is not waterlogged, is suitable, though sandy and chalky ones should be enriched with garden compost or peat and fertilizer.
Propagation: Perennials by division in early spring. Sow biennials in late spring in a cold frame. Thin and transplant seedlings as required,

putting them into their flowering sites in autumn.
Pests and diseases: Slugs and snails are fond of young shoots; apply slug pellets when growth starts in spring.

CATANANCHE
Cupid's Dart, C. caerulea, grows some 60cm (2ft) tall and has star-like purple-blue flowers in summer and early autumn that are not unlike cornflowers but with darker eyes. Anyone interested in flower arranging will find it useful for preserving.
General care: All well-drained soils in sunny sites are suitable. Dead-head regularly throughout the flowering season.
Propagation: Propagate from root cuttings taken in the autumn or from spring-sown seed kept in a cold greenhouse to germinate.
Pests and diseases: Generally trouble-free.

CELOSIA
Also known as Prince of Wales feather or cockscomb, celosia is useful and attractive as a pot plant and for bedding outside. Celosia argentea pyramidalis (syn. plumosa) is a half-hardy annual with an erect stem to 45cm (1½ft) tall. The upper third of this height is taken up by a plume of tiny silky yellow, red or pink flowers in summer. 'Fairy Fountains' grows to 30cm (1ft) only, while 'Geisha Mixed' is barely 30cm (8in) tall. C. a. cristata is a mutant form known as cockscomb, having the flower cluster condensed and flattened with a crested top. 'Jewel Box Mixed' is the best cultivar, bearing its elaborate crests on 15–20cm (6–8in) long stems.
General care: A sunny position and fertile soil which does not dry out is best.
Propagation: Sow seed in spring in warmth.
Pests and diseases: Generally trouble-free.

CENTAUREA

Cornflower, *Centaurea cyanus*, is an easy hardy annual for any well-drained, sunny site. It is a sturdy border and cut-flower plant, and may be either true cornflower blue or red, pink, purple or white. The taller varieties grow up to 90cm (3ft) high.

Another species is *C. moschata* or 'Sweet Sultan'. Its powder-puff flowers of yellow, pink, purple and white are sweetly scented and good for cutting. It grows to a height of 60cm (2ft).

General care: Well-drained, but not dry, soils of all types are suitable, adding organic matter to those which are sandy or chalky. Support tall cultivars with twiggy sticks, especially in exposed sites.

Propagation: Sow seeds *in situ* in spring, or autumn in mild areas if extra early flowers are desired.

Pests and diseases: Generally trouble-free.

CHEIRANTHUS

Wallflowers, *Cheiranthus cheiri*, are particularly popular as late spring and early summer flowering bedding plants.

There are numerous varieties to choose from; most of them make plants that grow 35–45cm (15–18in) tall and which should be spaced about 30cm (12in) apart. Recommended varieties are 'Fire King', a brilliant scarlet; 'Blood Red', with a colour that is true to its name; 'Vulcan', a deep crimson; and 'Cloth of Gold', a yellow variety. For really startling displays in many colours plus plenty of fragrance, try either 'Persian Carpet' or 'Colour Cascade'.

Seed of dwarf varieties that grow about 22cm (9in) high in the usual range of colours is available and these, of course, can be planted a little closer together.

Siberian wallflowers, *C. × allionii*, which grow about

Centaurea cyanus

30cm (12in) high and have brilliant orange spikes of flowers, can also be planted slightly closer together than the tall wallflowers.

General care: A well-drained soil is essential, and for the sturdiest growth it should be limy. A sunny site is also necessary for bushy plants and plenty of bloom.

Propagation: For best results sow the seed thinly in May/June, in shallow drills in a seed bed. When the seedlings are large enough to handle, transplant them into rows 15–20cm (6–8in) apart. At the same time, in order to ensure bushy plants, pinch out the tips of the growing points. In October lift the plants and plant them where you want them to flower, bearing in mind they prefer a sunny position.

Pests and diseases: Generally trouble-free, but plants can be damaged or killed in severe winters.

CHIONODOXA

Commonly known as glory of the snow, these early spring flowering bulbs, with their dainty small star-shaped flowers artistically arranged on slender stems, are natives of the high mountains in Asia Minor. *C. luciliae*, with its vivid blue, white-centred flowers, is one of the best. *C. luciliae* 'Rosea' has pure pink flowers and can be recommended, as can *C. gigantea*, which has large pale blue blooms. All are ideal for naturalizing in short grass or among shrubs.

General care: Practically all soils are suitable provided they are not waterlogged. Plant as early in autumn as

possible then leave undisturbed. Self-sown seedlings usually arrive to increase the colony.

Propagation: Divide clumps when dormant or sow seeds when ripe in a cold frame. Seedlings take 2–3 years to reach flowering size.

Pests and diseases: Generally trouble-free.

CHRYSANTHEMUM

This large genus can be divided into four groups: 1, the florist's hybrids with mainly double flowers. The best known, these are now available in pots all year round, but are still favourites as garden decoration, especially for cut flowers; 2, hardy border perennials as exemplified by the shasta daisy *C. maximum*; 3, perennial rock plants and 4, the popular annuals *C. coronarium*, *C. tricolor* (syn. *carinatum*) and their hybrids.

For garden decoration, spray varieties of florist's hybrids are best. These are allowed to grow naturally without disbudding. Recommended are: 'Pennine Bright Eyes', pink; 'Pennine Crimson', 'Pennine Orange', 'Pennine Yellow' and 'Pennine White', as well as some of the single spray varieties such as 'Pennine Dream', pink; 'Pennine Globe', gold; and 'Pennine Tango', a bronze. Most of these grow 90–120cm (3–4ft) tall. For the front of the border, 'Fairy' can be very colourful in late summer and early autumn. This is a dwarf pompom chrysanthemum which has numerous round rosy-pink flowers and grows to only 30cm (1ft).

Among shasta daisies with single flowers the 45cm (1½ft) tall 'Snowcap' takes some beating, while 'Wirral Supreme' is probably the most reliable double daisy of all.

Among rock or front of the border species *C. hosmariense* grows to about 15cm (6in) in height with silvery dissected leaves and white-rayed daisies off and on all the year in mild winters. Annual chrysanthemums come in a wide range of colours, often two or more contrasting shades or colours in each bloom. Seed strains are listed as 'Special Mixture', 'Flame Shades', 'Double Mixed' and 'Court Jesters'.

General care: With the exception of the rock garden species which need a fairly poor, well-drained soil, chrysanthemums in general must have fertile, moisture-retentive but not wet rooting medium. Poorer soils must be enriched with rotted manure, garden compost or peat and general fertilizer. In windy sites the taller ones will need support. Young plants of florist's and annual sorts should have their growing points pinched out at 10–15cm (4–6in) in height to promote branching.

Propagation: Sow seed of hardy annuals *in situ* in spring, the florist's varieties under glass in early spring. Divide hardy border perennials in spring and take cuttings of rock plants in spring or early autumn. Florist's varieties are usually propagated by cuttings taken from plants which have been dug up and overwintered in a cold frame. As soon as basal shoots are about 5cm (2in) long, these are severed and placed in equal parts peat and sand in a propagating case; March/April is the best time.

Pests and diseases: Aphids (greenfly) and capsid bugs attack and cripple young shoots and leaves, earwigs and caterpillars eat leaves and flowers. For all these pests, spray with malathion. Leaf miner causes white lines in the leaves, weakening and making them unsightly. Spray with HCH or trichlorphon, or hand-pick if the attack is slight. Mildew fungus produces a powdery coating, then the leaves turn yellow and die prematurely. Spray with benomyl or dinocap.

CLARKIA
Few hardy annuals are more elegant, colourful or easy to grow. *Clarkia elegans* grows up to 60cm (2ft) high and produces long double flower spikes in shades of purple, red, pink and orange to white. *Clarkia pulchella* grows to 45cm (18in) high and has double and semi-double flowers of white, violet and rose.

General care: Any reasonably fertile soil which is not waterlogged and gets plenty of sun is suitable.

Propagation: Sow in spring *in situ*.

Pests and diseases: Generally trouble-free.

COLCHICUM
Autumn flowering can be used to advantage in a shrub border or even in rough grass. The flowers are held on naked stems, and they do make an attractive splash of colour. While the flowers themselves take up only

ABOVE: *Colchicum speciosum*
BELOW: *Convallaria majalis*

a small space, the large though handsome leaves can smother nearby plants in the spring. They also look untidy before they die back. It is important therefore to choose the planting site carefully.

C. autumnale (sometimes called autumn crocus) is a European native, much appreciated by autumn visitors to France, particularly to the foothills of the Alps. Its crocus-like flowers are a soft rosy lilac. The hybrid 'Waterlily' is darker and fully double. *C. speciosum*, in its several forms – such as 'Album', a white, and 'Lilac Wonder', a pinkish lilac with a white throat – is probably best for garden planting.

General care: All garden soils that do not dry out when the plants are in full growth are suitable. A sunny site will ensure that the blooms open properly, but partial shade is acceptable. Plant the corms early, ideally in August.

Propagation: Separate offsets when dormant. Seedlings take up to 5 years to flower.

Pests and diseases: Generally trouble-free.

CONVALLARIA
Lily of the valley (*C. majalis*) is famed for its graceful 20cm

(8in) tall sprays of perfumed, bell-shaped white flowers in spring.

General care: A moisture-retentive fertile soil and partial shade are required for success. To ensure the right growing conditions, prepare the ground by digging in a liberal quantity of well-rotted compost. The best time to plant is September/October. When the bed becomes overcrowded – which it will after a number of years – lift and replant the rhizomes, having first replenished the ground with compost.

Propagation: Divide into single-budded crowns in September.

Pests and diseases: Generally trouble-free.

COREOPSIS

The best of the tickweeds are broad-petalled daisy flowers of quality. *Coreopsis grandiflora* is a robust species from the USA that grows 45cm (18in) high. Its leaves are narrow and deeply toothed and its bright yellow flowers, measuring up to 7cm (2½in) across and carried on good stems, are first class for flower arrangements. Recommended varieties are 'Sunray', which grows 45cm (18in) high and is very free flowering with double golden yellow flowers; 'Mayfield Giant', which grows 60cm (2ft) high and is a golden yellow; and 'Sunburst', also 60cm (2ft) high and a bright yellow, semi-double variety. 'Goldfink' is almost a miniature, rarely exceeding 25cm (10in) in height. *C. verticillata* 'Zagreb' grows to 40cm (16in), produces wiry stems, a froth of tiny grassy leaves and star-shaped bright yellow flowers.

General care: Ordinary fertile soil in sun is all that is needed for this hardy annual.

Propagation: Division in spring or seed at the same time in a frame.

Pests and diseases: Generally trouble-free.

COSMOS

This is a tall-growing elegant half-hardy annual with its very broad petalled daisy flowers and ferny foliage. It is very useful to bring colour to the back of the flower border. *C. bipinnatus* is the best known species with flowers in shades of rose, purple, pink and white on stems to 90cm (3ft); 'Sensation Mixed' is a recommended variety. *C. sulphureus* is shorter than *C. bipinnatus*, and produces flowers in a range of shades from yellow to orange-red.

General care: Fertile but not over-rich soil is required and a sunny site. If the plant is grown in an exposed site, some twiggy sticks for support will be needed.

Propagation: Sow seeds under glass in March or *in situ* in early May.

Pests and diseases: Generally trouble-free.

CROCOSMIA

This genus includes the well known montbretia *C. × crocosmiiflora*, which can be found growing naturally by roadsides in the north and west of the country. Sword-shaped leaves in clumps and sprays of small gladiolus-like flowers are the distinguishing features. 'Solfatare' has bronze-green foliage and apricot-yellow flowers, while *C. rosea* is soft pink. *C. masonorum* grows to 75cm (2½ft) with flame-orange flowers on arching stems, making a superb display from July to September, and it is excellent for cutting, too. A newer hybrid is *C.* 'Lucifer', which has even finer and more colourful flowers of an intense brilliant flame red. These appear in June/July and the plant grows to a height of 90cm (3ft).

General care: Well-drained fertile soil in a sunny site is necessary. In cold areas choose a sheltered site. Plant the corms 10–13cm (4–5in) deep in spring. Leave them until clumps form before lifting, separating and finally replanting.

Propagation: Divide congested clumps of corms in early spring.

Pests and diseases: Generally trouble-free.

CROCUS

The chalice-shaped flowers of crocus are well known to all as heralds of spring. There are many sorts however, some flowering in autumn and winter as well. While the large-flowered crocus may be the most spectacular, we should not forget the small-flowered species which flower in February/March. Try *C. chrysanthus* mixed, or *C. tomasinianus*; they will quickly multiply and give an increasing display as the numbers build up. The same can be said for the large-flowered varieties; such as 'Queen of the Blues'; 'Pickwick', pearly grey with dark centres and striped dark lilac; 'Jeanne d'Arc', snow white; 'Remembrance', a large pale violet purple; and 'Large Yellow'. For autumn flowering try *C. speciosus* in shades of purple to lavender-blue. *C. imperati*, violet from fawn buds, blooms at Christmas time if the season is mild and certainly in January.

General care: Any soil which is not waterlogged is suitable, plus a sunny site if the blooms are to open properly. Plant autumn flowerers in late summer or as soon as possible afterwards. The remainder can be planted in October.

Propagation: By separating clumps after flowering or when fully dormant. Seeds can be sown when ripe and take 2–3 years to bloom.

Pests and diseases: Generally trouble-free.

CUPHEA

Two tender members of this genus can be grown as annuals and provide something colourful and different for the summer border or as fillers elsewhere. *C. ignea* (*syn. platycentra*) is the cigar flower, a bushy slender-stemmed plant to 30cm (1ft) bearing a profusion of narrowly tubular scarlet flowers with purplish-brown and white tips. *C. miniata* is more robust to 45cm (1½ft) or more tall, having vermilion blooms bearing prominent rounded petals.

Crocus

Dahlia

General care: A sheltered sunny site is necessary for the best results but ordinary soil will do.
Pests and diseases: Watch for aphids.
Propagation: By seed in warmth in spring.

CYCLAMEN

The common hardy cyclamen (*C. neapolitanum*, syn. *C. hederifolium*) is a half-sized version of the familiar greenhouse pot plant and just as, if not more, charming. It starts to flower in late summer or early autumn before the leaves unfold and finishes 6–8 weeks later, surrounded by silvery-patterned leaves which persist all winter. Pink and white flowers are available.
General care: All well-drained soils are acceptable, ideally in a partially shaded site. Plant the corms in summer, making sure they are covered by about 5cm (2in) of soil. Roots appear only on the top side so this must be uppermost when planting.
Propagation: By seed, sown when ripe or in spring in a cold frame. Self-sown seedlings quite often appear.
Pests and diseases: Generally trouble-free.

DAHLIA

Familiar even to non-gardeners, this is one of the top favourite summer flowers. There are hundreds of different cultivars in a wide range of blossom shapes and colours. They are half-hardy, tuberous rooted perennials.
General care: Dahlias require a sunny position in rich fertile soil that is moisture-retentive and well prepared. As all parts of the plant are frost sensitive, planting must be delayed until the risk of spring frost has ended; this means late May/early June. Dahlia tubers can be planted out, but it is advisable to use tubers that have been started off in the greenhouse. How-

ever, best results of all are obtained with rooted cuttings, started in a warm greenhouse and hardened off before planting out. These methods are for the various decorative and exhibition types, which vary in height from 45cm–1.8m (18in–6ft). All but the shortest varieties need staking and tying during the growing season. Remove dead flower-heads throughout the season. When frost blackens the foliage, cut back to just above ground level, lift the tubers, wash off the soil and store in dry peat in a frost-free place.
Propagation: Take cuttings in spring from tubers that have previously been started into growth at about 16°C (60°F). Divide tubers that have been started into growth so that each tuber or group of tubers has at least one good shoot. Sow seeds in early spring in warmth.
Pests and diseases: Aphids (green- and blackfly), capsid bugs, caterpillars and earwigs can be troublesome. Spray with malathion.

DELPHINIUM

The genus *Delphinium* includes both the ever popular annual larkspur and the

Delphinium

queen of the herbaceous border with its statuesque spires in shades of blue, pink, cream, yellow and white. The latter is classified under *D. elatum* but is really a group of hybrids between at least three species. The tallest exceed 2.2m (7ft) in height and though a splendid sight need to be staked very securely against the wind. Shorter cultivars are now becoming more popular, the following being in the 1.2–1.5m (4–5ft) category: 'Black Knight' (dark blue), 'Blue Jay' (mid-blue), 'Astolat' (pink) and 'Galahad' (white). These are all Pacific hybrids and are raised from seed, though some nurserymen sell them as plants. More graceful, with slimmer branched stems, are the Belladonna delphiniums. Try the 1.2–1.5m (4–5ft) tall deep blue 'Lamartine', and shorter pinky-rose 'Pink Sensation'. Rocket larkspur *D. ajacis* syn. *D. ambiguum* and common larkspur *D. consolida* syn. *D. regale* are seldom listed by botanical name and are often confused in seed catalogues. Go for the double 'Stock-flowered Special Mix-

The popular sweet william, Dianthus barbatus

ture', at 90cm (3ft) tall, and the long-spiked 'Rocket Mixed' at 75cm (2½ft). For a front of the border site there is 'Dwarf Rocket' at 30cm (1ft) tall.

General care: A sunny site and moisture-retentive fertile soil are essential for really fine spikes of bloom. Light soils should be heavily enriched with decayed manure, garden compost or spent hops plus a general fertilizer each spring. When the first spikes have faded, remove them promptly and a second but poorer display often results. Larkspurs will thrive in less rich soils, but also need a sunny site.

Propagation: Divide or take cuttings of basal shoots in spring in a cold frame for the perennials. Sow seed in early spring under glass, or later outside. Sow larkspur seed *in situ* in autumn or spring.

Pests and diseases: Slugs are the main problem on perennial varieties; larkspur is usually trouble-free.

DIANTHUS

There are no less than 300 species of dianthus plus numerous hybrids and cultivars. Among these are some of the best loved and most familiar of garden flowers: garden pinks, carnations, sweet williams, and Chinese pinks.

Garden pinks come in two different kinds; Old-fashioned, with smallish single or double flowers derived from *D. plumarius*, and Modern, larger-bloomed, derived from crossing Old-fashioned with carnations. There are dozens of cultivars in a range of colours. The best known carnations are grown as greenhouse plants, but for the garden there are Border carnations. They are larger than Modern pinks and always double-flowered. They are best raised from seed strains, eg 'Chabaud Mixed', 'Vanguard' (a mixture of bi-colours) and 'Dwarf Fragrance Mixed', producing plants to 35cm (14in).

Sweet william *D. barbatus* is a short-lived perennial grown as a biennial. Its individual bi- or tricoloured flowers are small but gathered into broad, flattened clusters. They grow to about 45cm (1½ft) in height and are obtainable in mixed or single colours. 'Double Mixed' has fully and semi-double blooms while 'Dwarf Mixed' and 'Wee Willie' only grow to 15cm (6in) and

can be treated as annuals. Chinese pinks *D. chinensis heddewigii* is related to sweet william but has larger flowers in smaller clusters and lacks the clove scent. It is highly floriferous and usually grown as an annual. Modern cultivars grow 15–30cm (6–12in) tall and contain shades of red, pink and white, single or double.

General care: All dianthus need a sunny site and well-drained limy soil. All will grow in the heavier soils, but are then inclined to be short-lived.

Propagation: Pinks and carnations can be raised from cuttings or layers in summer or early autumn. They can also be grown from seed sown under glass in early spring. Chinese pinks are sown at the same time. Sweet williams are sown outside or in a cold frame in late spring unless the dwarf sorts are to be raised as annuals, when they must be sown early in warmth.

Pests and diseases: Generally trouble-free.

DICENTRA

Growing some 75cm (2½ft) high, *D. spectabilis* is a tall, graceful plant. The rows of rose-pink and white heart-shaped flowers (from which this flower takes its popular name of bleeding heart) dangle from arched stems and are at their best in May and June. They are equally attractive in the flower bed or in a flower arrangement, and are plants for that shady sheltered corner, away from the wind and the spring frosts.

General care: Moisture-retentive but well-drained soil is the ideal, liberally laced with organic matter, ideally leaf mould. Partial shade or full sun are acceptable.

Propagation: Root cuttings in late winter is the easiest way, or large plants can be divided at the same time.

Pests and diseases: Slugs, especially on the young

Dicentra spectabilis

shoots, are the primary pests.

DIGITALIS
Our native biennial foxglove is one of our most beautiful wild flowers and deserves a place in the garden. There are several fine selections stocked by seedsmen. Try 'Excelsior' at 1.5–6m (5–6½ft) with large spikes of white, cream or pink to purple flowers, all with delightfully spotted throats. The more recently introduced 'Foxy' strain is similar but not so tall.
General care: All but the wettest and driest soils are acceptable to foxgloves; the richer the grander are the flowers. Partial shade is ideal, but full sun is tolerated.
Propagation: May/June is the time to sow the very fine foxglove seed. Broadcast it over a well-prepared seed bed and lightly rake over the soil to cover the seed. When the seedlings are large enough to handle, space them out, 15cm (6in) apart. Plant them out in September.
Pests and diseases: Generally trouble-free.

DIMORPHOTHECA
Dimorphotheca aurantiaca is a bright daisy-like flower from South Africa known as star of the veldt.
General care: It loves a dryish border, but do not plant it in shade as its flowers only open in bright sunlight.
Propagation: Sow in *situ* from March to May.
Pests and diseases: Generally trouble-free.

DORONICUM
This is the showy spring-flowering yellow daisy or leopard's bane still to be seen in many cottage gardens. Modern cultivars are larger and finer, notably *D. caucasicum* 'Magnificum' at 60cm (2ft), and the somewhat shorter, double flowered 'Spring Beauty'. At 45cm (1½ft) or a little less is the very bright yellow, free-blooming single called 'Miss Mason', perhaps the most garden-worthy of them all.
General care: Sun or shade and ordinary soil are all that is required.
Propagation: Divide this perennial in autumn or late winter.
Pests and diseases: Generally trouble-free.

ECHINOPS
The globe thistles, with their round, prickly, ball-shaped flower-heads and dramatic grey and green foliage are always majestic plants during July and August. This is the time to cut and dry the flowers for winter use in flower arrangements.
'Taplow Blue' produces steel-blue flower-heads which turn silvery with age. It grows 1.2–1.8m (5–6ft) tall. *E. ritro*, growing to 1.35m (4½ft), is appreciated for its deep blue flower-heads.
General care: Any moisture-retentive soil in sun or partial shade will grow the best known species and varieties.
Propagation: Divide in early spring or sow seeds a little later in a cold frame or outside. Seedlings usually take 2 years to bloom.
Pests and diseases: Generally trouble-free.

ECHIUM
The hardy annual *Echium plantagineum* has a long flowering season. If sown early it will start to flower in late May and go on continuously until the autumn. Its flowers come in shades of blue, white and pink. *E. p.* 'Bedding Mixed' and 'Dwarf Hybrid', both about 30cm (12in) high, are recommended.
General care: All soils are acceptable, even dry poor ones, though the best growth is made on those of medium fertility and moisture content. Choose a sunny site although some shade is tolerated.
Propagation: Sow seeds *in situ* in spring or, for large, early blooming plants, also in autumn.
Pests and diseases: Generally trouble-free.

ERANTHIS
The winter aconite *E. hyemalis* is one of our earliest and brightest spring flowers. A wonderful bright golden yellow colour, they are rather like large buttercups on short stems, set in rings of leafy bracts. Grown in masses they are stunningly cheerful. Ideal for naturalizing under trees.
General care: Moisture-retentive soil while the plants are actively growing in spring is essential to the long-term success of this plant. Plant the corm-like, dark brown tubers in autumn; the earlier the better.
Propagation: Established clumps can be divided after flowering or when dormant. Large tubers can be cut or broken into two or more pieces. Seed sown when ripe *in situ* or in pots germinates freely but takes several years to reach flowering size.
Pests and diseases: Generally trouble-free.

ERIGERON
This ally of Michaelmas daisy bears flower-heads with many very slender ray petals which gives them a distinctive elegance. There are now many fine hybrid cultivars in shades of violet, lavender, and pink. All have a long flowering season, starting in June and continuing until the autumn. They last well when cut for indoor decoration.
The hardiest varieties include 'Darkest of All', which grows 45cm (18in) high and has deep violet flowers with golden eyes; 'Dignity', which grows 60cm (2ft) tall and has flowers that are deep blue turning mauve; and 'Sincerity', which grows 75cm (2½ft) tall and has flowers that are lilac mauve with a clear yellow centre. Those in the pink-rosy-carmine colour range include 'Foersters Liebling', growing to 60cm (2ft) tall with semi-double, rosy-carmine flowers and 'Gaiety', which grows to 75cm (2½ft) and has large pink flowers.
General care: A sunny site and any ordinary soil are the only necessities. Over-rich, moist soil will encourage soft, floppy growth.
Propagation: Division in spring is the usual method. Seed may be sown but does not come true to type.
Pests and diseases: Generally trouble-free.
See p. 34 for illustration

Erigeron; see p. 33 for entry

ESCHSCHOLZIA

Grown as a hardy annual, *E. californica* (Californian poppy) produces masses of orange-yellow poppy flowers from June to October. 'Ballerina' mixed is an interesting seed strain which has semi-double flowers with fluted petals in shades of orange, red, pink and yellow.

General care: Californian poppy does best in poorer sandy soils and is an ideal choice for a dry sunny border. Self-sown seedlings will flower well in succeeding seasons.

Propagation: Sow seed *in situ* in spring.

Pests and diseases: Generally trouble-free.

EUPHORBIA

Although about 2,000 different species of spurge are known, for the flower garden we are only concerned with the hardy herbaceous or sub-shrubby members of the genus. The flowers of euphorbia are small and insignificant; it is the surrounding petal-like bracts that give the plant its beauty.

E. polychroma (syn. *E.*

Fuchsia

epithymoides) is outstanding; growing to 45cm (18in), it produces brilliant yellow bracts in early spring akin to a touch of sunlight. *E. wulfenii* grows to 75cm (2½ft) and has glaucous foliage and yellowish-green spikes appearing in May. *E.*

griffithii 'Fireglow' grows to 45cm (1½ft) and has orange-red bracts and pinky foliage. It remains splendid through May/July.

General care: Ordinary soil will grow all these spurges well, though *E. griffithii* thrives best in the heavier or moisture-retentive ones. All will grow in sun or partial shade.

Propagation: Divide *griffithii* and *polychroma* in autumn or spring. Sow seeds of *wulfenii* when ripe or in spring in a cold frame.

Pests and diseases: Generally trouble-free.

FRITILLARIA

There are two species within this group of hardy bulbs that are of particular interest to the gardener: *F. imperialis* (crown imperial) and *F. meleagris* (snake's head). *F. imperialis* is a robust plant to 90cm (3ft) or more tall bearing a terminal cluster of

red or yellow bell flowers. *F. i.* 'Lutea Maxima' has deep yellow blooms and 'Rubra Maxima' has brick red flowers. The snake's heads, which are much lower growing at 25cm (10in) high, have charming solitary drooping bell flowers in many shades of purple with a dark chequered pattern.

General care: Moisture-retentive but reasonably well drained soils are preferred, though *meleagris* tolerates some waterlogging. The bulbs are fleshy, easily damaged and must be planted as fresh as possible from August to October. Plant crown imperials 15–20cm (6–8in) deep and snake's heads 10–15cm (4–6in) deep.

Propagation: Remove offsets or separate clumps as the leaves die down.

Pests and diseases: Generally trouble-free.

FUCHSIA

This must rank among the most popular of all plants. Although it is seldom used as a hardy perennial, with some extra care several varieties can be left in the flower bed during the winter.

'Mrs. Popple' is one of the hardiest varieties together with 'Riccartonii', but many others such as 'Celia Smedley', 'Madame Cornelissen' and 'Tom Thumb' do well.

General care: Any well-drained moderately fertile soil is suitable, preferably in a sheltered site. Put out young plants at the end of May, planting them as deep as is practicable. This is the best protection you can give the plant against winter frost damage. Cut them back in November and put a layer of sand or peat and if need be, bracken or straw, on top to protect the plants further. With nearly all varieties, new growth will come from the roots in April/May and plants will start flowering from July. Regular feeding

Galanthus

and watering during dry spells is essential for maintaining healthy and vigorous plants. They tolerate any soil as long as it is moisture-retentive.

Propagation: Take cuttings in late summer and grow the young plants in pots under cover until planting out time.

Pests and diseases: Generally trouble-free, but watch for aphids (greenfly) and capsid bug damage.

GAILLARDIA

Inelegantly known as blanket flower, *Gaillardia* × *grandiflora* is a startlingly showy daisy with broad ray petals of bright red-purple and yellow. Sometimes listed under one or other of its parent species (*aristata* and *pulchella*), there are several cultivar and seed strains. Try 'Suttons Large-flowered Mixed' which grows to 75cm (2½ft) or 'Goblin' (dwarf bedder), which is half the height at 38cm (15in), 'Mandarin' (rich orange-red) and 'Croft-way Yellow' (bright yellow).

General care: Blanket flowers do well in sun or light shade in almost any soil although a well-drained one is best.

Propagation: Sow seeds under glass in early spring to make sure of flowers the first season. Alternatively, sow in late spring outside and transplant in early autumn.

Pests and diseases: Generally trouble-free.

GALANTHUS

The fair maids of February, better known as snowdrops, are one of the first outdoor bulbs to flower and no garden is complete without them.

There are numerous varieties; *G. nivalis* is the common snowdrop and is usually chosen for naturalizing in the grass and in shade under shrubs. For open ground it is better to plant the

large-flowered varieties, such as *G. elwesii* or *G. nivalis* 'Viridapicis' with its green-tipped petals. Reliable are 'Samuel (Sam) Arnot' which has large single flowers and *G. nivalis plenus*, with large double flowers.

General care: Snowdrops succeed in moist soils, particularly in heavy loams. Left undisturbed they multiply freely until, if grown in a border, they may need lifting and dividing to maintain maximum flower production. The time to lift and replant snowdrops is a couple of weeks after flowering while the foliage is still green. If dry bulbs are bought they should be very fresh; plant them straight away.

Propagation: Separate offsets or divide clumps when replanting.

Pests and diseases: Generally trouble-free, but narcissus-fly is sometimes a nuisance.

GAZANIA

This is a half-hardy perennial from South Africa that loves sunshine; in fact its brilliant daisy flowers only open in direct sunlight. Seed mixtures are available which give flowers of yellow, pink and red shades as well as the more usual orange.

General care: Extremely well drained fertile soil and a sunny site are essential. In all but the mildest areas, plants to be overwintered must be lifted and kept in a frame or greenhouse. Alternatively, take cuttings in late summer and overwinter these. They can also be grown as annuals.

Propagation: Sow seeds in warmth early to mid-spring. Only set out the young plants when the threat of frost has passed. Take cuttings of non-flowering shoots in late summer or spring.

Pests and diseases: Generally trouble-free.

GENTIANA

The blue trumpets of gentians are the highlight of a garden display. Happily several of the best species are easily grown, provided the soil conditions are right.

Recommended are the dwarf *G. acaulis*, the blue trumpet gentian which flowers in May/June, *G. sino-arnata* with its brilliant

Gentiana

blue flowers in September/October, and the 60cm (2ft) tall willow gentian, *G. asclepiaedea*, which blooms in late summer and early autumn.

General care: *G. acaulis* needs a limy soil, *G. sino-ornata* an acid peaty one, while *G. asclepiadea* grows in any moisture-retentive rooting medium. Sun or partial shade is acceptable by all three.

Propagation: Plants can be propagated either from root cuttings taken in April/May or by division of plants in March (*G. acaulis* should be divided in June). Sow seeds when ripe or in spring in a cold frame. Fresh seed sown in late summer and subjected to winter freezing in a cold frame generally germinates well.

Pests and diseases: Generally trouble-free.

GERANIUM

Geranium is the botanical name for the cranesbill and must not be confused with the tender pot and bedding plants of that name which are technically members of the genus *Pelargonium*. Cranesbills are mainly hardy border and rock plants, some of which make splendid ground cover subjects.

G. psilostemon, growing to 75cm (2½ft) high, has numerous magenta red flowers with black centres and veins. In addition, it has beautifully coloured leaves in autumn. *G. pratense* (meadow geranium) grows 60cm (2ft) high and is available in several colours from white to violet blue; 'Flore Peno' has double blue flowers. *G. macror-rhizum* 'Ingwersen's Variety' is often used as ground cover as it only grows to 30cm (1ft) high. It has soft pink flowers and masses of aromatic leaves which colour beautifully in autumn. For the rock garden try the low-growing *G. cinereum* 'Ballerina' which reaches only 7.5–

Godetia

15cm (3–6in) high and has pale rosy purple flowers deeply veined with crimson.

General care: A sunny site is best, though *G. macror-rhizum* and *G. pratense* are happy in partial shade. Any reasonably well drained soil is suitable.

Propagation: Division in spring is easiest, though all species can be raised from seed when ripe or in spring.

Pests and diseases: Generally trouble-free.

GEUM

This genus of 40 evergreen and herbaceous perennials has long been a favourite for the flower border, with its basal pinnate leaves and flowers like small species roses. Among recommended cultivars are: 'Mrs. Bradshaw' growing to 60cm (2ft) with double flaming brick-red flowers; 'Lady

Stratheden' grows 60cm (2ft) high and has semi-double, warm yellow flowers and 'Fire Opal' grows 75cm (2ft) high and has semi-double flowers that are orange-scarlet with purple stems.

General care: Well-drained but moisture-retentive soil in sun or partial shade are the basic requirements.

Propagation: Plants can be raised from seed sown in a cold frame from April to July for planting out the following spring or by dividing the roots in spring.

Pests and diseases: Generally trouble-free.

GLADIOLUS

The gladiolus now takes its place in the top 10 of popular garden flowers. Thousands of cultivars have been raised in every colour of the rainbow except true blue. Best known are the large-flowered

cultivars with massive one-sided spikes 1–1.2m (3¼–4ft) tall. Better suited to general garden use and more graceful are the miniatures (Butterfly) and *Primulinus*. Many cultivars are available by mail order and from garden centres.

General care: Gladioli do best when planted in a sunny position where the soil has been well prepared. Some old compost or manure dug in also helps, as does good drainage. The corms are frost sensitive so plant in late March/early April. The depth is important — always plant at least 15cm (6in) or even deeper, so unstaked flower stems do not topple over, and if you are prepared to take a risk, the corms can be left in the ground through the winter. If not planted as deep as this, the corms need lifting in the autumn. Dry them off quickly indoors and store in a frost-free airy place.

Propagation: Separate the smaller daughter corms and very tiny cormets known as 'spawn' when lifting in the autumn. Spawn should be sown in rows in spring and will produce flowering-sized forms for the following year.

Pests and diseases: Generally fairly trouble-free, but look out for thrips on the blooms and leaves, dry rot, corm rot and core rot on the corms.

GODETIA

The colourful spikes of wide open four-petalled godetia have long been a standby among summer blooming hardy annuals. Best known is *Godetia amoena* var. *whitneyi* (*G. grandiflora* of seed catalogues) in one of its modern selections. Try 'Tall Double Mixed' which grows to 60cm (2ft) or 'Double Azalea-flowered Mixed' which grows to 35cm (14in).

General care: A sunny site and ordinary soil are the only requirements.

Propagation: Sow seed *in situ* in spring.

Pests and diseases: Generally trouble-free.

Gypsophila

GYPSOPHILA

Although it has the vernacular name of chalk plant it is seldom used and most people call it gyp or gypsophila. The wonderful froth of tiny blooms makes it a wonderful accompaniment to sweet peas and other large flowers when gathered for a bouquet or vase arrangement. A free-standing plant in full bloom becomes a glorious hazy cloud of colour.

'Bristol Fairy' which grows 1.2m (4ft) high is a favourite and is probably the best double white for cutting; it is also a good, strong grower. The pale pink-flowered 'Rosy Veil' is a different type; growing only 45cm (1½ft) high, it has a low, spreading habit. *G. elegans* is the popular annual with larger white or pink flowers.

General care: A sunny site and freely draining, limy, fertile soil is the ideal, but most soils are suitable for this tolerant plant.

Propagation: By basal cuttings in late spring in a frame or greenhouse for the perennials. Sow seeds *in situ* in spring for the annuals.

Pests and diseases: Generally trouble-free.

HELENIUM

This member of the daisy family has the same growth habit and appeal as the Michaelmas daisy. By planting several varieties, the flowering season can extend from July to October.

To start the season plant 'Moerheim Beauty', which flowers in July/August and reaches a height of 90cm (3ft). There is considerable warmth in its large, crimson-red, daisy-like flowers, which have a dark centre. Another for July/August flowering is 'Coppelia', which grows 90cm (3ft) high and has coppery-orange flowers. For flowering in August/September, 'Bruno' has really deep crimson-red flowers with a dark centre. It grows to 90cm (3ft). After that try 'Butterpat', which also grows 90cm (3ft) tall and has bright yellow flowers that remain into October. The earlier flowering varieties, such as 'Moerheim Beauty', will sometimes produce a second flush of flowers during October if they are cut down immediately after the first crop is finished.

General care: Ordinary garden soil that is reasonably moisture-retentive and a sunny site give the best results. Divide and replant every 3–4 years.

Propagation: Divide congested clumps in spring.

Pests and diseases: Generally trouble-free.

HELIANTHEMUM

For brightening up the rock garden, front of a border or dry bank, rock roses have no peer. Pleasant in foliage all year, they really come into their own in early summer when the leafy mats are obscured by abundant rose-like blossom.

Some of the best named varieties are 'Ben Afflick', which has orange and buff flowers; 'Beech Park Scarlet' which, true to its name, is a crimson scarlet; 'Wisley Pink', a delightful pink; and 'Wisley Primrose', a soft yellow. Planting out time is September to March when the soil is not frosted.

General care: Full sun and a sharply drained soil give the best results. After flowering, trim back to the leafy stem bases to maintain a compact habit.

Propagation: Take 7.5cm (3in) cuttings of non-flowering growth with a heel, June–August. Overwinter newly-rooted plants in a cold frame and plant out in March or April when it is warmer.

Pests and diseases: Generally trouble-free, but severe winters may damage or even kill the plants.

HELIANTHUS

True perennial sunflowers are indispensable border plants, especially *H. multiflorus* 'Loddon Gold' with fully double blooms on 1.5m (5ft) tall branching stems and the shorter, anemone-centred 'Morning Sun'. Among the annual sunflowers, *H. annuus* must be the most spectacular. Stems of 3.2–4m (8–10ft) topped by flowers measuring 30cm (12in) across are by no means unusual. The cultivar 'Giant Yellow' is one of the largest. Smaller-flowered and in a range of yellow, bronze and maroon shades is 'Sunburst' at 1.2m (4ft) tall. Shorter varieties are available and they will flower impressively in the centre of a bed or towards the back of the flower border, but remember the heads will always turn to face south.

General care: A sunny site is required for all. The perennials thrive in all but the wettest and poorest soils, but the annuals must have a humus-rich, well-drained but moisture-retentive rooting medium.

Propagation: Divide the perennials in early spring and sow seeds of the annuals *in situ* mid to late spring.

Pests and diseases: Generally trouble-free.

See p. 38 for illustration

Helianthus; see p. 37 for entry

HELICHRYSUM

The strawflower, *H. bracteatum*, is certainly attractive in the garden as a hardy annual bedding plant, but its great value is to the flower arranger for drying. The flowers are daisy-like in shape but the petal-like bracts are shiny and somewhat like straw. Flowers are produced from July to September and blooms for drying should be cut just as they are opening. If they are cut when fully open, seed development continues and the flower centres are spoilt. Try growing 'Hot Bikini', a bright red and 'Bright Bikini', a colourful mixture, both of which grow to 30cm (12in) high.
General care: A sunny site and ordinary soil are the only requirements.

Propagation: Usually best sown under glass in early spring, but can be sown *in situ* in late spring.
Pests and diseases: Generally trouble-free.

HELIOTROPIUM X HYBRIDUM

Heliotrope or cherry pie is an evergreen shrub which responds to culture as an annual. It bears an abundance of somewhat forget-me-not-like flowers from May to October. The dark green to almost purple foliage of some varieties makes a useful contrast both to its own flowers and to other foliage 'Marine', which grows 38cm (15in) high, is outstanding.
General care: A sunny sheltered site and well-drained fertile soil give the best results, but most ordinary soils are adequate. Plants can be lifted and potted and grown in a greenhouse or sunny window if desired.
Propagation: Sow in the greenhouse at a temperature of 15–20°C (60–68°F) in February/March and plant out when fear of frost has passed. Cuttings can be taken in late summer, and the young plants overwintered in warmth, or taken in spring from overwintered plants of the previous season.
Pests and diseases: Generally trouble-free.

HELIPTERUM ROSEUM

This is often listed by seedsmen as acroclinium. It has delicate daisy flowers like those of helichrysum but in shades of pink and white. 'Sandfordii' is an attractive yellow variety, growing 30cm (12in) high. A delightful annual for the summer flower border and for drying for winter decoration.
General care: Sunshine and well-drained soil are essential. Avoid over-rich soil which will encourage soft, floppy growth.
Propagation: Sow seeds directly into their flowering position in April/May. Can also be sown earlier under glass.
Pests and diseases: Generally trouble-free.

HELLEBORUS

The hellebores are supreme among hardy perennials in producing their attractive bowl-shaped blooms in winter and early spring. It is such a thrill to have two or three Christmas roses (*Helleborus niger*) as a centre-piece on the dinner table at Christmas time that it is worth all the trouble of using cloches and dealing with the slugs to get them in bloom for that special occasion.

There are several forms of the Christmas rose, some with very much larger flowers than others. The best is 'Potter's Wheel', which has pure white, broad petals with no pink flush on the back of them. *Helleborus orientalis* and its hybrids, the Lenten rose, produce several large nodding flowers on each stem from February to April. They vary in colour from deep purple to creamy white with or without spots inside. *Helleborus corsicus* grows to 60cm (2ft) and makes quite a large shrubby plant. Its strong stems carry creamy-green flower trusses from early February until May. Not only are the flower-heads sought after by flower arrangers but the seed pods that follow are just as interesting for the same purpose. *Helleborus foetidus*, stinking hellebore, grows to 45cm (18in). A native of this country, it produces its flower-heads from February to April, followed again by attractive seed pods.
General care: Sun or partial shade are acceptable and ideally a humus-rich soil that does not readily dry out.
Propagation: Sow seeds when ripe in a cold frame. (Dry seeds may take a year to germinate.) Divide clumps in spring as flowers fade.
Pests and diseases: Slugs can be a nuisance in mild winters.

HEMEROCALLIS

Day lilies are easily grown plants of great appeal. They have a unique flower production system; a single flower on each stem opens in the morning and dies at night to be followed by a new fresh bloom on the same stem the next day. This flowering routine goes on without a break for 6–8 weeks and by growing several varieties of the best garden hybrids it is possible to have these beautiful lily flowers from June/July to September.

To start the flowering season in June, plant 'Gold Dust' which grows to 45cm (18in) tall and has yellow flowers with a dark reverse. Follow with 'Tejas', which grows to 75cm (2½ft). Its bright coppery-crimson flowers appear in June/July. If you like

The Christmas rose, Helleborus niger

a bright clear yellow flower, grow 'Hyperion' instead; it grows to 90cm (3ft). For July/August you could choose from 'Bonanza', which grows to 45cm (18in) high and has flowers that are buff yellow with a dark brown throat, or 'Mrs. John Tigert', which grows 75cm (2½ft) tall and has coppery-red flowers with a dark centre.

General care: Ordinary soils of moderate fertility and retentive of moisture are suitable; even wet soils are tolerated. A sunny site is best, but partial shade is acceptable.

Propagation: Propagation is by division of roots between October and March. Once planted take care not to disturb the roots. Seeds can be sown in spring, but cultivars do not come true to type.

Pests and diseases: Slugs and snails attack young leaves.

HOSTA

The bold, spade-shaped leaves of the plantain lilies or funkias in many shades of grey, green and sometimes almost blue or golden yellow, with or without contrasting margins, make hostas great plants not only for the gardener but also for those interested in flower arranging. In addition they grace the garden with upright spikes of delicate lilac, lily-like flowers.

There are certainly too many varieties of hosta to list here, but two outstanding ones are: *Hosta fortunei* 'Albopicta', which has yellow leaves edged with pale green (in fact, there are several *fortunei* varieties in different combinations of green and yellow) and *Hosta sieboldiana* with lovely blue-grey crinkled and deeply veined leaves.

General care: Partial shade and humus-rich, moisture-retentive soils provide the best conditions.

Propagation: Divide the clumps in spring and replant immediately. Hosta can also be grown from seed sown in spring, but seldom come exactly true to type.

Pests and diseases: Slugs and snails are a primary nuisance on shoots, leaves and flowers.

HYACINTHUS

The sturdy dense flower spikes of forced hyacinths at Christmas or bedded out in spring are a familiar and cheering sight. There are several cultivars, all derived from *Hyacinthus orientalis* and strongly fragrant.

Recommended are: 'Anna Marie' (pale pink); 'Carnegie' (pure white); 'Delft Blue' (light blue); 'Ostara' (deep blue); 'Jan Bos' (red).

General care: Ordinary soil, ideally enriched with organic matter, and a sunny site are all that is required. In the poorer, drier soils hyacinths tend to dwindle away.

Propagation: Separate long-established clumps or remove offsets when dormant.

Pests and diseases: Generally trouble-free.

IBERIS

Candytufts have long been gardening favourites, being of very easy culture and freely producing spiky, head-like white, pink or purple flowers. Among the low, shrubby perennials, *Iberis saxatilis* reaches 10–15cm (4–6in) in height and is a spreading plant. It is well suited for a rock garden. The white flat flower-heads make a good show in May/June. *Iberis sempervirens*, growing 15–23cm (6–9in), is taller and makes a larger spreading plant, reaching anything up to 60cm (2ft) across. It is more suitable for planting on top of a dry wall or for general open situations. Two good varieties are 'Little Gem' and 'Snow Flake', growing 15cm (6in) and 23cm (9in) tall respectively. Both have white flowers. Best known of the annuals is common candy-tuft, *I. umbellata*, bearing many clusters of pink, white or purple flowers. 'Giant Hyacinth', a white, and 'Red Flash', a vivid carmine red, are both successful varieties.

General care: A sunny site and well-drained soil are essentials. Poor soil is tolerated, but moderately fertile soil is recommended for the annuals.

Propagation: Take cuttings of the perennials, choosing non-flowering shoots in summer and placing in a cold frame. Sow seed of the annuals *in situ* in spring.

Pests and diseases: Generally trouble-free.

IRIS

There are 300 species of iris and many more hybrids and cultivars. Some have rhizomes, others bulbs and among their ranks are some of the loveliest flowers for the garden. Among the many bulbous irises the best known is probably *I. reticulata*, which grows 15–20cm (6–8in) tall. It is often planted with good effect in rock gardens, and it produces its purple-blue flowers in February/March. The variety 'Cantab' is a lighter blue than 'J. S. Dijt', which is a near purple. *Iris danfordiae* has vivid yellow flowers in February. The tall Dutch iris which grows 75cm (2½ft) high is excellent for cutting in June. If left undisturbed it will flower for years provided it has been planted about 12.5cm (5in) deep. In fact, the same is true of the Spanish and English iris. Best known of the rhizome-bearing sorts is the huge assemblage of large-flowered bearded or flag irises, derived from I. *pallida* and allied species. These come in all colours of the rainbow and bloom in June and July. There are so many varieties to choose from that it is best to consult a specialist's catalogue, or better still make a visit to a nearby nursery in June to see those that they have in flower. In addition to the taller varieties and hybrids there are many dwarf ones, some of which only grow to 10cm (4in) high.

General care: A sunny site and well-drained fertile soil are essential for the success of the bulbous and rhizomatous irises mentioned here. Plant bulbous species in autumn, rhizomatous sorts after flowering in autumn or spring. Divide and replant rhizomatous irises every third year to maintain vigour.

Propagation: Divide rhizomatous irises after flowering or in spring. Separate clumps of bulbous irises or remove bulblets when dormant.

Pests and diseases: Slugs and snails damage flowers and leaves, leaf spot spoils the foliage and bulbs and rhizomes are attacked by soft rot.

KNIPHOFIA

The brightly-hued flower spikes and grassy foliage of red hot pokers have long assured their popularity in gardens as something different and desirable. Of the many varieties, 'Samuel's Sensation', which grows 1.5m (5ft) high, is outstanding with its bright scarlet blooms. 'Bressingham Torch', growing to 90cm (3ft), is also spectacular and has orange-yellow spikes.

General care: Although some

shade is tolerated, a sunny, sheltered site and well-drained but moisture-retentive soil provide the best growing conditions. Plant in spring and subsequently protect the crowns with straw or bracken during the winter in cold areas.

Propagation: Divide established clumps in spring or sow seeds at the same time under glass.

Pests and diseases: Generally trouble-free.

LATHYRUS

The sweet pea, L. *odoratus*, is familiar to all and has long been a great favourite. From June to September the lovely flowers in shades of red, pink, salmon, blue, lavender and white are a delight in the garden and for indoor flower arrangements. The tall Spencer group of varieties all need sticks or some form of support as does 'Jet Set' (mixed colours) which grows 90cm (3ft) tall. 'Snoopea' (mixed) is 30–

38cm (12–15in) tall and needs no support, making it excellent for a border.

General care: For the finest sweet peas, a rich, moisture-retentive soil and a place in the sun are required. Dress the poorer soils with rotted farmyard manure, garden compost or peat and fertilizer, and if it is acid apply lime.

Propagation: Sow seed January–March under glass at a temperature of 15–20°C (60–68°F) or in April/May in open ground.

Pests and diseases: Generally trouble-free, but look out for thrips, slugs and snails and downy mildew disease.

LAVANDULA*

The English lavender *Lavandula angustifolia* (*spica*), grown for its fragrant essential oil, is still popular in spite of the fact that its height – it grows to 90cm (3ft) – means it needs plenty of space. Its blue-purple flower spikes open from July to Sep-

The sweet pea, Lathyrus odoratus

tember. The dwarf variety, 'Munstead', growing to 45cm (18in) is ever a favourite with its lavender-blue spikes of flowers, and it is undoubtedly good for an average-sized garden. 'Hidcote' is another compact variety and has violet flowers. If you want to dry stems of flowers, cut these when the flowers are just showing colour but not fully open. The fragrance is then retained at its best.

General care: All but the wettest soils grow lavenders, but for long-lived, healthy specimens a well-drained, fertile, limy soil in a sunny site is best. Remove old flower spikes and at least a few centimetres (2–3in) of stem each spring to keep the growth of the plant compact.

Propagation: Take 7.5cm (3in) cuttings of ripe non-flowering shoots in late summer and when rooted overwinter them in a cold frame. Plant out in March or April.

Pests and diseases: Generally trouble-free.

LAVATERA

The annual mallow, L. *trimestris*, is an erect annual plant which grows to around 75cm (2½ft) tall, branches naturally and is a good space filler. The wide petals of its pink or white flowers form a beautiful open trumpet up to 10cm (4in) across and appear from July to September. Recommended varieties are 'Silver Cup', which grows 60cm (2ft) tall, and 'Mont Blanc', which is white and a little shorter at 50cm (20in) tall.

General care: Ordinary, reasonably fertile, well-drained soil and a sunny site are all that is required.

Propagation: Sow seed *in situ* in spring.

Pests and diseases: Generally trouble-free, but look out for aphids (greenfly).

LEUCOJUM

The hardy snowflakes, with their snowdrop-like flowers, are welcome additions to the spring garden. *L. aestivum* grows 50cm (20in) tall and in spite of its common name – summer snowflake – actually flowers in April. It has pure white bells on each stem. *L. vernum*, smaller at 15cm (6in) tall, is the spring snowflake, and it flowers soon after the snowdrop.

General care: Although snowflakes will grow in ordinary soils, they thrive best where it is really moist, or even wet, during the growing period. Sun or partial shade is acceptable.

Propagation: Divide clumps or separate offsets, either just after flowering or when dormant. Seed may be sown when ripe (germinating the following spring), but takes several years to reach flowering size.

Pests and diseases: Generally trouble-free.

LILIUM

The majestic lily has never been more popular, mainly as the result of the arrival of many new vigorous hybrid cultivars which are freely available commercially. There are two broad types of lily, those with trumpet-shaped flowers and those with reflexed petals, sometimes known as Turks-cap. Best known in the latter group is *L. martagon*, an easy-going purple-flowered species to 1.2m (4ft) tall. A very familiar trumpet lily species is *L. regale* with fragrant red-purple budded white blooms. A long-lived and very easy Turks-cap with orange flowers in late summer is *L. henryi* which, when well grown, can attain 2m (6½ft) in height. The following trumpet hybrids can be recommended: 'Pink Pearl' (shades of pink); 'Royal Gold' (rich yellow); 'Green Dragon' (white from chartreuse-green buds); and 'Olympic Hybrids' (mixed colours). Among the Turks-caps, try the mixed coloured 'Harlequin Hybrids', 'Citronella' (yellow) and 'Connecticut Yankee' (orange). There are many lily cultivars which are halfway between the trumpet and Turks-cap, most with upward facing blooms. Recommended in this group are: 'Enchantment' (brightest orange-red);

Lilium regale

'Destiny' (lemon yellow); and 'Snow Princess' (ivory white).

General care: Ordinary, well-drained soil is suitable, ideally laced with leaf mould, garden compost or peat. Plant about 15cm (6in) deep, ideally in late autumn, though any time to March is satisfactory. Sun or partial shade is accepted, but if in a sunny position place them in among dwarf shrubs or perennials to shade the soil and keep the bulbs cool. Staking may be needed in windy sites.

Propagation: Divide clumps or remove offsets when dormant. Some species and cultivars, eg *L. tigrinum* (tiger lily) and 'Enchantment' produce aerial bulbils on the stem. Remove these in late summer and treat as seeds. Sow seeds when ripe or as soon as received and put them in a cold frame. Some species, eg *L. martagon*

The annual mallow, Lavatera trimestris

germinate and form minute bulbs but no top growth until after they have been chilled by winter cold. This could mean 6–12 months before obvious 'germination' occurs.

Pests and diseases: Slugs and snails damage young shoots, viruses may mottle and stunt growth and aphids (greenfly) deform shoot tips and flower buds.

LIMONIUM

Statice (*Limonium sinuatum*), a half-hardy annual, bears sprays of small yellow, pink, lavender, blue and white flowers from July to September. They are excellent for drying if you cut them just as they begin to open. 'Rainbow' mixture is a recommended variety: it grows 45cm (18in) tall.

General care: Any ordinary soil is suitable for this plant with a position in the sun.

Propagation: Sow at a temperature of 15–20°C (60–68°F)

for planting out at the end of May. Alternatively, sow *in situ* in early May for a late display.

Pests and diseases: Generally trouble-free.

LOBELIA

The Oxford and Cambridge blue *Lobelia erinus* has been a popular bedding and edging plant since Victorian times. Other colours are now available, eg 'Rosamond' (crimson and white) and 'String of Pearls' (mixed). *L. e. pendula* has prostrate stems and is useful for hanging baskets. Try 'Blue Basket' (violet-blue) and 'Red Cascade' (purple-red).

General care: Ordinary, reasonably well-drained soil and sun or partial shade suits these half-hardy annuals. Plant out only when threat of frost has passed.

Propagation: Sow seeds in warmth in early spring.

Pests and diseases: Generally trouble-free.

LOBULARIA

This small, ever-popular edging plant, sweet alyssum (*Lobularia maritima* syn. *Alyssum maritimum*), is suitable for growing in the rock garden and in the crevices of paving or as an edging. A hardy annual, it flowers continuously throughout the summer. It grows to a height of 10–15cm (4–6in) and popular varieties are 'Little Dorrit', white; 'Snowdrift', white; 'Rosie O'Day', pink; and 'Royal Carpet', purple.

General care: Grow in any ordinary well-drained soil in full sun.

Propagation: Sow under glass in February/March and keep at 10–15°C (50–60°F). Sow in open ground in April/May.

Pests and diseases: Generally trouble-free.

LUNARIA

Honesty, *Lunaria annua*, is a must for the flower arranger's garden, and the real interest

LEFT: *Lunaria annua*
ABOVE: *Russell lupins*

will be in the stems of silvery seed pods produced at the end of the summer. These are always in great demand for dried winter floral arrangements. While the variety with purple flowers is generally the most popular, there are others which have white or pink flowers. The colour of the flowers, incidentally, make no significant difference to the quality of the seed pods. You will only need to sow honesty once if you allow the seed to shed; in fact, seedling production is so prolific that it can become a weed. The plant is a biennial however and easily kept in check.

General care: Any ordinary soil and a site in sun or shade is suitable.

Propagation: To make a start sow the seed outside in May/June where you want it to flower. Thin out to 30cm (12in) apart.

Pests and diseases: Generally trouble-free.

LUPINUS

Although 200 species of lupin are known, only the hybrids derived from *L. poly-phyllus* can be described as first-rate garden plants. The world famous Russell strain has 1m (3¼ft) tall strong stems, plenty of vigour and a wide colour range. Many cultivars have bi-coloured flowers. Recommended are: 'Chandelier' (yellow shades); 'My Castle' (red shades); 'Noble Maiden' (white and cream); 'The Governor' (blue and white); and 'Dwarf Lulu' (mixed colours on stems up to 60cm (2ft) in height). These can all be raised from seed or bought as plants. Russell lupins grow to about 105cm (3½ft) and flower in June/early July. If the dead flower spikes are removed before seed forma-tion, flowering will resume in a limited way.

General care: Ordinary fer-tile soil which does not dry out and a sunny or slightly shaded site produce fine lupins; over-rich conditions promote extra tall soft stems liable to wind damage.

Propagation: Divide clumps in late winter, take cuttings of basal shoots in spring in a cold frame and sow seeds in a nursery row outside or in a cold frame in late spring.

Pests and diseases: Generally trouble-free, but powdery mildew can sometimes be a nuisance.

MALCOLMIA

The 20cm (8in) high drifts of small rose, lilac and white sweet-scented flowers of Virginian stock *M. maritima* appear very quickly after sowing the seed of this hardy annual. It is a perfect stop-gap plant, for example for covering the sites of spring bulbs and for edging beds and borders.

General care: A sunny site and all well-drained soils are suitable.

Propagation: Sow seeds *in situ* in spring, or 4–6 weeks before a display is required.

Pests and diseases: Generally trouble-free.

MATTHIOLA

The well-known night-scented stock *Matthiola bi-cornis* is not much to look at during the day but at night it opens its pale lilac flowers and gives out a sweet, heavy scent. This hardy annual is especially fragrant on a still, warm evening. Mix it with the similar-sized Virginian stock to provide daytime colour. Sow seed from March to May where you want it to flower in any garden soil in sun or partial shade.

General care: Ordinary, reasonably fertile soils and a sunny or slightly shaded site are all that is required.

Propagation: Sow *in situ* in spring and again in early summer to extend the dis-play into autumn.

Pests and diseases: Generally trouble-free.

MECONOPSIS

This genus of largely Hima-layan poppies is famed for its blue-flowered species. The best known and easiest to grow are: *Meconopsis beton-icifolia* (syn. *M. baileyi*), the Himalayan blue poppy, which has delightful sky blue flowers and bright yel-low anthers and is well worth trying in every garden. It is a short-lived perennial and often only biennial. It reaches a height of 90cm (3ft). *M. grandis* produces gentian-blue flowers and is a more re-liable perennial. The yellow and orange-red *M. cambrica* (Welsh poppy) is attractive but can become a nuisance as it seeds very freely.

General care: The blue pop-pies require a humus-rich soil which is moist but not waterlogged. In limy soils they are mauve-blue unless treated with iron sequestrene. A partially shaded site is best, but full sun is tolerated. It is recommended that the first flower spike on home raised plants of *M. betonicifolia* be pinched out when young. This ensures a better floral display the following year and sometimes results in the plant persisting for several years.

Propagation: Sow seed as soon as ripe if possible, over-wintering the small plants in a frame. Alternatively, sow under glass in spring, prick off into boxes and plant out as soon as each young plant has 5–6 good-sized leaves.

Pests and diseases: Generally trouble-free.

Meconopsis cambrica

MESEMBRYANTHEMUM

The Livingstone daisy *Dor-otheanthus bellidiformis* syn. *Mesembryanthemum crini-florum* is a sun-loving, suc-culent-leaved native of South Africa which spreads brilli-ance over the driest of sunny sites. Masses of bright red, pink, and white daisy flow-ers appear continuously from June to August. Try growing 'Sparkles', which grows to 10cm (4in). *D. oculatus* is similar in appear-ance but has yellow flowers.

General care: Sun and well-drained soil, preferably not too rich, are the basic re-quirements of this half-hardy annual.

Propagation: Sow seeds early to mid spring under glass and set out young plants when the threat of frost has passed.

Pests and diseases: Usually trouble-free, but in a wet season slugs and snails can eat leaves and flowers.

MIMULUS

The strikingly coloured mon-key flowers with their some-what antirrhinum-shaped blooms can be used as bed-ding annuals and in a bed of perennials. Species names are rarely mentioned in seed catalogues, but the various seed strains are hybrids known as *M. × variegatus*. 'Giant Mixed' has large yel-low to red, darker blotched flowers. 'Royal Velvet' has en-tirely mahogany-red blooms with yellow throats. The new 'Malibu Orange' is a clear vivid orange on com-pact plants.

General care: Humus-rich soil which does not dry out and a sunny or slightly shady site are required for the best results. Pondside or other wet sites are ideal as monkey flowers are always associ-ated with water in the wild.

Propagation: Divide estab-lished plants in spring. To grow as an annual, sow seed in early spring under glass.

Pests and diseases: Generally trouble-free.

MOLUCELLA

The tall flower spikes of bells of Ireland *M. laevis* reach up to 90cm (3ft) and consist of tiny white flowers, each surrounded by a light green large shell-like calyx. These half-hardy annuals are highly valued by flower arrangers for drying and cut flower use.

General care: Ordinary fertile soil that is reasonably well-drained and a sunny position are all that is required. For drying, cut the stems just as the flowers appear and hang up in bunches in an airy place out of direct sunlight.

Propagation: Sow seeds under glass in early spring and plant out in early summer or sow *in situ* in late spring.

Pests and diseases: Generally trouble-free.

MUSCARI

With their little inverted grape-like clusters of rounded bells, the grape hyacinths are so different and cheerful they demand a place in every spring garden. Try the 10–15cm (4–6in) tall

Nemesia

Muscari botryoides with deep blue flowers, and its pure white form 'Alba'. Vigorous and very free-flowering is *M. armeniacum*, which grows to 20cm (8in). The best forms are 'Cantab' (sky blue), 'Early Giant' (deep blue) and 'Blue Spike', the latter having crowded double flowers of flax blue.

General care: Ordinary soil that is reasonably well-drained is perfectly adequate and, ideally, a sunny site, though some shade is tolerated. Plant in autumn. Lift and replant when clumps get congested as soon as the leaves yellow and die down.

Propagation: Divide clumps or separate offsets or bulblets when re-planting.

Pests and diseases: Generally trouble-free.

MYOSOTIS

Forget-me-nots are everyone's favourites and make a splendid accompaniment to tulips and other spring bulbs. Even when grown without the company of other plants, the dainty flowers carried on thin stems are a delight in April and May. Species names are only rarely given in seed cata-

logues, but the taller, 25–30cm (10–12in) tall cultivars are referrable to *M. sylvatica*, the wood forget-me-not, and the dwarf sorts to *M. alpestris*, alpine forget-me-not, or are otherwise hybrids. 'Royal Blue', which has rich dark blue flowers and grows 30cm (12in) tall, is an excellent choice. 'Dwarf Royal Blue' grows only 18cm (7in) tall and has a more bushy habit. 'Miniature Blue' reaches only to 12.5cm (5in) in height. Varieties in colours other than blue are 'Carmine Red' and 'Victoria White'.

General care: Ordinary well-drained soil is satisfactory in sun or shade. To avoid hordes of self-sown seedlings, which can be as bad as weeds, pull up the plants as the last flowers fade, or before if possible.

Propagation: Sow seed outside around midsummer and plant into permanent sites in autumn.

Pests and diseases: Generally trouble-free, though mildew is sometimes a nuisance.

NARCISSUS

These are the hardy flowering bulbs which are such a delight in spring and easily

recognized by even the non-gardener. To many people the terms 'daffodils' and 'narcissus' mean two different plants, but botanically they are both members of the genus *Narcissus*. True daffodils have a trumpet equal in length to the petals. Outstanding large golden-yellow trumpet daffodils include 'Golden Harvest' and 'Rembrandt', but there are long lists to choose from in the bulb catalogues. Among the pure white-flowered sorts old 'Mount Hood' is one of the best. Among large-cupped *narcissus cultivars*, try 'Carbineer' (yellow and orange-red); 'Ice Follies' (white and cream); 'Stadium' (yellow and white). Small-cupped sorts are 'Blarney' (white and salmon-orange) and 'Verger' (white and scarlet). For the rock garden or front of beds and borders do not neglect the small wild species such as: *N. bulbocodium* (hoop petticoat daffodil); *N. asturiensis* (syn. *minimus*) (a perfect miniature trumpet daffodil); and *N. triandrus albus* (the creamy white angels' tears).

General care: Practically all soils will grow narcissus, but they must be moist during the growing season. Sun or shade is equally acceptable.

Propagation: Divide clumps or separate offsets when dormant or when in full leaf after flowering.

Pests and diseases: Generally trouble-free, but narcissus fly attacks the bulbs and viruses cripple the whole plant.

NEMESIA

This early flowering annual, which resembles a small, broad-flowered antirrhinum in a wide colour range, puts on a show from the end of May to August. Growing to a height of 20–30cm (8–12in) it is a good subject for beds and borders. 'Carnival Mixed' produces compact plants of glorious colours. Keep the soil moist if the plants are to flower well for a long time.

General care: Sunshine and a fertile soil which is well-drained but not dry provide ideal conditions.

Propagation: Sow seeds in warmth in spring and plant out as soon as the threat of frost has passed.

Pests and diseases: Generally trouble-free, but watch for aphids (greenfly).

NEMOPHILA

The hardy annual N. insignis (syn. N. menziesii) has a useful spreading habit and from June to August it forms a carpet of bright blue, white-centred saucer-shaped flowers. It makes a lovely edging to a bed or can be sown to cover gaps where spring bulbs have died down. It also looks choice enough to be grown on the rock garden.

General care: Ordinary well-drained soil and a site in the sun are all that is required.

Propagation: Sow seeds in situ in spring.

Pests and diseases: Generally trouble-free.

NEPETA

This attractive aromatic plant, with its blue-grey foliage and misty mauve flower spikes, is often used as an edging plant. It does well on light soils in full sun but tends to die out fairly quickly on heavy, cold, poorly drained soils.

Nepeta faassenii (syn. N. mussinii), which grows to 45cm (18in) high, is the commonly grown catmint, but the variety 'Six Hills Giant', which grows to 60cm (2ft) and has violet-blue flowers, makes a better and more positive display.

General care: A sunny site and well-drained soil are the basic requirements; even poor soils are suitable.

Propagation: Divide in spring or take cuttings of basal shoots at the same time or in late summer in a cold frame.

Pests and diseases: Generally trouble-free.

NICOTIANA

The beautiful trumpet-shaped scented white flowers of the tobacco plant are borne from late June to September. Older varieties open in the evening only, while newer varieties open during the daytime as well. Nicotiana alata grandiflora (syn. N. affinis) is a tender perennial to 90cm (3ft) tall grown as an annual. Seed strains with pink and red flowers are hybrids known as N. × sanderae. Choose from 'Evening Fragrance', mixed colours growing 90cm (3ft) tall; 'Crimson Rock', growing 45cm (18in) tall; and 'Lime Green', growing to 75cm (2½ft) tall.

General care: For the best results, choose a sunny site and provide a humus-rich soil that is drained but does not dry out.

Propagation: Sow seeds under glass in March at 15–18°C (60–65°F) for planting out in late May.

Pests and diseases: Generally trouble-free, but look out for the crippling yellow mottle caused by virus.

PAEONIA

There are several different types of peonies, including the old-fashioned, cottage garden types with their green foliage and fully double flowers. The double Chinese peonies are now very popular; they have a greater range of delightful colours and the added virtue of being scented.

Among the old cottage peonies (P. officinalis), which grow to 45cm (18in) tall, there are 'Alba-plena', a double white; 'Rosea-plena', a double pink; and 'Rubra-plena', a double crimson. All flower in May/June. Among the many excellent double Chinese peonies, all of which flower in June, are: 'Adolph Rousseau', a crimson; 'Alex Fleming', bright rose-pink; 'Kelway's Glorious', pure white; and 'President Wilson', pale cream

Double white peonies

pink. Single bloom varieties include 'Globe of Light', a pink with a large cream-yellow centre; 'Jan van Leeuwen', pure white with a golden centre; and 'Soshi', rose with a yellow centre.

General care: A moisture-retentive but not wet soil, well laced with organic matter is necessary for the best results. Sun or partial shade are equally acceptable. In windy sites the taller cultivars will need support.

Propagation: Divide the roots in October or early spring. Once planted, on no account disturb them.

Pests and diseases: Generally fairly trouble-free, but grey mould (botrytis) can be a nuisance on flower buds if the season is damp and cool.

PAPAVER

The boldly colourful bowl-shaped flowers of poppies have a perennial charm and have long graced our gardens. Best known is the oriental poppy P. orientale and its hybrid cultivars with their massive flowers on 1m (3¼ft) stems and hairy, coarsely ferny leaves. Try 'Glowing Embers' (orange-red, ruffled petals); 'Beauty Queen' (buff apricot-orange); 'Midnight' (salmon-pink); and 'Perry's White'.

The common annual field poppy P. rhoeas has given rise to 'The Shirley', a strain of mixed shades of red, pink and white, often with picotee edges. It can attain 90–120cm (3–4ft) in height.

General care: A sunny site and ordinary fertile soil are required. Over-rich soil promotes tall, soft stems liable to wind throw.

Propagation: Divide perennials in early spring or take root cuttings at the same time in a frame or cool greenhouse. Sow annuals *in situ* in spring.

Pests and diseases: Generally trouble-free.

PELARGONIUM

This genus contains several kinds of popular plants generally called geraniums. They are bright and showy, and thrive equally well grown as window ledge pot plants or in beds outside in summer. Best known is the so-called zonal geranium, *P.× hortorum*, a hybrid race containing hundreds of cultivars with rounded clusters of five-petalled or double blooms in shades of red, white and pink for most of the year. The rounded leaves may or may not have a ring-like bronze zone, and several cultivars are strikingly variegated; eg 'Mr Henry Cox'. Most *hortorum* geraniums grow 45–60cm (1½–2ft) tall, but there is a dwarf race about 20cm (8in) or under; eg 'Red Black Vesuvius'. Best grown as a pot plant is the regal or show geranium *P.× domesticum*. It has larger, often bi-coloured flowers mainly from spring to autumn. Useful for hanging baskets is the trailing *P. peltatum* or ivy leaved geranium. The various cultivars have almost fleshy, lobed leaves and single or double blooms in reds, pinks, mauves and white. Mainly less showy but grown for their aromatic leaves are the so-called scented geraniums. Several different species are involved, among them rose-scented *P. capitatum*, lemon-scented *P. crispum* and peppermint-scented *P. tomentosum*.

General care: Any standard compost or ordinary well

Physalis

drained soil is suitable and as much sun as possible.

Propagation: Take tip cuttings in warmth in late summer, early autumn or spring.

Pests and diseases: Watch for aphids, caterpillars and rust disease.

PENSTEMON

These graceful plants, with their 60–90cm (2–3ft) tall spikes of flowers like large, open-mouthed antirrhinums appearing from July to September, are well worth a place in any garden. They are short-lived, however, so frequent replacement is necessary. 'Garnet' is just about the hardiest. It makes a neat bushy plant and produces spikes of deep red flowers. 'Firebird' has the same growth habit, but its flowers are bright scarlet. 'Sour Grapes' has flowers of a

unique purplish hue. Various seed mixtures are available, such as 'Grandiflorum Excelsior' which grows to 75cm (2½ft), or 'Skyline', which has a more bushy growth habit. Both have a lovely mixture of colours.

General care: A sheltered sunny site and well-drained but not dry humus-rich soil give the best results.

Propagation: Take cuttings of non-flowering shoots in late summer and overwinter the young plants in a frame. Sow seeds in warmth in early spring and grow on without a check to growth (ie don't starve or allow to become dry) for flowers the same year. Sow seed outside in a seed bed from June to August and transplant to flowering positions in October. The plants

will flower the following season.

Pests and diseases: Generally trouble-free, but watch for aphids (greenfly) and caterpillars. Severe winters can damage the plants.

PETUNIA

The wide range of dazzling colours, a long and prolific flowering season and ease of cultivation have put petunias well up among the top favourite annual flowers. Some are self-coloured, others bicoloured in radiating stripes. A few seed strains are double-flowered. Some of the newer varieties are earlier, freer flowering and more weather resistant than their predecessors. Try 'Resisto Rose' and 'Red Joy', plus other colours in the same series. Also recommended are the purple and white 'Telstar', red and white 'Star Jay', yellow 'California Girl' and the mixed doubles 'Super Fanfare Mixed'.

General care: Ordinary fertile soil and a sunny site are necessary.

Propagation: Sow seeds thinly in early spring in warmth. Prick off the tiny seedlings with care and grow on without a check. Plant out when the threat of frost has passed.

Pests and diseases: May be subject to attack by aphids, but generally trouble-free.

PHACELIA

The California bluebell *P. campanularia* is a bushy annual growing only 23cm (9in) high and flowering from June to September. The freely borne flowers are a wonderful gentian blue and bell-shaped, and the foliage gives off a fragrance when lightly bruised.

General care: This plant does best in a light well-drained soil and is well suited for small informal sowings towards the front of the border.

Propagation: Sow seeds *in situ* in spring.
Pests and diseases: Generally trouble-free.

PHLOX

The bright clean colours and sturdy, reliable growth of border phlox *P. paniculata* make them indispensable for a late summer display. Their erect, almost woody stems never need staking and bear terminal trusses of flowers which, individually, resemble primroses in shape. Recommended are: 'Cinderella', which has lilac-pink flowers with rose eyes and grows to 90cm (3ft) tall; 'Firefly', which grows to 75cm (2½ft) tall and has pink flowers with crimson eyes; 'Rembrandt', which is pure white and grows 90cm 3ft) tall; and 'San Antonio', which is claret red and grows 75cm (2½ft) tall. The only variegated type, with pale mauve flowers, is 'Norah Leigh', which grows 60cm (2ft) tall. A bright addition to the border, it is less vigorous than the others.

Similar in flower shape, but with bushy annual growth up to 30cm (1ft) in height, is *Phlox drummondii*, which is first-rate as a bedding plant and for patio containers. Try the 15cm (6in) tall 'Beauty Mixed', the starry flowered 'Twinkles' at 18cm (7in) and the full-sized 'Large Flowered Mixed'.
General care: Although phlox will perform reasonably well in ordinary soil, they respond well to a humus-rich rooting medium which does not dry out. Sun or shade are acceptable.
Propagation: Divide established clumps in spring or take root cuttings in late winter in a frame or greenhouse. Sow seeds of annuals in warmth in spring, planting out when fear of frost has passed. They can also be sown *in situ* in late spring.
Pests and diseases: Generally trouble-free, but look out for stem eelworm and powdery mildew.

PHYSALIS

Chinese lanterns *P. alkekengi* (syn. *P. franchetii*) is grown for the ornamental calyx, which looks like an orange lantern. If cut while the colour is still good, the stems of lanterns can be dried for winter indoor decoration, but remove the foliage first.
General care: All but the wettest soils are acceptable and a site in sun or shade. Physalis is likely to become invasive, especially in the richer soils, and it is usually best to keep its roots confined with vertically sunk slates or tiles.
Propagation: Divide any time from late autumn to spring.
Pests and diseases: Generally trouble-free.

POLYGONATUM

Solomon's seal, *P. × hybridum* (syn. *P. multiflorum* of gardens) forms elegant colonies of erect, unbranched stems with arching tops 60–90cm (2–3ft) in height. In May and June, the white, waisted flowers hang gracefully down in clusters of two or three almost along the full length of each stem. They are set off by a background of equi-spaced oblong mid-green leaves, which turn a lovely shade of yellow in the autumn.
General care: Partial shade and ordinary soil which does not dry out readily provide the ideal conditions.
Propagation: Propagation is by division of rhizomes in March/April or from small rhizome eyes potted on and kept in a cold frame or greenhouse until large enough to be planted out.
Pests and diseases: Generally trouble-free, but in some areas Solomon's seal sawfly can strip the leaves.

PORTULACA

This somewhat neglected half-hardy annual deserves wider use. It is a neat plant with succulent foliage that enables it to withstand a degree of drought. It can really only be said to grow 15cm (6in) tall as the stems tend to lie along the ground. Semi-double flowers with prettily ruffled petals in shades of most colours (except blue) appear successively from June to September. The flowers wait for sunlight before opening fully and then form a complete carpet of colour and decorative foliage. Recommended varieties are *P. grandiflora* 'Double Mixed' and 'Calypso'.
General care: A sunny site and well-drained, even poor, soil are essential for a good floral display.
Propagation: Sow in warmth, early to mid-spring. Handle the fleshy seedlings with care and allow the compost to almost dry out between waterings.
Pests and diseases: Generally trouble-free.

PRIMULA

There are no less than 400 species of primroses, mainly from Asia and Europe. Five are native to the British Isles and of these, primrose and cow-slip are among our most favourite wild flowers. Primrose (*Primula vulgaris*) is also much grown in gardens, especially in its mixed colour seed strains, eg 'Juliet'. The large bloomed and variably coloured hybrid between primrose and cowslip (*P. veris*), known as polyanthus, has long been a popular garden plant and there are many first-rate seed strains, eg 'Triumph', available mixed or in separate colour shades of white, yellow, pink, red and purple-blue. The extra large flower 'Pacific' strain is also good, especially the low-growing 'Pacific Dwarf Jewel'. The claret-crimson *P. × 'Wanda'* has long been a favourite. It is derived from the dwarf *P. juliae* and *P. vulgaris* and is like a smaller, rounder-leaved primrose in habit. Very popular is the drumstick primrose, *P. denticulata*, a Himalayan species with small lilac to purple flowers aggregated into dense, spherical heads.

Some of the finest border primulas belong to the Candelabra group. These have erect stems to 60cm (2ft) tall with several whorls of flowers. *P. japonica* is red-purple, *P. bulleyana* light orange, *P. pulverulenta* red, and *P. helodoxa* yellow. Even taller is the so-called giant cowslip *P. florindae*, with its large, loose, terminal

Primula

cluster of bright yellow, sometimes red-flushed, fragrant flowers.

Many primulas are small or very small and are among standard plants for the rock garden. Best known is the easy going *P. auricula* and its many hybrid cultivars in almost every shade of the rainbow. Also recommended and well worth trying are *P. marginata* (blue-lilac), *P. frondosa (rosy-lilac)*, *P. × pubescens* 'Falconside' (crimson) and *P. rosea* (bright pink).

General care: With the exception of *P. auricula*, *marginata* and × *pubescens*, which require moist but well-drained soil, all other species need constantly moist soil to really thrive, though they will grow in ordinary soil that is watered during dry spells. The Candelabra group and *P. florindae* grow best in waterside or bog conditions. Divide clumps at least every third year to keep them vigorous and floriferous.

Propagation: Divide after flowering, late summer or spring. Sow seeds when ripe or in spring in a cold frame.

Pests and dieases: Vine weevil grubs may attack the roots, bryobia mites brown or bronze the leaves and birds shred the flowers.

PULSATILLA
Pasque flower, *P. vulgaris*, sometimes known as *Anemone pulsatilla*, is a rare English plant of grassland, mainly in eastern England. It has long been valued in gardens for its froth of ferny foliage and large silky-purple cup-shaped flowers. Several colour forms are known, mainly shades of red, pink and white, all of which are little less vigorous than the original purple sort.

General care: A sunny site and well-drained, fertile but not rich, limy soil is the ideal, but some shade and acid soils are acceptable.

Propagation: Sow seed when ripe or as soon as purchased in a cold frame. Dried packeted seed may take up to 12 months to germinate.

Pests and diseases: Generally trouble-free.

PYRETHRUM
With leaves more finely cut than most ferns and large, brightly hued, golden centred daisy flowers in early summer, the pyrethrum has long been a favourite perennial. *P. roseum* is the basic species (now classified by botanists as *Chrysanthemum coccineum*). Only cultivars are commercially available. Recommended are: 'E. M. Robinson', a pale pink; 'James Kelway', a crimson red; and 'Marjorie Robinson', a deep pink. Try also the double pink 'Princess Mary' and the carmine 'Red Dwarf' at only 30cm (1ft) tall.

General care: A sunny site and fertile, moisture-retentive but well-drained soil provide ideal conditions. The support of twiggy sticks is advisable as stems bearing flowers in full bloom are likely to collapse in strong wind and heavy rain.

Propagation: Propagation is by division of the roots in the spring, which is also the time for planting bought-in stock. Autumn planting can result in considerable losses. Large flowered hybrids can be raised from seed sown in June/July outside or in a cold frame.

Pests and diseases: Generally trouble-free, but watch for aphids (green- and blackfly).

RUDBECKIA
Popularly known as cone flowers because of the thimble-shaped centres to their daisy-like flowers, rudbeckias are indispensable perennials for late summer and autumn colour. Try 'Goldquelle' which, with its bushy habit, grows 90–120cm (3–4ft) high and has large double yellow flowers that open from July to October; 'Goldsturm', which grows to 60cm (2ft) and has flowers with long, deep golden yellow petals surrounding a black centre, appearing from July until September; and *R. newmanii* (syn. *R. fulgida speciosa*), the original black-eyed Susan, having yellow flowers with black centres, which appear on branching stems from July to October.

General care: Ordinary soil

Pulsatilla vulgaris

is adequate, provided it does not dry out unduly. A sunny site is best but partial shade is tolerated.

Propagation: Divide in spring or autumn immediately flowering ceases. Some sorts are easily raised from seed sown in a frame in spring.

Pests and diseases: Generally trouble-free.

SALPIGLOSSIS
Sometimes known as painted tongue, *S. sinuata* is so beautiful and exotic to look at that it gives the impression it is harder to grow than it really is! Trumpet-shaped flowers, some attractively veined, are carried on slender stems and open in succession from July to September. At a height of 60–75cm (2–2½ft) it is a striking mid-border plant; try growing F_1 'Splash', 'Suttons Triumph' or the 30cm (1ft) tall 'Ingrid', all in shades of red, purple, blue and yellow.

General care: A sunny site and ordinary fertile soil are all that is required. Support the tall sorts with twiggy sticks.

Propagation: Sow seed under glass in February at 18°C (65°F) to plant out at the end of May.

Pests and diseases: Generally trouble-free.

SALVIA
With their freely produced dense spikes of tubular, hooded flowers, the annual and perennial sages are undoubtedly worthy of a place in the flower border. The most familiar annual is the brilliant scarlet *S. splendens*. Recommended varieties are 'Carabiniere', scarlet-red, growing 38cm (15in) tall and 'Volcano', an intense bright red, which grows to the same height.

Salvia haematodes grows to a height of 90cm (3ft) and has graceful branching spikes of lavender blue flowers. It is one of the most popular varieties for June/July flowering. It is best as a biennial and is naturally short-lived. Salvia × superba grows to a height of 75cm (2½ft) and is fully perennial. It makes a bushy plant with violet-purple flowers that appear in July/August. Salvia superba 'Lubec' at 45cm (18in) tall is a shorter, more compact plant. S. uliginosa reaches 1.5m (5ft) in height, producing long spikes of sky-blue flowers in autumn.

General care: Reasonably fertile soil that is drained but

[handwritten note: RUDBECKIA Black-eyed Susan]

autumn. The ever-popular 'Clive Greaves', which grows 90cm (3ft) high, produces a constant supply of large lavender blue flowers on long stems which do not require staking. 'Miss Willmott' with its white flowers has a similar growth habit. Very different is the mauve-flowered S. graminifolia, which blooms at the same time on 30cm (1ft) tall stems above wide mounds of silvery grassy foliage.

General care: Ordinary, fertile, preferably limy soil and a site in the sun are basic requirements.

Propagation: Propagation is by dividing roots in the spring or by cuttings taken

with a heel after flowering. Planting out should always be done in the spring.

Pests and diseases: Generally trouble-free.

SCILLA

This genus of mainly spring blooming bulbous plants includes the squills and the familiar bluebell. The dwarf squills are well worth a place in any rock garden.

There is a choice of several varieties; S. sibirica 'Spring Beauty', which grows 15cm (6in) tall and is a bright blue; S. tubergeniana, which has bluish-white flowers and _ y 10cm (4in) high; _lia, bearing bright _e flowers on 10– –6in) stems. S. _n. Endymion non- _s the English blue- its elegantly nodd- r spikes of narrow s; pink and white available. S. cam- (syn. Endymion _s) is the Spanish _a similar plant but _e bells and a straight ; stem. Bulbs under e in catalogues are hybrids between and Spanish and e characteristics of

care: Ordinary soil ; moist during the season is all that is Sun or partial shade is tolerated.

Propagation: Divide clumps or separate offsets when dormant. Sow seeds when ripe in a cold frame; several years elapse to flowering.

Pests and diseases: Generally trouble-free.

SEDUM

At least 500 species of stonecrop are known. Most of them are smallish and the hardy ones are best for the rock garden, eg Sedum album (white), S. cauticolum (rose-purple), S. floriferum (yellow), S. spathulifolim 'Purpureum' (yellow with grey-purple leaves) and S. spurium (pink or red).

Among taller sorts for the perennial border are the grey-leaved S. spectabile with wide heads of pink flowers on 40cm (16in) stems. Its variety, 'Autumn Joy', is salmon pink and grows to a height of 60cm (2ft). The dwarf variety, 'September Ruby', growing only to 30cm (1ft), has deep rose-pink flower-heads. S. maximum 'Atropurpureum' is undoubtedly the most striking stonecrop with stems to 75cm (2½ft) tall, bearing dark red-purple leaves and reddish flowers.

General care: A sunny site and almost any well-drained soil are suitable.

Propagation: Divide the deciduous clump-formers in spring and take cuttings of non-flowering shoots of the rest, any time from spring to early autumn.

Pests and diseases: Generally trouble-free.

SOLIDAGO

For a patch of frothy bright yellow in late summer and autumn, golden rods have no peer. The old varieties were inclined to be weedy, but the newer cultivars which follow are all desirable and recommended: 'Cloth of Gold', which grows to 45cm (18in) and makes a robust plant with deep yellow flower-heads; 'Crown of Rays', which grows to the same height and has attractive horizontal golden spikes; 'Golden Thumb', which grows to 30cm (1ft) and is a neat plant with yellow fluffy flower-heads; and the tall 'Mimosa', which grows 1.5m (5ft) high and is a trouble-free plant with yellow flower-heads.

General care: For the best golden rods choose a sunny site with moisture-retentive fertile soil.

Propagation: Divide roots in March/April. Plants can also be grown from seed sown in a cold frame in March.

Pests and diseases: Generally trouble-free, but mildew can sometimes be a nuisance.

TAGETES

Best known as African and French marigolds, tagetes are top-ranking half-hardy annuals of great popularity. Tagetes erecta, the African marigold, is the tallest and largest flowered. It usually begins its flowering a little later than the smaller types. It provides large lemon-yellow to bright orange blooms from June until the first frosts and is always splendid. Try 'Cracker-jack Mixed' which grows 60cm (24in) tall. T. patula, French marigolds, are compact, bushy and very free-flowering. They flower from late May until the first frosts and can completely clothe the planting area with masses of individual, long-lasting blooms. There are singles, doubles and variants in plenty; try 'Queen Sophia', which is an outstanding double. Among the new Afro-French hybrid marigolds 'Suzie Wong', 'Moll Flanders' and 'Nell Gwynn' are all excellent, and grow to a height of 30cm (12in). Tagetes tenuifolia var. pumila (syn. signata) is the plant commonly known as tagetes. Small bushy plants with finely cut foliage are covered with small, single gold, lemon or mahogany daisy-like flowers from July to September. It is a particularly good edging plant; try 'Golden Gem' at 18cm (7in) tall.

General care: A sunny site and ordinary well-drained soil are suitable.

Propagation: Sow all types in the greenhouse in March at a temperature of 15°C (60°F) for planting out at the end of May.

Pests and diseases: Generally trouble-free.

TROPAEOLUM

To provide a quick temporary screen of attractive leaves and flowers, the common nasturtium, Tropaeolum majus, takes some beating. For a few weeks in early summer this hardy annual will cover banks, fences or any 'eyesore' with great efficiency. It blooms from June to September with minimum demands on soil or gardening skill. Try 'Mixed Tall Single' a climbing variety which grows up to 1.8m (6ft). The dwarf varieties will grow happily in any sunny spot in need of colour. Best are the 'Gleam' hybrids, which have double flowers and grow 38cm (15in) tall.

General care: Ordinary soil and sun are quite adequate, but for fastest growth a humus-rich, well-drained but moisture-retentive rooting medium is best.

Propagation: Sow seeds *in situ* mid to late spring. For an earlier display, sow singly in 9cm (3½in) pots under glass in March.

Pests and diseases: Generally trouble-free, but in some seasons the caterpillars of large and small white butterflies can strip leaves.

TULIPA

The tulip ranks high in the top 10 of favourite bulbs. It has graced English gardens for centuries and its beauty and simplicity ensures its continued popularity. There are well over 50 wild species, and thousands of cultivars have been raised in a wide range of colours; only true blue is missing. In height

Tulipa

they range from about 15cm (6in) to 75cm (2½ft). Because of this variation, it is important to find out about the growth habit of the different types. While most hybrid tulips, such as the tall Darwins and May-flowering varieties, deteriorate if left in the ground from season to season, some of the species persist well, and in fact will multiply freely. For long-term planting, try *T. fosteriana* 'Madame Lefeber', which grows 45cm (18in) tall and is a striking vivid scarlet, *T. greigii* 'Red Riding Hood', which grows 15cm (6in) tall or *T. kaufmanniana* (Water-lily tulip) 30cm (12in) tall. 'The First' is a very early variety with pure white blooms tinted carmine-red on the reverse of the petals. It grows to 20cm (8in).

To make your choice, look through a bulb specialist's catalogue, which always has dozens of different cultivars and several species.

General care: A sunny site and well-drained fertile soil are required. Bulbs used for bedding can be lifted after flowering while in full leaf, and if replanted in a spare corner can still be expected to bloom the following year though not so splendidly.

Propagation: Separate offsets when dormant.

Pests and diseases: Generally fairly trouble-free but beware of tulip fire (botrytis) and grey bulb rot.

Veronica gentianoides, speedwell

VERBASCUM

Although somewhat short-lived the mulleins always capture attention, especially when they flower majestically as individual plants in a garden. They are so stately, often towering above their surrounding neighbours to show off their long, thick and sometimes woolly spires of flowers which appear in July/August, and are a must for any flower garden. Of perennial duration is *V. phoeniceum*: 'Cotswold Queen' grows 1.3m (4½ft) high and has branching stems and buff-orange flowers. 'Gainsborough' grows 1.2m (4ft) high and is the most beautiful of them all with its graceful spikes of clear yellow flowers. 'Pink Domino' is the same height and is rose-pink, a rare colour in the mulleins.

General care: Sun and ordinary soil are the basic requirements. Over-rich conditions will encourage taller, softer stems prone to wind blow.

Propagation: Take 7.5cm (3in) long cuttings of named varieties in March for rooting in a cold frame, or from root

cuttings taken in December/January. To grow from seed, sow 'Choice Mixed' in a frame in April/June for flowering the following year.

Pests and diseases: Generally trouble-free.

VERBENA X HYBRIDA

The heads of these half-hardy annual, primrose-like flowers come in shades of red, pink, blue and white, and are often faintly scented. They are borne in profusion by sturdy little plants from June until the first frosts. Outstanding varieties are 'Derby Salmon Rose' and 'Derby Scarlet'; 'Springtime' is a reliable mixture.

General care: For most satisfactory growth a humus-rich, well-drained but not dry soil and a sunny place are required.

Propagation: Sow seed under glass in February at temperatures of 15–20°C (60–68°F) for planting out at the end of May.

Pests and diseases: Generally trouble-free.

VERONICA

Among the 300 species of speedwell are several first-rate border plants, mostly in shades of blue, purple and mauve. *Veronica gentianoides* grows 60cm (2ft) high and is sometimes planted for ground cover. It produces slender spikes of palest blue flowers in April/May. *Veronica incana* 'Saraband' grows 45cm (18in) high and has beautiful grey foliage followed by violet-blue flowers that appear from June to August. *Veronica spicata* 'Barcarolle', grows to 45cm (18in) and makes a neat carpet of dark foliage punctuated with narrow spikes of deep rose-pink flowers in June/July. *V. spicata* 'Red Fox' grows to 37cm (15in) and has red flowers from June to September.

Veronica teucrium 'Shirley Blue' grows to 30cm (1ft) tall and bears a profusion of bright blue flowers from May to July. *V. t.* 'Trehane' has golden green leaves.

General care: Ordinary fertile reasonably well drained soil and a sunny position produce excellent results.

Propagation: Divide established clumps in spring or early autumn. Sow seeds in late spring in a cold frame.

Pests and diseases: Generally trouble-free.

VIOLA

This large genus of 500 species includes both the viola and the garden pansy (*V. × wittrockiana*), which is still the most popular.

The superb strain of Swiss giant pansies called 'Roggli Giant Mixed' is well known and a packet of seed will have many colours. 'Tiara Mixed', which has large flowers, is a good variety as is 'Engelmann's Giants'. The lighter coloured faces of 'Love Duet Mixed' are simply charming. Among the faceless pansies, 'Azure Blue', which is a clear blue with a yellow eye, is excellent and 'Golden Champion' and 'Clear Crystal Mixed' also deserve a mention. There are many more.

Bedding violas or tufted pansies, *V. × williamsii*, make compact plants with somewhat smaller flowers freely produced throughout the spring and summer in a wide range of mainly self colours. They are fully perennial. Try 'Irish Molly' (copper-yellow), 'Maggie Mott' (silvery blue), 'Nora Leigh' (light violet blue). True violets are well worth a place in every garden. Sweet violet, *V. odorata*, is best known, but also good are the horned violet, *V. cornuta*, the heavily blue-purple freckled white *V. cucculata* 'Freckles' and the purple leaved *V. labradorica* 'Purpurea'.

General care: Ordinary fertile soil that does not dry out is essential for all the violas mentioned here. Sun is best for pansies and bedding violas, partial shade for the violets.

Propagation: Divide violets and bedding violas in spring or early autumn. Take cuttings of bedding violas in late summer in a cold frame and over-winter there. Favourite pansies can be propagated in the same way but they are usually raised from seed sown in spring under glass or outside in early summer. There are also seed strains of bedding violas, which are dealt with in the same way. True violets are also raised from seed, ideally sown when ripe or as soon after as possible and placed in a cold frame.

Pests and diseases: Generally trouble-free, but watch for aphids (greenfly).

XERANTHEMUM

The immortelle *X. annuum* is one of the best plants to grow for the production of everlasting flowers. Growing to a height of 60cm (2ft), the strawy-petalled white, pink, lilac or purple daisy-like flowers keep their true colours for years if cutting and drying are carried out properly (see under *Helichrysum bracteatum*, page 38).

General care: Sun and ordinary soil are all that is required.

Propagation: Sow seed *in situ* in spring.

Pests and diseases: Generally trouble-free.

ZEA

The half-hardy annual ornamental maize, *Zea mays* 'Japonica', produces an ornamental corn cob which can be cut when fully ripe for drying and winter decoration. *Z. m.* 'Japonica Variegata' has white-striped leaves. Try 'Strawberry Corn' which grows to 60cm (3ft) and produces small, broad strawberry-shaped cobs.

General care: A sunny sheltered site and humus-rich moist but not wet soil is required for the best results. Set out the plants in groups of not less than three together to ensure cross-pollination.

Propagation: Sow under glass in March at a temperature of 15–20°C (60–68°F). Plant out at the end of May.

Pests and diseases: Generally trouble-free.

ZINNIA

The half-hardy annual zinnias are highly distinctive members of the daisy family with very broad ray petals. Modern seed strains are mostly semi- or fully double in a wide range of bright clear colours and open from July to September. The large-flowered popular cultivars are derived from *Z. elegans*. Some varieties are quite tall, growing up to 90cm (3ft), but the strong stems and firm flower-heads are excellent for cutting. Try 'Ruffles Mixture' or select separate colours; they grow 60cm (2ft) high. 'Thumbelina' to 15cm (6in) and 'Persian Carpet' to 25cm (10in) tall form bushy plants with many small flowers. They are derived from *Z. haageana*.

General care: Humus-rich, moisture-retentive but well-drained soil and a sunny site give the best results. Tall cultivars may need support, especially in windy places.

Propagation: Sow in the greenhouse in March at a temperature of 15–18°C (60–68°F) for planting out at the end of May.

Pests and diseases: Generally trouble-free, but watch for grey mould during cool, wet summers.

Viola

SHRUBS AND CLIMBING PLANTS

Both in actuality and in many classic paintings, the idealized country cottage invariably has a rose, clematis or similar climber on its walls. The blank brick walls of starker, modern suburbia cry out for the same treatment, and yet all too many home owners are either dubious or actually against the idea. There are stories that roots get into and damage foundations and brickwork and that a covering of vegetation on the walls encourages 'creepie-crawlies'. There is no real evidence to support these assertions. The roots of most climbers are either deeply delving or widespreading and remain of a small diameter. Even the trunk-like stems of 100-year old wisterias have not been reported as doing any damage. In fact, climbers mould to their supports. To undermine and weaken them would be self-defeating. The aerial stem roots of ivy are surface stickers and are more likely to hold up a wall than break it down. Many a picturesque ruin owes its unchanging existence to a mantle of ivy, which very effectively protects its support from rain, heat and cold. Foliage on a wall will, of course, provide a home for wildlife, and a few extra little creatures may find their way into the home. None should cause alarm. Indeed spiders, for example as eaters of flies, should be positively encouraged.

House and garden should be harmoniously merged whenever possible by planting climbers and shrubs where they meet. In the USA this is known as foundation planting, an apt and descriptive term. Shrubs and climbers go hand-in-hand. All the less hardy shrubs benefit for being grown against or trained to walls, and some of the hardy ones have just the right shape for this treatment; eg garrya and *Cotoneaster horizontalis*. Free-standing shrubs in groups or as solitary specimens are essential in the garden to create that furnished, mature look which is the essence of good gardening. Like the climbers, if chosen with care they can be colourful and attractive in their own right while also providing a background for the smaller annuals and perennials.

Before choosing what you need, look around and see what is being grown in your area and then browse around the nurseries and garden centres nearby. The latter usually have a wide selection of suitable plants. The tables on p. 61 are arranged in useful categories to cover most parts of the garden. When choosing climbers and shrubs make sure that some are evergreen so that the garden does not have that dreary, bare look in winter. There are also shrubs and a few climbers which flower during mild winter spells; look in the A–Z section for *Jasminum nudiflorum*, chimonanthus, *Cornus mas*, garrya and chaenomeles.

Soil

All the plants described in the A-Z will grow in the ordinary soil of your district. Ideally it should not be dry or water-logged. The latter situation is practically non-existent where modern houses are built and even the older properties are adequately drained in the vicinity of the building. If it does hang a bit wet on the surface, work in coarse sand or grit or

1   2

LEFT: *Climbers have a built-in means of clinging to a support. Some twine themselves round a frame or wires by their growing tips (**1**) or tendrils (**2**).*

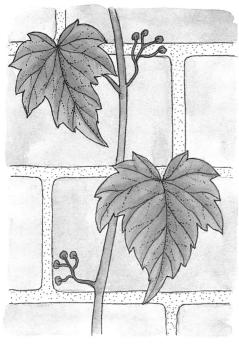

raise the surface about 10–15cm (6in) by digging out paths and placing the soil on the adjacent beds. Dry soils must be laced with decayed manure, garden compost or peat using at least one 9lt (2gal) bucketful per sq m (yd). Fork over the surface to remove perennial weeds or treat with a weedkiller well before the planting time.

Supporting

Climbers and taller wall shrubs will need support for life which must be provided before planting is carried out. Secure horizontal galvanized wires at 45cm (1½ft) intervals to walls and fences, using eyed bolts (vine eyes)

embedded in rawl plugs. If wooden trellis is preferred, or a wood arbour or pergola is to be created, make sure it is treated thoroughly with a preservative. Ideally, poles or posts should not be less than 10cm (4in) in diameter and deeply set in a concrete base.

Planting

Containerized shrubs and climbers purchased from a garden centre can be planted at any time of the year provided the soil is not too wet or frozen. If you live in the east of the country where spring or early summer droughts are likely, try to plant evergreens in

*Not all climbers need support and can use their aerial roots to climb by themselves (**top**), in the case of the Virginia creeper (**left** and **above**) by means of adhesive pads that will attach themselves to any rough surface.*

autumn, the earlier the better, so that they can get established. Many nurseries still sell plants 'bare root', that is dug direct from the nursery soil. Such plants are only available from late autumn to early spring – which is the traditional time for planting hardy trees and shrubs. Some of the finest wall shrubs are not reliably hardy, especially in hard winters and when young. These

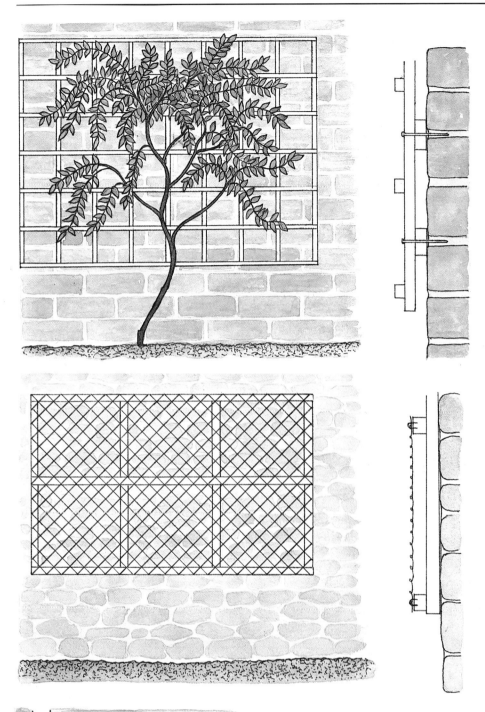

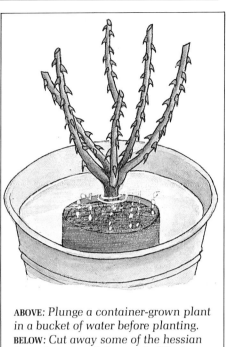

ABOVE: *Plunge a container-grown plant in a bucket of water before planting.*
BELOW: *Cut away some of the hessian from the sides of the root-ball before filling in.*

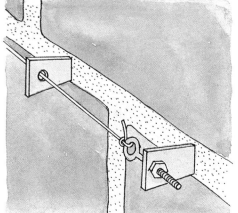

*To support climbers, fix wooden trellis away from the wall (**top**) and away from direct contact with the soil. Stretch mesh over panels made with battens (**above**), fixing the mesh with staples. Fix the panels to the wall or fence. Wire laced through vine eyes (**below left**) provides strong support for permanent planting.*

are always sold in containers and should not be set out until spring after the worst of the frosts is over. If you buy plants from a garden centre, choose the healthiest and best-looking specimen available. Look for vigorous, leafy growth with unblemished foliage of a good green (not yellowish). Buying a good plant will make all the difference to the way it performs, at least initially.

Whether in containers or bare root, dig out a hole somewhat larger than the root system in both width and depth. For containers make the depth a few centimetres (1–2in) more than the root ball. For bare root specimens look for the soil mark on the stem and make the hole deep enough to just cover it when filled in with soil. Once the plant is in place, spade or trowel the soil around the roots. Bare root plants should be gently bumped up and down a few times to work the soil among the roots.

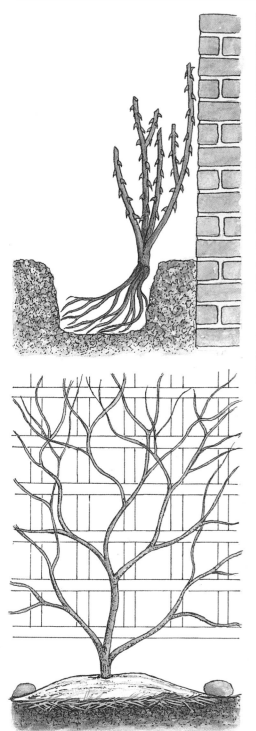

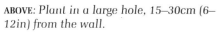

ABOVE: *Plant in a large hole, 15–30cm (6–12in) from the wall.*

BOTTOM: *Protect half-hardy plants with a mulch covered with plastic sheeting.*

When the hole is loose-filled, firm with fists or feet, then top up and firm again. Finish off so that there is a shallow saucer-shaped depression around the stem base to facilitate watering.

There is no set distance apart at which to set climbers and shrubs. So much depends upon what sort of effect is desired,

whether each species is to be treated individually or several are to be grown harmoniously intermingling. In the latter case climbers and wall shrubs can be set 1–2m ($3\frac{1}{4}$–$6\frac{1}{2}$ft) apart and shrubs at about half their ultimate height. For specimen status, space shrubs at a distance apart equal to their ultimate (catalogue or book) height. Climbers should be spaced at about two thirds this distance.

Aftercare and maintenance
For the one to two years following

ABOVE: *Pyracantha and Cotoneaster planted together provide a colourful and effective screen.*

planting, watering, weeding and training must be regularly attended to. During all dry spells, water thoroughly once or twice a week. In the spring following planting, apply a mulch of peat, strawy manure, composted bark, etc and repeat this a year later. If growth seems slow, apply a light dressing of a general fertilizer. Climbers and tall-growing wall

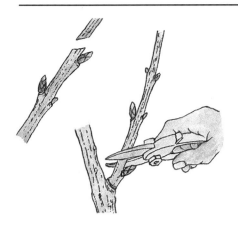

RIGHT: *To prune climbing and wall plants, make a clean, slanting cut across the stem, just above a bud if you are trimming back a branch (**right**) or where a side branch joins the main stem (**above**).*

shrubs will need an initial tie to the first supporting wire. If the climber is a twiner, vertical strings secured to the wires will aid its ascent.

Pruning
Both climbers and shrubs will be more effective if they branch fairly close to ground level. The spring following planting, reduce the height of the young plants by two thirds to a half. This will stimulate growth low down and create bushy shrubs and well branched climbers. The growth which results after this pruning will become the main framework of the mature plant. Thereafter, climbing plants should be pruned annually after flowering, when spent blooms are removed and crowded stems lightly thinned, and in winter when further thinning is well worthwhile. Wall shrubs need little pruning other than to remove stems which grow too far forward from the wall. Most free-standing shrubs can also be allowed to grow naturally, though it pays to thin out congested growth. Vigorous summer bloomers such as philadelphus (mock orange) and weigela greatly respond to an annual thinning after the first two or three years from planting. Remove whole flowered branches back to near the base to encourage young replacement stems. Spring flowerers such as forsythia, kerria and ribes should be pruned only immediately after blooming; winter pruning destroys potential flowers. Where a particular plant has special pruning requirements, mention is made in the A-Z section.

Forsythia planted with Clematis

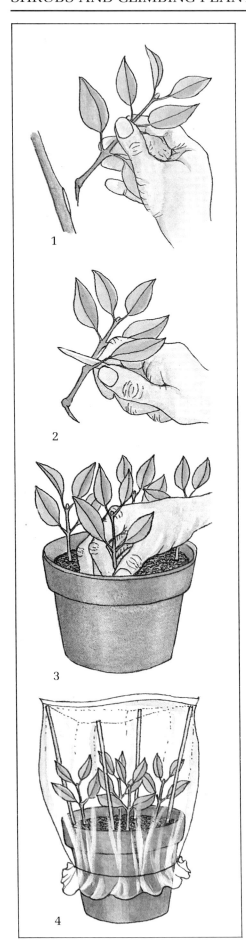

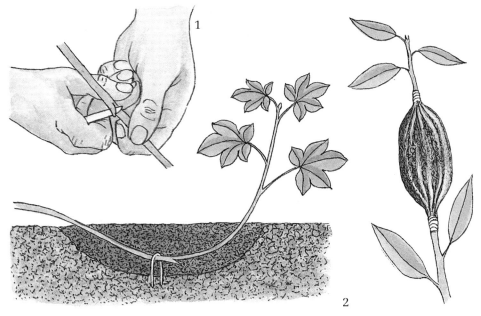

Propagation

There are various ways of propagating shrubs and climbers, the easiest being suckers, layering and hardwood cuttings. Semi-hard and softwood cuttings and seeds require more skill and patience.

Suckers: A few shrubs and climbers, eg berberis, hydrangea, kerria, mahonia, ribes and viburnum often produce shoots from below ground level at or near the base of the plant. These are suckers. When one or two years old they usually have some roots of their own and can be removed and planted independently. Remove the soil down to where the sucker is attached and carefully pull or cut it free. Do this between autumn and early spring and replant immediately. Cut back the top by half.

Layers: Practically all woody stemmed plants can be layered. Firstly, in late summer or spring a low branch is pulled down to soil level and pinned or tied in position. Next, one-year old stems from this branch are bent into a U-shape so that the bottom of the U can be buried shallowly with the free tip erect. Loosen the soil with a fork and then make a shallow hole. Work some coarse sand into the bottom of the hole if the soil is not free-draining. Nick the stem at the bottom of the U, dust with hormone rooting powder and bury it about 5cm (2in) deep. Secure the free end to a short cane. Keep moist in dry weather and

LEFT: Semi-hardwood cuttings are taken from shoots removed with a 'heel' attached (1). Remove the lower leaves (2) and place cuttings to root round the rim of a pot (3). Cover with a plastic 'tent' (4) to increase humidity.

ABOVE LEFT: To increase a plant by layering, 'nick' the underside of the chosen shoot (1) and peg the shoot into the soil (2) with the nick still on the underside.

RIGHT: For air-layering, dip the stem in rooting compound, wrap it in moist sphagnum moss and cover it tightly with clear polythene, ensuring that the nick in the stem remains open. Once the roots push through the moss, remove the covering and sever the new plant below the level of the wrapping.

one year later sever and dig up the rooted layer and replant immediately.

Hardwood cuttings: All deciduous shrubs and climbers and some of the evergreens (eg euonymus and ligustrum) root easily from hardwood cuttings. These are mature stems of the previous season severed in autumn or early winter. Each stem must be cleanly cut above and below a bud and should be 20–30cm (8–12in) long. Any leaves are removed from the lower part, the end is dipped in rooting powder and the cutting inserted two-thirds deep in sandy or sharply drained ground in a sheltered, partially shaded site. One year later the rooted cuttings can be lifted and replanted in permanent sites.

Semi-hardwood and softwood cuttings: For these techniques some kind of propagating case is necessary. This can be improvised from a seed tray covered with plastic sheeting supported by U-shaped lengths of galvanized wire. Single pots can be placed in polythene bags. Best of all are the custom-made propagators with a clear rigid top and a heating element in the bottom. Semi-hardwood cuttings can also be placed in a shaded cold frame. Softwood cuttings are sappy, recently formed stems with active growing tips. They are taken in spring and summer, severed with 5–7.5cm (2–3in) of stem and cut beneath a node (bud or leaf). The lower leaves are cut or nipped off, the base dipped in rooting powder and inserted one-third deep in pots of equal parts sand and peat, or perlite. A case or polythene bag is needed, and bottom heat around 18–21°C (65–70°F) hastens rooting. Semi-hardwood cuttings are the current season's stems starting to become woody at the base. They are taken in late summer and early autumn, severed at the base and trimmed to 7.5–10cm (3–4in) by reducing the top. With some shrubs (eg ceanothus, cistus, elaeagnus, ilex, pyracantha) this kind of cutting roots more successfully if it has a heel of parent stem. The cuttings are carefully pulled or sliced off to leave a shield-shaped base of older wood. The tail of tissue from this shield is pared off and the cutting is then treated as described above. A propagating case is needed and bottom heat is an advantage.

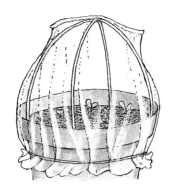

ABOVE: *When sowing seeds in a pot, cover with a plastic bag until the seeds have germinated.*

Seeds: Many shrubs and climbers can be raised from seed, but if they are hybrids or selected forms they will not come true to type. Most of them germinate and grow well but the seedlings usually take several to many years to reach flowering size. Easy genera to try are: berberis, buddleia, chaenomeles, cotoneaster, potentilla, pyracantha, rosa, syringa, viburnum and weigela. The seed is best sown when ripe or as soon afterwards as possible. Dried, packeted seed may take more than a year to germinate. As usually only a few new plants are needed, use 7.5–10cm (3–4in) pots. Fill these with a standard seed compost then sow the seed thinly. If it is large enough to handle with the fingers or tweezers then space sow at 1cm (½in) apart each way. Seed embedded in berries (berberis, cotoneaster and pyracantha) should be squeezed or tweezed out of the surrounding pulp and sown immediately. When sown, press the seeds into the surface of the compost, cover with 1cm (½in) of grit, water, and put outside in a sheltered place or a cold frame. Many shrub and climber seeds, especially those from berries, need a period of low temperature (winter) before they can respond to spring warmth. Pots left outside all winter are best put in a frame or greenhouse in early spring and the seeds should soon germinate.

CLIMBERS AND SHRUBS FOR SPECIAL PURPOSES

CLIMBERS		SHRUBS FOR WALLS		SHRUBS FOR THE OPEN GARDEN	
Sheltered north walls:		**Sheltered north walls:**		**Shady sites:**	
Celastrus	Parthenocissus	Camellia (E)	Garrya	Berberis (some E)	Prunus (some E)
Clematis (some)	Polygonum	Cotoneaster	Kerria	Cornus	Ribes
Hedera (E)	Rosa (some)	Daphne (some E)	Mahonia	Cotoneaster	Salix
Hydrangea	(partially E)	Euonymus (E)	Ribes	Elaeagnus (some E)	Skimmia (E)
Jasminum	Tropaeolum	Forsythia	Skimmia (E)	Forsythia	Spiraea
Lonicera	speciosum			Ilex (E)	Symphoricarpus
				Kerria	Viburnum
				Mahonia (E)	(some E)
South walls:		**South walls:**		**Sunny sites:**	
Campsis	Rosa (some)	Abutilon	Garrya (E)	Buddleia (some E)	Potentilla
Clematis (some)	(partially E)	Buddleia (some)	Magnolia (E)	Chaenomeles	Prunus (some E)
Ipomoea	Tropaeolum	Ceanothus	Pyracantha (E)	Cistus (E)	Santolina (E)
Lathyrus	tuberosum	Chimonanthus	Santolina (E)	Conifers (E)	Senecio (E)
Passiflora	Wisteria	Choisya (E)	Senecio (E)	Cytisus (E)	Spiraea
		Cistus (E)		Erica (E)	Syringa
		Escallonia (E)		Philadelphus	Weigela
East and west walls:		**East and west walls:**		**Exposed sites:**	
All those for north walls plus:		All those for north walls plus:		Berberis (some E)	Potentilla
Campsis	Wisteria	Buddleia (some E)	Magnolia (E)	Buddleia davidii	Ribes
Lathyrus		Chimonanthus	Rhododendron (E)	Conifers (E)	Santolina (E)
		Choisya (E)	Viburnum	Cotoneaster (some E)	Senecio (E)
		Elaeagnus (E)	(some E)	Cytisus (E)	Spiraea
		Escallonia (E)	Weigela	Elaeagnus (E)	Viburnum
				Erica (E)	(some E)
*E = Evergreen				Ilex (E)	Weigela

SHRUBS AND CLIMBING PLANTS

ABUTILON

Abutilon is mostly tropical in origin, and is usually grown as a greenhouse, conservatory or pot plant in this country, but two of the species can be grown outdoors in favoured sites in the south and west of England, and are well worth attempting for the sake of their beautiful, exotic-looking flowers. *A. vitifolium* is the

Abutilon

hardier, and if grown as a wall shrub in a sheltered position could even succeed in areas farther north. It grows to 1.8m (6ft) – more if on a good site – and produces masses of large mauve flowers from May to September, or later in good years. 'Album' is a white cultivar. *A. megapotamicum* is less hardy, but is worth attempting for its unusual flowers, produced from late April right through the summer, red and yellow and pendant,

looking like fuchsia flowers. It can grow to 2.4m (8ft) in good conditions. *A. M.* 'Variegatum' has yellow and green leaves.

General care: Abutilon prefers a sunny site, as sheltered as possible, preferably against a wall. Any garden soil will do. Depending on the site, it will probably need protection from frost or cold with bracken or straw in anything but the mildest winter, and in any case the young plants should be given routine winter protection until they are fully grown. Little pruning is needed, apart from removal of dead or diseased shoots in the spring.

Propagation: All the species can be raised from seed, which is freely produced. Sow in pots in spring at 18°C (65°F). But named varieties will only come true if raised from semi-hardwood cuttings. Take shoots any time in the summer and strike in pots of a 50–50 mixture of peat and sand.

Pests and diseases: Generally disease-free, but mealy bugs cause sticky brown patches on the leaves. Spray with malathion.

BERBERIS

Berberis is a trouble-free, easy shrub grown for its striking flowers and berries. It will succeed almost anywhere, and does not need the protection of a wall, but is often placed near one because it looks so good there. *B. darwinii* is one of the most splendid species, growing

to 3m (10ft), evergreen, with tiny holly-like leaves, masses of dark yellow or orange flowers followed by blue-purple berries. It makes a fine screen or hedge plant. Flowers in May. Another good screen shrub is *B. gagnepainii*, evergreen, up to 1.8m (6ft) in height, with an upright growth habit. Also May-flowering. *B. thunbergii* is deciduous, with brilliant red autumn colours. The variety 'Atropurpurea' has purple leaves.

General care: Berberis is easy to look after, and is tolerant of poor soil conditions. Plant in March and, if using for screen or hedging, set about 60cm (2ft) apart. *B. aggregata* needs a sunny site for good autumn leaf colour, but the rest will succeed anywhere. No pruning is needed, except for trimming of hedges.

Propagation: Berberis grows readily from seeds sown in spring in a cold frame or from berries collected in autumn.

Pests and diseases: Generally trouble-free.

BUDDLEIA

Buddleia davidii, the so-called butterfly bush, is too often seen to need a description and too easy to grow to waste a wall on, but many of the buddleias are half-hardy, or only just hardy, and are worth growing with the protection of a wall. *B. fallowiana* grows to about 2.7m (9ft), has downy white shoots, and produces very fragrant lavender flowers

plant needs some shelter from cold north and east winds, and because it can bear its flowers as early as February, it should be away from the early morning sun or the flowers will be frost-damaged.

A vast number of cultivars are available which, like those of roses, are constantly being added to. They can be red, pink, white or bi-coloured, and single, double, or semi-double and the safest way of buying is to see the camellias in flower, rather than choosing from a catalogue or description. Camellia 'Leonard Messel' is a hybrid with a complex par-

LEFT: *Berberis thunbergii* 'Atropurpurea'
BELOW: *Buddleia*

entage, growing to about 3m (10ft), hardy on a wall everywhere, with large semi-double flowers in March and April. *Camellia × williamsii* has a number of named varieties, and has the merit of giving a succession of blooms from February right through the spring. *C. reticulata* and its named cultivars are less hardy than the others, and should be attempted outdoors only in the south of the country, and against a wall.

General care: Camellias hate dry, limy soils. Before planting, the site should be dug over and plenty of compost or peat added, with extra nourishment given in the form of mulches after planting. They like cool roots, so a south wall should be

from July to September. It can be cut right down by frost, but usually grows again from the base. *B. crispa* has white down over all its leaves, giving them a silvery appearance. It grows to 3m (10ft), and produces lilac flowers from July to September. *B. globosa*, 2–3m (6½–10ft) is evergreen in most winters, and is hardy in a sheltered site. Its clusters of orange ball-shaped flowers are a charming sight in early summer.

General care: Plant buddleia in March; half-hardy ones against a west- or south-facing wall. They are happy in most soils, including chalk, but like a sunny position. Prune back *B. fallowiana* and *B. crispa* in the spring.

Propagation: Take semi-hardwood cuttings in August and strike in a 50–50 mixture of peat and sand.

Pests and diseases: Generally trouble-free.

CALLUNA (HEATHER)
See under Erica

CAMELLIA
This is one of those exotic looking plants that is easier to grow than it looks. Introduced into this country in the eighteenth century, camellias were treated as tender plants, and the Victorians devoted whole greenhouses to their culture. Gradually it was realized that many could live happily outdoors, especially in a wall environment. All camellias are evergreens, and hate lime soil.

C. japonica, the common camellia, can grow to 6m (20ft), although 2–3m (6½–10ft) is more usual. It is generally hardy, although it benefits from the protection of a wall, especially in the north. The site should be chosen carefully, since the

ABOVE: *Camellia*
BELOW RIGHT: *Ceanothus*

CAMPSIS

Campsis, or trumpet vine, is a deciduous climber producing orange and red trumpet flowers in August and September. It grows up to 12m (40ft) under ideal conditions and will climb a wall by means of its tiny aerial roots. *C. radicans* is the most common species, and the hardiest, but *C.* × *tagliabuana* 'Mme Galen' has finer flowers.

General care: To give of its best, campsis needs a sunny, warm, sheltered site and a humus-rich, well-drained soil. Plant out in the winter or early spring. The plant will have to be tied to the wall until it produces its own aerial shoots. Once it is established on the wall, campsis has to be pruned every winter to encourage the flowers: cut back the previous season's growth to within a few buds of the old wood. The flowers appear at the end of the current season's shoots.

Propagation: Campsis can be propagated readily by layering long shoots in the autumn and separating them from the parent a year later and also from semi-hardwood cuttings taken in August and grown in a cold frame.

Pests and diseases: Aphids attack tender young shoots, causing flower loss. Spray with dimethoate (systemic), formothion (which can be watered in and taken up by the roots), malathion and menazon (systemic).

Flower bud drop is caused by low temperatures and dry roots. Guard against the latter by a generous mulch.

CEANOTHUS

A native of California, ceanothus can be grown in the open on only the warmest sites in this country, and usually needs the protection of a wall. *C. dentatus* is one of the species most commonly grown. It can grow up to 3m (10ft) on a good wall site, and it produces its bright blue spikes of flowers in May and June. *C. thyrsiflorus* is about the hardiest of the evergreen species, and will grow anywhere in Britain, given the protection of a wall. It produces masses of light blue flowers in May and June, is very floriferous, and grows to

avoided. The best aspect is west, or north if the wall is sheltered. Plant in March and give support until the plant is established on the wall. Young plants should be given plenty of water during the summer, and good frost protection in the winter. Keep the soil round the plant well mulched. Camellias do not need any routine pruning.

Propagation: Take semi-hardwood cuttings in the summer and strike in pots of a 50–50 sand and peat mixture.

Pests and diseases: Frost damages the buds. Leaf discoloration is probably caused by too much lime in the soil. Treat with chelated iron.

6m (20ft) on a good site. *C. impressus*, 2.7m (9ft), bears masses of dark blue flowers in May and June. 'Autumnal Blue' is a hybrid of uncertain parentage. It is a vigorous grower, up to about 2.7m (9ft), is evergreen and hardy and as its name suggests, produces its dark blue flowers from late summer through to the autumn.

General care: Ceanothus likes a sunny site, preferably a west- or south-facing wall. It does best in a light, well-drained soil. The spring-flowering species need only light pruning when flowering is over, but 'Autumnal Blue' should have the previous year's growth cut back in spring.

Propagation: From heeled cuttings taken in late summer and struck in pots of a 50–50 peat and sand mixture with bottom heat.

Pests and diseases: Generally trouble-free.

CELASTRUS

This is a deciduous shrub which climbs by twisting its stems. Its flowers are inconspicuous, and it is grown for the beauty of its fruits, which split open in the autumn to reveal scarlet seeds behind which the inner yellow surface of the seed capsule appears like the petals of a flower. Luckily the fruits do not seem attractive to birds, so they last for months, sometimes well into the new year.

Celastrus is a vigorous grower, and the most popular species, *C. orbiculatus*, can reach 12m (40ft). It usually has male and female flowers on separate plants, in which case you have to grow one of each to get berries. There is however a hermaphrodite form, with male and female flowers on the same shrub, and you should be sure to choose this form if you are growing only one.

General care: Celastrus grow well in most garden soils, but they do not like chalk or excesses of wet or dry. Being

vigorous growers, they need a lot of feeding, and like regular mulches. Dig in plenty of compost before planting, which can be carried out any time in the winter. Celastrus do not need regular pruning, merely a tidying-up of the old wood in the winter.

Propagation: Best by layering one-year-old shoots in the autumn, choosing a hermaphrodite parent plant. Or you can root semi-hardwood cuttings in the summer, or hardwood cuttings in the winter, using a 50–50 peat and sand mixture.

Pests and diseases: Generally trouble-free.

CHAENOMELES

This is the flowering quince, and is a hardy, deciduous wall shrub. It is related to the common quince and its fruits can be eaten. *C. speciosa*, the Japanese quince, is the most commonly planted, and is the one which often starts flowering before Christmas, although its main flowering comes in March and April. It is a spreading, rather untidy

LEFT: *Chaenomeles japonica*
BELOW: *Celastrus orbiculatus*

shrub, up to about 3m (10ft) tall on a wall. The flowers of the species are red, but it has been cultivated for centuries, and there are at least a dozen varieties still available, with different coloured flowers: 'Cardinalis' (dark red), 'Moerloosii' (pink and white), 'Nivalis' (white), 'Phyllis Moore' (semi-double pink), 'Umbilicata' (salmon-pink). C. japonica is not, as you might think, Japanese quince; it is Maule's quince, and to add to the confusion the true Japanese quince is sometimes sold under the Latin name Cydonia japonica. Maule's quince is low and spreading compared with the true Japanese quince – it seldom grows higher than 90cm (3ft) – and has orange-red flowers. C. × superba is a cross between these species, and has a number of named varieties in shades of red, pink and orange.

General care: Chaenomeles

is happy in any garden soil, prefers sun but will tolerate shade, and likes a wall or fence against which to grow. Prune after flowering, tidying up the shoots as far as possible and reducing the previous year's growth to a couple of buds.

Propagation: Most successful from heeled cuttings, taken in the summer and struck in a 50–50 peat and sand mixture.

Pests and diseases: Generally trouble-free.

CHIMONANTHUS
Winter sweet is a shrub which is not planted as often as it deserves to be. It has many merits. It bears its exotic looking, fragrant flowers right through the winter, from November onward, and will provide cut flowers for the house. Its only fault is that it takes some years to come into full flowering. C. praecox is deciduous and

hardy, although it does best on a wall, where it can reach 3m (10ft). The species flowers are yellow, with purple inner petals. C. praecox 'Grandiflora' has larger flowers, but with less scent, and C. praecox 'Luteus' is pure yellow.

General care: Chimonanthus likes a south or west wall, but will tolerate any soil conditions provided they are well-drained. Plant in the spring. Once it is established and flowering, prune it every spring by removing most of the shoots that have just flowered, leaving only a few buds on each.

Propagation: Can be raised from seed, but you may have to wait 10 years from seed sowing before you get flowers. Layering in September is the easiest way of propagating, but wait two years before severing the shoot from the parent plant.

Pests and diseases: Generally trouble-free.

CHOISYA
The Mexican orange blossom bears its white, orange-blossom-like scented flowers on and off right through the summer, and even into the winter if it is mild; its main flowering is in May. It is evergreen and hardy, but should be grown as a wall shrub in the north, and even in the south it does better on a wall, reaching a height of 2–3m (6½–10ft). Not only the flowers are fragrant: the leaves, too, give off scent when crushed.

General care: Choisya is tolerant of most soils, but not heavy clay. In the north it should be given a south-facing wall. In the south it is not so fussy and will tolerate some shade, but shelter is important. Plant in April. Regular pruning is not needed, but any tidying up should be done in June. Any frost-damaged shoots should be cut right out in the spring.

Choisya ternata, Mexican orange blossom

Propagation: From semi-hardwood cuttings taken in the summer and struck in a 50–50 sand and peat mixture.

Pests and diseases: Generally trouble-free.

CISTUS
The sun rose is among the most colourful and attractive of evergreen shrubs and bears a profusion of single rose-like flowers in summer. It grows in poor, dry, sandy and chalky soils to perfection, but must have plenty of sun and freedom from severe frost. One of the best is C. × purpureus which bears large, rose-purple, chocolate-blotched flowers on grey green rounded bushes to 90cm (3ft) in height. Somewhat hardier is C. ladanifer, the so-called gum cistus, bearing white, crimson-purple blotched flowers on dark green erect bushes to 2m (6½ft) or more tall. Hardiest of all is the similar C. laurifolius, which produces slightly smaller, white, yellow blotched blooms. Also fairly hardy are the pink-flowered 'Anne Palmer' and the white C. salvifolius, both of which are about 60cm (2ft) in height.

General care: It does not require pruning and is best without it, except for removing untidy or dead shoots. The sun rose must have a sheltered site and must be protected from freezing winds. On the whole it is only worth growing in the south and west of the British Isles, especially in the coastal 10-mile zone.

Propagation: From heeled cuttings taken in late summer and inserted in pots of 2 parts sand and 1 of peat in a case with bottom heat.

Pests and diseases: Generally trouble-free.

CLEMATIS
There are a great many species and hybrids of clematis. All climb readily by twisting their leaf stalks

Clematis 'Nellie Moser'

round the nearest available support. The hybrids, which produce large, exotic-looking blooms, are easier to grow than they look. Each variety keeps to a timetable for blooming, so by planning you can have a succession of clematis flowers right through the summer. All of the following are deciduous.

C. *montana* is vigorous, hardy, and easy to grow. It climbs as high as 9m (30ft), producing small white flowers, slightly scented, in May and June. The main problem is to keep it under control. C. *alpina*, growing to 2.4m (8ft), is not a strong grower, but produces delightful, bell-shaped blue flowers in April and May.

C. *jouiniana* grows to 3m (10ft), but needs tying to supports to help it climb. Produces lilac flowers from August to October.

C. × *jackmanii*, bred by Jackman's of Woking in Victorian times, has justifiably retained its popularity to this day. Easy to grow and vigorous, growing to 6m (20ft), it produces masses of large purple flowers, with a darker stripe, from July onward. Similar in appearance, but not in the same grouping, are the large-flowered hybrids such as 'Nellie Moser' (pink and mauve flowers in May and September), 'The President' (purple, June and September), and 'Ville de Lyon' (carmine red, June and September). All grow to about 3m (10ft) tall. Clematis gives a mass of growth starting from a small base, so a lot of plants can be put into quite a small plot.

General care: Clematis is tolerant of a lot of different growing conditions but prefers its roots in the shade in moisture-retaining soil with some chalk. Its top growth likes the sun but some flowers, such as 'Nellie Moser', bleach in sunlight and should be planted on a north wall. Heavy clay soil should be lightened with

peat or leaf mould. Clematis does not like its roots disturbed, so always use container-grown plants, putting them in at any time during the winter.

Correct pruning is essential if clematis is to give of its best in flowers. C. *montana* blooms on the previous year's growth so pruning, if done at all, should be carried out just after flowering. C. *alpina* seldom needs pruning, C. *jouiniana* may need some top growth cut back after a few years to encourage basal shoots. C. × *jackmanii* flowers on the current year's growth, and should be cut right back in February to encourage young shoots. 'Ville de Lyon' needs the same

treatment, but 'Nellie Moser' and 'The President' need only light pruning to tidy the plant.

Propagation: Clematis can be raised from seed, but the offspring are often not as good as the parents. Cuttings can be taken in July and rooted in a 50–50 mixture of peat and sand, but the most reliable way of propagating on a small scale is to layer shoots in the spring, and separate them from the parent a year later.

Pests and diseases: Clematis wilt causes shoots – often a whole young plant – to wilt and die rapidly but fresh shoots may appear from the base later. There is no reliable cure.

CONIFERS

Pines, firs, spruces, redwoods, hemlocks, cedars, larches, cypresses, junipers and yews are all described as conifers. In the main they are forest trees and too large for the average garden. However, many of them have produced smaller or really dwarf mutations which collectively are known as dwarf conifers. Those, by reason of their neat architectural shapes, wide range of foliage colours and textures, have become popular garden plants in recent years. The most useful of all are the many junipers, most of which are normally bushy or prostrate shrubs. They make splendid ground cover which, when established, requires virtually no maintenance. For this purpose, *Juniperus sabina* 'Blue Danube', *J. squamata* 'Blue Carpet' with grey-blue-green foliage, and the rich green *J. communis* 'Green Carpet' are to be recommended. Among taller junipers look out for the 2m (6½ft) tall deep green *J. chinensis* 'Kaizuka', the spreading grey-green *J. virginiana* 'Grey Owl' and the golden 'Old Gold', both about 1.2m (4ft) in height. Among small pines, try the 2m (6½ft) tall *Pinus parviflora* 'Glauca' with blue-green leaves or the 30cm (1ft) tall *P. mugo* 'Ophir' with bright gold leaves in winter. Long known and still one of the best dwarf spruces is *Picea glauca* 'Albertiana Conica', which forms a dense wide cone eventually to 2m (6½ft) or more. Among the firs, *Abies balsamea* 'Hudsonia' ('Nana') has long graced our gardens. It develops into a compact, rounded green bush to 30cm (1ft) or so in height. A most satisfying dwarf spreading and weeping conifer is the Canadian hemlock (*Tsuga canadensis*) known as 'Jeddeloh'. Eventually it can exceed 30cm (1ft) in height and double this in width. It combines well with the dwarf Lawson cypress (*Chamaecyparis lawsoniana*) called 'Ellwood's Pillar'. Blue-grey in leaf, it eventually forms dense columns to about 60cm (2ft) tall. Best known of all conifers nowadays is Leyland cypress (× *Cupressocyparis leylandii*). It has a potential height in excess of 30m (100ft) but stands clipping well and makes a good windbreak or hedge. There are green, greyish and yellowish foliaged sorts to choose from. **General care:** With the exception of the firs (*Abies*) which are best in an acid soil, all the conifers mentioned here will grow in most soils provided they are not waterlogged. For wet ground, try the deciduous dawn redwood (*Metasequoia glyptostroboides*). Except for hedging, conifers do not need pruning and are best without it.

Propagation: Dwarf conifers and those of hybrid origin (eg Leyland cypress) must be propagated by heel cuttings in early autumn in a cold frame. True species of pine, spruce, fir, cypress, etc come easily from seed sown in autumn or spring in a frame. Some of the really small varieties of pine and spruce are difficult and very slow to root, and nurserymen graft them on to seedlings of true species.

Pests and diseases: Generally trouble-free.

CORNUS

Although collectively known as dogwoods, the genus *Cornus* is a varied one, including trees and shrubs grown either for summer flowers, autumn fruits and foliage or coloured winter stems. All the hardy species are deciduous. Their flowers are small, borne in compact rounded heads and are not showy. In the so-called flowering dogwoods however, each flowerhead is surrounded by four or more large, coloured, petal-like leaves known as bracts. The best known and most reliable of this sort is *C. kousa*, a large shrub to 3m (10ft) or more with profusely borne white bracts followed by pendant strawberry-like fruits and good autumn colour. *C. florida* is even better, with bracts of white, pink or red, but it is not so easy to grow. Coloured twigged dogwoods are *C. alba* 'Sibirica' (red) and *C. stolonifera* 'Flaviramea' olive-yellow). *C. mas* is the cornelian cherry and provides a profusion of yellow (bractless) flowers on naked twigs in spring followed by edible fruits in late summer. **General care:** Coloured twigged dogwoods will grow in any soil, even wet ones. Cornelian cherry is also adaptable but the soil must be well drained. Flowering dogwoods need moisture retentive acid land, though *C. kousa* will stand some lime. Coloured twigged species are best pruned back to 30cm (1ft) above ground each spring. All the others are best left to grow naturally, except for removing untidy stems in late winter or after flowering. **Propagation:** Cuttings with a heel in late summer for all species, also hardwood cuttings in the open ground in October for the coloured twigged sorts. *Cornus mas*, *C. florida* and *C. kousa* can also be layered in autumn or raised from seed sown as soon as ripe in a cold frame; germination sometimes takes 15 months or more.

Pests and diseases: Generally trouble-free.

COTONEASTER

Cotoneaster is an easy-to-grow, red-berried shrub that includes species suitable for screening and hedges, as well as for training on walls. The two varieties most suitable for screening are both semi-evergreen: *C. × watereri* and *C. × 'Cornubia'*, both of which can reach 3m (10ft) or more, and spread almost as wide. When used as a screen, *C. × watereri* should be planted 1.5m (5ft) apart, and *C. × 'Cornubia'* 2.1m (7ft) apart, at least. These planting distances will give a very thick screen, and can be exceeded and still give satisfactory screening eventually. Another semi-evergreen is C.

Cotoneaster horizontalis

simonsii, seldom growing above 2.1m (7ft) but, because of its upright habit of growth, suitable for a screen or hedge. Plantings for the latter use should be 30cm (12 in) apart. *C. horizontalis* is a deciduous species whose shoots and laterals form a regular herringbone pattern which looks very effective when trained on a wall or wooden fence and as it is deciduous, you get the bonus of the autumnal tints before leaf-fall. It will reach a height of 1.8m (6ft) to 2.4m (8ft) when trained in this way. The prostrate evergreen *C. dammeri* and 'Skogholm' provide good ground-cover on banks and between shrubs.

General care: Cotoneaster is not fussy about site or soil, and in fact seems to prefer poor soil. Plant any time in the winter and, if growing for hedging, shorten the shoots to encourage a bushy growth habit. Routine pruning is not needed, but hedges should be trimmed.

Propagation: It can be grown easily from seed harvested in the autumn, but is unlikely to grow true to type. It is

better to use heeled cuttings, taken in late summer and struck in a 50–50 peat and sand mixture, or to layer some shoots, which can then be separated from the parent a year later.

Pests and diseases: Birds often eat the berries. Aphids can be sprayed with malathion. Fireblight, which is on the increase, can affect cotoneaster. Its symptom is dark brown, shrivelled leaves, caused by a bacterium. There is no chemical cure. Infected branches should be cut back well below the infected area and burned, and the secateurs should be disinfected afterwards. (Fireblight is a notifiable disease.)

CYTISUS

Cytisus is the well-known and popular garden broom (*Cytisus scoparius*). There are many cultivars, in shades of yellow, pink, red and white. Well worth growing as a wall shrub is the very different *C. battandieri*, the pineapple or Moroccan broom, so-called from the scent of its flowers which are

Daphne

bright yellow and borne in June and July. It is a spectacular shrub that will grow up to 4.6m (15ft) on a wall, its light green leaves covered in silky hairs looking particularly good against red brick. It is evergreen, but may lose most of its foliage in a severe winter.

General care: A sunny site and rather poor soil are preferred. Some chalk is tolerated. Use container-grown plants, putting them in in September or March. Prune in the summer, removing the shoots which have just finished flowering and you will get young shoots to provide next year's flowers.

Propagation: Best grown from seed. Leave some pods on the plant to ripen, and harvest when they turn brown. Keep in a cool place throughout the winter, and sow seeds in 9cm ($3\frac{1}{2}$in) pots of soil-less compost in April.

Pests and diseases: Generally trouble-free.

DAPHNE

Renowned for its scented blossom, daphne contains no less than 70 species, few of which are in general cultivation. They are small shrubs, some evergreen, others deciduous, usually freely bearing their clusters of small tubular flowers. Best known is the erect 90–120cm (3–4ft) tall, deciduous, mezereon (*D. mezereum*) with rose-purple flowers on naked twigs in winter and spring. *D. m.* 'Alba' is white-bloomed. About the same height but more widespreading is *D. odora*, a splendid evergreen with red-purple buds opening to almost white in late winter or spring. The commonest form has narrowly yellow-margined leaves ('Aureomarginata'). Mat-forming and magnificent when well grown is *D. cneorum*, aptly known as the garland flower. It is not a very distinguished evergreen until early summer when every shoot tip bursts into a little posy of

Cytisus battandieri, pineapple broom

rich pink, highly fragrant blossom.

General care: Almost any well-drained soil is acceptable provided it is neither too dry nor too wet. *D. cneorum* must have a sunny site; the other two will stand partial shade. *D. odora* is not totally hardy and needs a position sheltered from cold winds.

Propagation: By taking cuttings with a heel in late summer for the evergreen species or by layering in autumn or spring and leaving for at least a full year. *D. mezereum* is easiest by seed, which must be sown when ripe in a cold frame if germination is to occur in the next spring. Seedlings may flower the second spring and certainly the third.

Pests and diseases: *D. mezereum* in particular is prone to virus infection which causes a yellow mottling and crippling of the leaves, then dieback and death. It is best to destroy any plant as soon as the virus symptoms are recognizable. All daphnes are liable to die suddenly though this is not as common an occurrence as statements in the popular gardening press would suggest. Virus infection may be a contributing or major cause of death.

DEUTZIA

This genus of carefree shrubs is prolific with its trusses of five-petalled white or pink flowers. *D.* × *rosea* forms rounded bushes to 1.2m (4ft) in height with pink flowers. *D.* × 'Montrose' is almost twice as tall and bears purplish-rose blooms. *D. scabra* is erect and can exceed 4.2m (8ft). The pink-tinted buds open pure white. *D. s.* 'Flore Pleno' is double white tinted rose-purple.

General care: Ordinary soil and sun or partial shade are all that are needed.

Propagation: Take hardwood cuttings in autumn or semi-hardwood cuttings in late summer.

Pests and diseases: Generally trouble-free.

ELAEAGNUS

Grown for its decorative foliage, elaeagnus is particularly

Elaeagnus pungens

useful for screening or hedging, especially near the sea, owing to its ability to stand up to salt-laden winds. Some elaeagnus are deciduous, but the two sorts described and recommended here are evergreens. *E.* × *ebbingei*, introduced from Holland in the 1930s, is particularly useful because of its speed of growth. It will reach a height of 2.7–3m (9–10ft) a few years after planting. Its leaves are deep glossy green above, silvery beneath and there is a named variety, 'Gilt Edge', which has yellow leaf margins. *E. pungens*, which can grow to the same height but is slower to do so, has a number of named cultivars that do not grow so tall or so fast as the species: 'Dicksonii' (broad yellow leaf margins), 'Frederickii' (yellow leaves with green margins) grow only to 1.8m (6ft), 'Maculata' (variegated yellow and green), to 2.4m (8ft).

General care: Elaeagnus is very accommodating as to site and soil, being happy in poor, thin conditions, and tolerant of chalk. Plant container-grown specimens in April, 45cm (18in) apart if grown for hedging, 90cm (3ft) apart if for screens. Shorten the shoots to encourage bushy growths. No routine pruning is needed, but hedges should be trimmed in mid-summer. Remove any all-green shoots as soon as they appear on variegated varieties.

Propagation: From semi-hardwood cuttings taken in summer.

Pests and diseases: Generally trouble-free, though *E.* × *ebbingei* is heir to a die-back of branches, occasionally the whole plant, caused by coral spot fungus. Remove and burn dead stems promptly.

ERICA and CALLUNA

The heaths (erica) and heathers (calluna) are inseparable in their garden value and so close botanically as to have once been classified together. Those mentioned here are hardy, wiry-stemmed shrubs with tiny leaves and a profusion of little bell-flowers throughout the year. They provide

Erica

ground cover which is highly decorative in its own right. Beds or whole gardens devoted to them have become popular as a labour-saving device during the past 20-30 years. There are hundreds of cultivars of calluna, some with coloured foliage and producing flowers in a wide range of red, pink, purple and white shades. Only a few can be mentioned here, many more being found in garden centres and nurseries. All grow about 30cm (1ft) in height and bloom in late summer and early autumn. 'Anne Marie' has fully double pale pink and cerise flowers. 'Anthony Davis' has grey foliage and white flowers. 'Beoley Gold' bears white flowers above bright gold foliage. 'Darkness' is dark green with crimson blooms. 'Golden Feather' is yellow in summer, reddish-orange in winter and produces unremarkable mauve flowers. 'Robert Chapman' has purple flowers and foliage which changes from gold to bronze to red. Following true heather is the so-called winter heath *Erica carnea*, which flowers mainly in winter and spring and rarely exceeds 25cm (10in) in height. 'Anne Sparkes' has bronze and orange-red tinted foliage and red-purple flowers. 'January Sun' is half the normal size with pink flowers and gold-green leaves. 'King George' is an old cultivar but still one of the best pinks. 'Ruby Glow' has a compact habit and ruby-red blooms. 'Springwood White' is mat-forming and vigorous, producing its white flowers freely. The best summer ericas are *E. cinerea* and *E. vagans*. The latter grows to 45cm (1½ft) or more in height with a greater spread. 'Lyonesse' is white, 'Mrs D. F. Maxwell' rose-crimson and 'St Keverne' salmon pink. The bell heather (*E. cinerea*) forms spreading bushlets to 20cm (8in) tall. 'Foxhollow Mahogany' has dwarf foliage

and mahogany red flowers. 'Hookstone' is a strong-growing white. 'Pink Ice' is a glowing pink. 'Stephen Davis' has blooms of a startlingly bright magenta. The white 'Rock Pool' is largely grown for its gold foliage, which takes on coppery-bronze hues in winter.

General care: Well-drained soil and sun are essential for the heaths and heathers and, except for *E. carnea*, lime-free soil is needed. Pruning is controversial but cutting off the spent flower spikes does promote compact, floriferous plants of lawn-like neatness.

Propagation: Cuttings in late summer in a cold frame in 50–50 peat and sand is the easiest method, but for a few extra plants, layering in spring is recommended, severing one year later.

Pests and diseases: Generally untouched by pests but dieback can be a nuisance in some areas. Foliage yellows and looks small and thin, dying first in patches, then whole plants. Destroy infected plants promptly. In future make sure the site is well-drained and keep watering, feeding and mulching to a minimum.

ESCALLONIA

This South American shrub is much favoured for its pretty red or pink flowers which are sometimes borne right through the summer and autumn. It is hardy only in the south and west: elsewhere it needs the protection of a wall. The most popular of the evergreen species is *E. rubra* and, in the south and west near the sea, its variety *macrantha*, a favourite for hedging and screening and in seaside towns for its ability to stand up to salt-laden winds. More useful is its cultivar, 'C. F. Ball' which is hardier and bears red flowers. Hybrid cultivars suitable for hedges or screening include 'Donard Seedling' (1.8m [6ft], pink fragrant flowers in June and July), 'Crimson Spire' (1.8m [6ft], quick-growing red flow-

ers), and 'Slieve Donard, (2.1m [7ft], pink flowers in June, probably the hardiest of all).

General care: Escallonia is happy in any well-drained soil, including chalk. It likes a sunny site. Plant in April, 45cm (18in) apart if it is being used for hedging, and 75cm (30in) apart for screens. Routine pruning is not needed, and hedges should be lightly sheared once after flowering only, or you will get few flowers the following year.

Propagation: From heeled cuttings, taken at the end of the summer, and struck in 50–50 peat and sand mixture.

Pests and diseases: Generally trouble-free.

EUONYMUS

The form of euonymus grown on walls is the evergreen *E. fortunei*, also known as winter creeper. Like ivy, it climbs by the roots which appear along its stems. Flowers and fruits are insignificant and the plants are grown for their foliage. The species plant, which has dark green leaves, grows to a height of 5m (15ft), but the named cultivars are usually lower growing. 'Colorata', which reaches the same height as the species, has unusual foliage that turns purple in winter and changes back to green in

Euonymus 'Emerald 'n' Gold'

spring. 'Emerald 'n' Gold' and 'Emerald Gaiety' are cultivars from the United States, both with green leaves edged with yellow and are low climbers. 'Variegatus', also known as 'Gracilis' and 'Argenteomarginata', has white bordered leaves and can attain 3m (10ft) in height.

General care: Plant in April in any ordinary soil. Will tolerate chalk and any aspect. A poor soil often produces better leaf variations and colourings. No pruning is needed, apart from what is necessary to keep the plants going in the right direction. Like ivy, they sometimes need encouragement to start them climbing.

Propagation: Either soft or semi-hardwood cuttings pulled from the plant in late summer and pushed into a 50–50 peat/sand mixture.

Pests and diseases: Aphids, especially blackfly, can be troublesome and should be sprayed with malathion or a systemic insecticide.

FORSYTHIA

Springbells is an easy-to-grow, popular shrub whose brilliant yellow flowers appear in spring before the foliage. Some forsythia are especially suitable as wall shrubs, or for hedging or screening. *F. suspensa*, the weeping forsythia, is suitable for a north or east wall, where it can reach 3m (10ft). It has a number of varieties: *F. suspensa fortunei* is the tallest; *F. suspensa sieboldii* has thin, very pendulous shoots; *F. suspensa atrocaulis* has pale, lemon-yellow flowers and stems that are purple when young. *F. × intermedia*, a hybrid of *F. suspensa*, is most suitable for hedging or screening. It grows to 2.4m (8ft) or more, and carries masses of flowers. It is most commonly grown as the cultivar 'Spectabilis' but 'Lynwood' has richer hued flowers.

General care: Forsythia is very easy to grow and is happy with any soil and aspect. It is especially successful in town gardens where its bright yellow flowers brighten a dull corner. Plant

Garrya

any time in the winter. If using *F. × intermedia* as hedging, space the young plants 45cm (18in) apart; if for screening 75cm (30in) apart. Prune *F. suspensa* and its varieties as soon as they have flowered, cutting back the laterals to leave a couple of buds on each. *F. × intermedia* grown as a hedge or screen should be clipped lightly only after flowering. Too-vigorous pruning of forsythia will reduce next year's flowers.

Propagation: Cuttings 30cm (12in) long of the current year's growth, taken in the autumn and pushed into the soil, will be ready for transplanting a year later.

Pests and diseases: Birds eat the flower buds, especially in country gardens. Spray with a bird repellent if you can find an effective one; if not, net. Otherwise trouble-free.

FUCHSIA

For grace, beauty and eye-catching colour the fuchsias are hard to beat. Excellent as pot plants, many are also surprisingly hardy and can be used as hardy perennials or shrubs. Hardiest of all is the Chilean species *T. magellanica gracilis* with slender red and purple blooms. Its variegated form 'Versicolor' has greyish leaves splashed pink and white. Best known are the many large-flowered cultivars, some double, in shades of white, pink, purple, almost blue and red. Recommended for garden use are 'Alice Hoffman' (pink and white single), 'Brilliant' (red and purple double), 'Mme Cornelissen' (red and white single), 'Mrs Popple' (red and purple with cerise veins, single).

General care: Ordinary soil ideally enriched with humus, and sun or partial shade give good results.

Propagation: Take cuttings in spring, summer or autumn, either soft tips or more mature growth.

Pests and diseases: Watch for capsid bugs and aphids.

Forsythia

GARRYA

The evergreen garrya is grown for its long, pendulous catkins, which it bears from February or earlier, until April. It is hardy in the south, but needs the protection of a wall in the north. *G. elliptica* is the only species commonly grown in Britain. The green-grey male catkins, about 20cm (8in) long, are the most spectacular, and male plants are the ones usually available at nurseries and garden centres. If a female plant is bought and planted nearby, it will produce brown-purple berries. 'James Roof' is an American cultivar with especially long catkins, about 30cm (12in) long. Garrya does not like damp sites. It will tolerate any aspect, but a south-facing wall produces the best catkins.

General care: Garrya hates being transplanted, so make sure the site is right before you plant, and use container-grown specimens. Garrya grows in any soil, but it must be well-drained. Give some protection to the young plant in the first winter or two, especially if they are hard, by means of straw or bracken, or some glass leaning up

against the wall. Tidying up is the only pruning needed.

Propagation: Take semi-hardwood cuttings at the end of the summer and root them in 9cm (3½in) pots of a 50–50 peat and sand mixture.

Pests and diseases: Generally trouble-free, but any frost-damaged shoots should be pruned away in the spring.

HEDERA

Hedera (ivy) is a vigorous, evergreen climber which clings to walls by means of aerial roots. Old ivy plants which have reached the top of their supports cease to produce the aerial roots, but change to an adult form of the plant with flowers and fruits. *H. helix* is the common English ivy, with plain dark green leaves. *H. colchica* (Persian ivy), and *H. canariensis* (Canary Island ivy) have larger more handsome leaves, the former being the best and hardiest. Cultivars of all these species are available, with variegated leaves, including mixtures of yellow, cream, silver and white. They are known by various different names, some confusing to the non-expert, and the safest and easiest way of getting the variations you want, since the plants are evergreen, is by looking before you buy.

General care: Ivies are very tolerant of soil and site conditions, but a sunny wall encourages them to produce the best colour variations in their leaves. Plant out in the spring, pegging the stems flat to the soil with the growing tips pointing towards the wall.

Propagation: From cuttings, taken in summer and put into pots with a 50–50 peat and sharp sand mixture, or by layering at any time. But if you want climbing plants, take your material from the juvenile shoots with aerial roots. If you propagate them from the adult growth, the plants will become ivy bushes.

Pests and diseases: Generally trouble-free.

HIBISCUS

Although mainly a tropical genus, there are two hardy hibiscuses, *H. sinosyriacus* and *H. syriacus*. Both are similar deciduous shrubs of rounded habit to 2m (6½ft) in height. In late summer and autumn they bear single or semi-double blooms in a range of colours. *H. sinosyriacus* 'Ruby Glow' is white and cerise. *H. syriacus* 'Bluebird' is violet-blue, 'Pink Giant' has large rose-pink blooms, and 'William R. Smith' is pure white.

General care: Ordinary, even poorish soil is acceptable but the site must be sunny.

Propagation: Take cuttings with a heel in late summer.

Pests and diseases: Generally trouble-free.

HYDRANGEA

Hydrangea petiolaris is the climbing version of the common hydrangea. It is deciduous, hardy and vigorous, and can reach as high as 15m (50ft). It climbs like ivy, by aerial roots on its stems. In June it produces masses of flat, white lacy heads of flowers. It likes a shady site – a north wall is ideal.

General care: Plant in the spring in well-drained soil which has had plenty of compost added to it. Secure the stems to the wall to give the growing tips a chance to cling firmly, and water during dry spells. Once they are established they need very little attention beyond light pruning in the winter or spring to keep them tidy. A well-established plant is self-supporting.

Propagation: Cuttings of non-flowering shoots, about 7.5cm–10cm (3–4in) long, taken in summer and put in a 50–50 mixture of peat and sand will root by autumn. Layering in spring is even more certain.

Pests and diseases: Generally trouble-free.

HYPERICUM

The flowers of St John's wort have something of the appeal of a rose but always in a shade of cheerful yellow. *H. calycinum* is widely used for ground cover and can be invasive. *H.* 'Hidcote' is a true, almost evergreen shrub eventually 90cm (3ft) or more tall and blooms over a long period. *H. prolificum* forms a slightly smaller, rounded bush with flowers having long, dense stamen brushes of great charm.

General care: Ordinary fertile soil and sun or partial shade are basic requirements.

Propagation: Divide *H. calycinum* in autumn and spring. Take cuttings of the rest in late summer.

Pests and diseases: Generally trouble-free.

ILEX

Ilex is the botanical name for holly. The evergreen forms are very useful for hedging and screening, especially as they are tolerant of quite hard pruning and trimming. *I. × altaclarensis* is hardy and evergreen, and will in time attain a height of 9m (30ft). It is particularly useful in seaside areas, owing to its ability to stand up to salt-laden gales. *I. aquifolium* is our native English holly. It does not grow quite so tall – 7.6m (25ft) – but has the advantage of yielding the familiar red berries for Christmas decorations.

Male and female flowers are borne on separate plants and the berries appear only on the female plants, but some male plants must be grown nearby to fertilize the females. There are also one or two hermaphrodite varieties of *I. aquifolium* that can produce berries without males. There are a large number of named varieties of both these species of holly, with variegated leaves and different colours of berries.

General care: Holly will tolerate any aspect and soil, although it prefers some moisture at its roots. Plant in May, about 60cm (2ft) apart for hedging and at least 1.2m (4ft) for screening. Make sure you plant some males to fertilize the females if you want berries. If you are planting on an exposed site, erect small screens of polythene sheeting or hessian to protect against the prevailing wind until the young plants are established. Trimming and pruning should be done in April.

Hydrangea petiolaris

Ilex aquifolium 'Aureo-Marginata'

Propagation: Take small heeled cuttings in autumn from that year's growth and strike in a 50–50 mixture of peat and sand. Alternatively, layer some shoots in October or November. In either case, wait two years before putting the young plants into their permanent positions.
Pests and diseases: Birds take the berries, and are difficult to stop. Brown blotches on the leaves are caused by holly leaf miner. Spray with HCH at intervals in May and June to prevent further infection. Later use a systemic insecticide, eg dimethoate.

IPOMOEA
Ipomoea is the Latin name for morning glory, so called because its flowers open in the morning sunshine but fade by the end of the afternoon. It looks and behaves like our own convolvulus, and is related to it, but comes from South America, and is not hardy in this country. 'Heavenly Blue' is the most popular variety – a cultivar of *I. tricolor* which produces purple and blue flowers from July to September. It grows to about 3m (10ft). *I. purpurea* is similar but has smaller flowers and is slightly

hardier. The species flowers are purple, but there are different coloured cultivars, including 'Alba' with white flowers and 'Rosea' with pink flowers.
General care: Ipomoea likes a warm, sunny, sheltered site, although *I. purpurea* will tolerate some shade. It is treated as an annual in this country. It can be grown up a south-facing wall or fence, or up sticks or poles in a sheltered corner. It likes a compost-rich soil, and needs plenty of water during the growing season. Plant out 30cm (12in) apart in late May, when all danger of frost has passed, but in a cold spring delay planting until the weather warms up.
Propagation: Germinate the seeds at a temperature of 18°C (65°F) in a soil-less compost after soaking for 24 hours. Prick out into 10cm (4in) pots, and harden off carefully.
Pests and diseases: The young shoots may be attacked by aphids, leafhoppers or thrips. Spray with malathion at once. Generally disease-free.

JASMINUM
There are 200–300 species of jasmine but most are suit-

Ipomoea, morning glory

able only for a conservatory or glasshouse, or occasionally for warm and sheltered positions in the west and south. The two jasmines most commonly grown in this country are *J. nudiflorum*, producing yellow flowers at intervals throughout the winter, and *J. officinale*, the common jasmine, producing fragrant white flowers from mid summer to early autumn. They are both tolerant of shady sites, and need only ordinary, well-drained garden soil. *J. officinale* climbs by twisting its stems, is a vigorous grower, and will go up to 9m (30ft) if it can find the support. It is deciduous, but will retain its leaves in a mild winter or position. *J. nudiflorum*, which can reach a height of 4.6m (15ft), is not a climber and must have its leading shoots fixed to the wall or fence. The laterals will curve downwards by themselves.

General care: *J. officinale* should not be pruned unless it is necessary to keep it in shape, and pruning too hard will cause it to miss a year's flowering. But *J. nudiflorum* needs a lot of pruning to encourage plenty of flowers in the winter. As soon as it has finished flowering, prune the laterals back to within a few centimetres of the leading shoots, to encourage the new growth which will bear the coming winter's flowers. Cut old wood back to the ground from time to time to encourage young basal shoots.
Propagation: Take semi-hard cuttings at the end of summer and root in a 50–50 peat and sand mixture, or layer one-year old stems in spring.
Pests and disease: Generally trouble-free.

JUNIPERUS
See under Conifers

Golden privet, Ligustrum ovalifolium 'Aureum'

KERRIA

Kerria, or Jew's mallow, is a 1.2m (4ft) tall deciduous shrub with green stems, bearing bright yellow flowers in April and May. It is most commonly seen in its double-flowered cultivar, 'Pleniflora', or bachelor's buttons, which grows much taller than the single-flowered species, reaching 2m (6½ft) or more. It is quite hardy, but in cold northern sites it is happier grown against a wall.

General care: Kerria is happy with any ordinary soil, and a sunny or half-shady site. Plant any time during the winter. Cut back the flowered shoots of 'Pleniflora' to promote the new growth on which the plant will flower next year. At the same time remove a few of the old shoots at ground level to promote new basal growth. The original species is best left to develop its normal spreading and shapely habit.

Propagation: The easiest way is to divide the clump of shoots any time during the winter. Alternatively, take cuttings from the lateral growths at the end of the summer, and strike them in 50–50 sand and peat.

Pests and diseases: Generally trouble-free.

KOLKWITZIA

This very hardy deciduous shrub can attain 3m (10ft) tall on good soil. In early summer, every twig is wreathed in a cloud of exquisite pink fox-glove-shaped flowers and it then fully merits its vernacular name, beauty bush.

General care: Ordinary soil which does not dry out is suitable and a site in partial shade or sun, the latter assuring a heavy crop of bloom.

Propagation: Take cuttings with a heel in late summer or sow seed in spring.

Pests and diseases: Generally trouble-free.

LATHYRUS

This is the group which includes sweet peas and everlasting peas. All are hardy. *L. odoratus* is the familiar garden sweet pea, an annual producing fragrant flowers from June to September. There are many named varieties in a vast range of colours, but not all are fragrant. They climb by tendrils to a height of up to 2.7m (9ft), depending on variety and growing conditions. Among the perennial species are *L. latifolius*, height to 2.4m (8ft), purplish flowers from June to September; and *L. rotundifolius*, the Persian everlasting pea, height to 2m (6½ft), pink flowers from June to August. Lathyrus like full sun, and a rich, well-drained soil with some chalk.

General care: Plant annuals 25cm (10in) apart, and perennials 60cm (2ft) apart. Grow up pea sticks, mesh, trellis, etc. Sweet peas need plenty of nourishment: dig a lot of compost into the site before planting, and give a weekly feed of a liquid fertilizer while they are in flower. Annuals and perennials should have the seed pods removed as they appear, to encourage repeat flowering.

Propagation: Nick the seed coats to encourage germination. Annuals sown in September for the following year give the earliest flowers. Sow in seed boxes of compost, or direct into the site. Otherwise, sow in March, in boxes or into the soil. Perennials should be sown in boxes in a cold frame in March, potted on, and planted out in October.

Pests and diseases: Aphids and thrips should be controlled with malathion.

Lathyrus are subject to a number of fungal diseases. Some cause the leaves to brown and develop white patches and the plant to wilt. Spray with fungicide.

LIGUSTRUM

This is the familiar privet, grossly over-planted since its introduction to Britain in Victorian times, but still useful for situations where nothing else will grow, such as poor soil, or in atmospheric pollution. *L. ovalifolium* is the common privet with glossy oval green leaves and short panicles of creamy flowers produced in July. It will grow to 4.6m (15ft), but is usually kept lower by clipping. Cultivars include 'Aureum', the golden privet, and 'Variegatum', which has cream leaf margins. They do not grow so tall.

General care: Privet is very easy to grow, and will put up with poor soil and other adverse conditions. Plant 45cm (18in) apart in April and cut back all shoots by half. Each autumn reduce new shoots by half to encourage the shoots at the base and to prevent the plant becoming leggy. Privet will take any amount of clipping.

Propagation: By hardwood cuttings taken in the autumn and struck in the open ground.

Pests and diseases: Generally trouble-free.

LONICERA

A range of honeysuckles, which include Britain's native wild plant. All climb by twining, but not all are fragrant. *L. periclymenum*, our wild species, is usually grown as are its cultivated varieties, which give a longer flowering period – 'Belgica' (or early Dutch honeysuckle) and 'Serotina' (or late Dutch). By planting these two you can have flowers from May to October. They are deciduous, and grow to about 4.6m (15ft). *L × brownii* (scarlet trumpet honeysuckle) grows to about 3.6m (12ft), and flowers from June to October. It is evergreen in mild winter conditions, and is available in a number of striking named varieties, but it has no scent. *L. caprifolium* (goat-leaved honeysuckle) is similiar to our native honeysuckle, but is more vigorous, growing up to 6m (20ft), and more heavily scented. It is sometimes found naturalized in the south. *L. japonica* (Japanese honeysuckle) is the most vigorous species of all, climbing sometimes to 9m (30ft). It is evergreen, and produces very sweetly fragrant flowers in summer and autumn but they are not as large as those of most of the other honeysuckles.

General care: Plant deciduous climbers in the winter, evergreens in April. Honeysuckles need a good soil, with plenty of humus. They will grow in sun and shade. Prune lightly to remove old wood and tidy the plant up. Too-heavy pruning will reduce flowering.

Propagation: Raise from cuttings taken in the autumn or by layering shoots bent down in October, which can be severed and planted out a year later.

ABOVE: *Lonicera*
LEFT: *Magnolia grandiflora*

Pests and diseases: Aphids can stop the plant from flowering. Spray with malathion or a systemic insecticide. Dust powdery mildew with sulphur.

MAGNOLIA

If you have a south-facing house wall, there is no finer thing you can plant against it than a *Magnolia grandiflora*, a magnificent wall shrub introduced from the southern United States in the eighteenth century. Given time, it will grow to 7.6m (25ft) or more. An evergreen, it flowers from July to September, with — as its name suggests – the biggest blooms of any magnolia, creamy white, heavily fragrant, and up to 22.5cm (9in) across the bowl. Unlike some magnolias, it is not a lime-hater. Among the cultivars available are two which get over one of the disadvantages of magnolias by producing flowers on young plants. They are 'Exmouth' and 'Goliath' which, as its name suggests, has bigger flowers than those of the species.

General care: Plant in April, and provide shelter from cold winds, especially when the plant is young. Put in stakes for its support until it is established on the wall, and give a spring mulch of compost or leaf mould. Only its main shoots need to be tied to the wall. In spring cut out basal shoots that are facing away from the wall.

Propagation: Layering is the most successful method. Peg the shoots down in the spring, but allow at least two years before separating from the parent.

Pests and diseases: Generally trouble-free, but frost-damaged shoots may become diseased. Guard against this by cutting back the damaged shoots in spring.

MAHONIA
Glossy, large, evergreen leaves which are handsome in their own right, and showy yellow flowers from autumn to spring are the hallmark of this genus. Best known is the Oregon grape (*M. aquifolium*), a suckering species to 1.2m (4ft) or more tall with leaves which often take on red or bronze tones in winter. Its rich yellow flowers borne in early spring are followed by blue-black edible berries. Finest of the hardy larger sorts is the hybrid 'Charity', an erect shrub to 2m (6½ft) or more with leaves 45-60cm (1½– 2ft) in length, and long trusses of yellow flowers in autumn and early winter. Less statuesque but still very good garden value is

Mahonia

M. *japonica* (one of 'Charity's' parents). Slower growing but eventually to the same height, it has somewhat shorter leaves and paler flowers which open successionally from autumn to the following spring.

General care: Mahonias will grow in any well-drained, but not dry, fertile soil. Enrich sandy and chalky soils with plenty of organic matter, eg peat, garden compost or leaf mould. Pruning should be restricted to the removal of dead or untidy stems.

Propagation: True species are easy from seed sown when ripe in a cold frame but seedling growth is fairly slow. M. *aquifolium* is best divided in spring or early autumn; suckers can be removed from 'Charity' and *japonica* at the same time.

Pests and diseases: Generally trouble-free.

PARTHENOCISSUS
This group of vigorous climbers includes the Virginia creeper, and that name is often applied to the whole group. They are deciduous, climb by tendrils which often have sticky pads on the ends, and are grown for their ornamental leaves, which change colour spectacularly in the autumn. P. *quinquefolia* is the true Virginia creeper from North America, which has been cultivated for centuries. Since it can climb to 21m (70ft), it can be difficult to control, and is best left to clamber up tall trees. P. *tricuspidata* is often called 'Virginia creeper' – wrongly, since it comes from Japan. It is the Boston ivy, commonly planted on walls, where it can go to 15m (50ft) or more, and give a marvellous display of crimson foliage in the autumn. P. *henryana* (Chinese Virginia creeper) grows to 7.6m (25ft) and has distinctive rich green, silvery-veined leaves in summer which also turn red in autumn. It needs a sheltered site.

General care: Dig a large planting hole – about 45cm (18in) square and fill with a humus-rich soil. Use container-grown plants, as par-

thenocissus does not like root disturbance. Support it with sticks until it climbs by itself. Once established, it needs little attention.

Propagation: Take hardwood cuttings in late autumn and push them into the ground to root; or layer long shoots. Semi-hardwood cuttings can be taken in late summer and rooted in pots.

Pests and diseases: Generally trouble-free.

PASSIFLORA
There are hundreds of species of passion flowers, but only two are hardy enough to be grown outdoors in this country, and even they must have sheltered sites. Frost may cut the tops to the ground, but the plant usually grows back in the spring. P. *caerulea* (the blue or common passion flower) is the one most often planted in this country. It climbs to about 7.6m (25ft). The species flowers are blue, purple and white, but there is a cultivar, 'Constance Elliott', which is entirely white; both open from mid to late summer into autumn. Egg-shaped, pale orange yellow fruits may follow.

General care: Find a sheltered site, preferably with full sun. Plant in ordinary garden soil when danger of frost has passed, and while the plant is young give it winter protection with bracken, straw, glass or plastic sheeting. Help the young plant to climb by tying it to a trellis or mesh until it has started to pull itself up. Confine pruning to tidying up and removing weak growth.

Propagation: Take semi-ripe cuttings in summer and root them in pots of 50–50 peat and sand mixture, or grow from seed, germinating at a temperature of 21°C (70°F) and planting out in May after hardening off.

Pests and diseases: Generally trouble-free.

See p. 76 for illustration

ABOVE: *Passiflora caerulea; see p. 75 for entry.*
BELOW: *Philadelphus*

wet soils, though light sandy or chalky ones should be enriched with organic matter. To build up shapely, free-blooming shrubs, cut back flowered stems by two thirds once the last blossom has faded.

Propagation: Take semi-hardwood cuttings in late summer in a propagating case. Take hardwood cuttings in late autumn when they can be inserted in the open ground.

Pests and diseases: Generally trouble-free.

PHOTINIA

The evergreen members of this genus of shrubs and small trees make splendid specimen plants and hedges with a difference. One of the best is *P. × fraseri* 'Red Robin' which grows 1.8–2.4m (6–8ft) in height. The glossy leaves start bright red and are produced in flushes in spring and summer. There is also a bonus of clustered small white flowers in summer.

General care: Most soils which do not dry out are suitable, including those containing chalk.

Propagation: Take cuttings in late summer, ideally with bottom heat.

Pests and diseases: Generally trouble-free.

POLYGONUM

Polygonum baldschuanicum, or Russian vine, is about the fastest-growing climber in captivity. It can put on 4.9m (16ft) per season

BELOW: *Polygonum baldschuanicum, Russian vine*

PHILADELPHUS

Mock orange has long been a garden favourite with its profusion of white, sweetly scented flowers in summer. There are a few species and several good hybrids readily available from garden centres and nurserymen. All are vigorous, deciduous shrubs, the smaller cultivars being best value in the garden. Recommended are: 'Belle Etoile', of compact habit to 2m (6½ft) tall, bearing white flowers with a purple eye. 'Beauclerk', semi-spreading habit to 2.5m (8½ft) tall with large, milky flowers with a faint purplish eye. *P. coronarius* 'Aureus' is a spectacular yellow-leaved rounded shrub to 2.5m (8½ft) in height with heavily scented creamy-white flowers. It makes a particularly fine accent plant in the garden.

General care: Mock orange grows well in all but really

and cover a small house in a couple of summers. The problem is keeping it in check. It is a deciduous, twining climber, producing masses of long panicles of pale pink or white flowers from June to September. *P. aubertii*, which has similar, white flowers is very like *P. baldschuanicum*, and is often sold under that name – in fact, most of the Russian vines growing here are *P. aubertii*. It will tolerate any soil, even chalk, and any site.
General care: Plant in March. Some care of the young plant is needed, including twiggy support to start it climbing, and pinching out the leading shoots to encourage side growth, but once it is established all the Russian vine needs is controlling.
Propagation: Take semi-hardwood cuttings in August and root them in a 50–50 mixture of sand and peat.
Pests and diseases: Generally trouble-free.

POTENTILLA

The shrubby cinquefoil, *Potentilla fruticosa*, is a twiggy, bushy plant of variable habit but seldom above 90–120cm (3–4ft) in height. It has small, neat, fingered leaves and a long succession of five-petalled flowers like small dog roses but in shades of yellow, pink, red and white. Totally hardy and requiring virtually no maintenance, it is a perfect shrub for the casual or uncommitted gardener. Among the best are: 'Abbotswood', with greyish leaves and pure white flowers; 'Goldfinger' has deep, glowing yellow blooms; while 'Katherine Dykes' is primrose yellow. Pink fading to almost white typifies the new 'Princess'. 'Red Ace' is red but fades badly in hot sun. 'Tangerine' has a low spreading habit and reddish-copper flowers which contrast nicely with the cream ones of 'Tilford Cream', an equally low-growing but more compact sort.

General care: Shrubby cinquefoils grow in practically all soils, even those which are seasonally wet. Pruning is not required except to keep them shapely. Untidy specimens can be cut down to a few centimetres above soil level and will soon regenerate.
Propagation: Easy by seed sown in spring, but plants so raised from cultivars will not come true to type. Semi-hardwood cuttings taken in late summer or autumn and placed in a cold frame will root readily.
Pests and diseases: Generally trouble-free.

PRUNUS

Prunus is a genus of plants that includes apricots, peaches and cherries. *P. triloba* does best on a wall, preferably fan-trained, as it is doubtfully hardy in some districts, and in any case produces far more flowers on a sunny wall. The species carries single flowers and is seldom seen. The Chinese cultivar 'Multiplex' is the variety commonly available. It grows to 3.6m (12ft) or more on a sunny wall and carries masses of large double pink flowers from the end of March. *P. cerasifera*, the cherry plum, is an excellent screen tree, growing to 6m (20ft) or more. It carries white flowers in February and March and eventually small cherry-plums. The cultivars, which can be mixed in with the species in the screen, have different colours: 'Atropurpurea' has purple adult leaves, and 'Nigra' purple leaves and pink flowers. The cherry plum is deciduous, but another prunus, *P. laurocerasus*, the cherry laurel, is evergreen, and therefore more commonly planted for screening. It is fast-growing to 3m (10ft) or more and produces candles of white flowers in April, and fruit similar to cherries which are red at first and turn black as they ripen. Among a number

Potentilla

of named cultivars is *P. l.* 'Otto Luyken', a low-growing plant which makes excellent ground-cover.
General care: Prunus are happy in any ordinary, well-drained garden soil, and most prefer a trace of chalk in it. The evergreen species should be planted in April,

the remainder in autumn and winter. For hedging, plant 60cm (2ft) apart, and for screening 1.5m (5ft) apart, cutting back the tips of the shoots if planting for hedging. Prune back hard as soon as the flowers are finished on *P. triloba* as well as the screening prunus, to encourage young flowering shoots for next year, and use secateurs to trim the screening prunus if they need it, rather than hedge trimmers.

Propagation: All are easiest from cuttings taken in August and rooted in a 50–50 sand and peat mixture.

Pests and diseases: Birds eat the flower buds. Try net, or cotton. Blackfly should be sprayed with malathion. Peach leaf curl may be controlled by spraying with Bordeaux mixture in the winter.

PYRACANTHA

Pyracantha, or firethorn, is a popular wall shrub grown chiefly for its fire-coloured berries, although its flowers are not unattractive. It is evergreen and hardy, so does not need the protection of a wall, but it does seem to go

Pyracantha

naturally with a wall, being erect growing and easy to train, and having dense vegetation which can be used to cloak an unsightly support. *P. coccinea* is the most popular species. It grows to a height and spread of 3.6m (12ft), and provides a profusion of white flowers in June and July followed by bright red berries in the autumn. 'Lalandei' is the most popular cultivar, and with its erect habit of growth it is more suitable for a wall or fence. It can reach 6m (20ft), has larger leaves than those of the species, and its berries are more orange. *P. crenulata* 'Rogersiana', generally known as *P. rogersiana*, grows to 3m (12ft). Its large white flower clusters are borne in June, and are followed by orange berries. Among its cultivars is 'Flava', which has yellow berries. *P.* 'Mohave' is an American hybrid with orange-red berries from mid-August onwards. Another very popular hybrid is the

Dutch *P.* 'Orange Glow' which makes an excellent specimen plant, very vigorous and free-fruiting. Both these are said to have some resistance to scab.

General care: Pyracantha are happy with almost any soil, including chalk, but not those which are waterlogged. Both sunny and partially shaded sites are acceptable. Plant container-grown specimens in March, watering in well and making sure that they do not dry out. Tie to wires or trellis as they grow up the wall. Trim back the current year's growth in June.

Propagation: Pyracantha will grow readily from seeds harvested in the autumn, but if the seed is from hybrids the resulting plants are unlikely to grow true. It is safer to take semi-ripe cuttings of the current year's growth in the summer, and strike in a 50–50 sand and peat mixture.

Pests and diseases: Birds take the berries, especially of *P. coccinea*. Try cotton

strung between the shoots. Scale insects should be sprayed with diazinon when seen. Pyracantha scab causes a brown coating on leaves and fruit. Spray fortnightly with captan. Fireblight, a bacterial disease causing leaves to turn dark brown and wither, is on the increase. Cut away the shoots well beyond the infection and burn, and disinfect the secateurs. (Fireblight is a notifiable disease.)

RHODODENDRON

Queen of the evergreen flowering shrubs, the rhododendron has much to offer those who are lucky enough to garden on acid soil. Apart from prodigious displays of blossom in practically all colours of the rainbow some sorts also have foliage which is attractive at all times. In stature they range from mats and buns under 30cm, (1ft) in height to large shrubs up to 3m (10ft) plus, some trees eventually to three times

Rhododendron

this. About 800 true species are known, and literally thousands of hybrid cultivars have been raised, so it is impossible to do justice to them here. All the species and cultivars stocked by nurserymen at garden centres are good and worth trying in the garden.

Depending on the height required, look out for the following:

Under 30cm (1ft): *campylogynum* 'Crushed Strawberry' (pink), *hanceanum* 'Nanum' (yellow), *keleticum* (purple-crimson), *pemakoense* (lilac pink).

30-120cm (1–4ft): 'Blue Tit' (lavender blue), 'Cilipinense' (white flushed pink), 'Elizabeth' (scarlet), 'Bow Bells' (shell-pink, darker buds), 'Chikor' (yellow).

Under 2m (6½ft): 'Don-caster' (scarlet), 'Pink Pearl' (pink), 'Blue Peter' (lavender blue), 'Cunningham's White' (white), 'Yellow Hammer' (yellow; can eventually exceed 2m).

General care: Plant in March, in lime-free soil which has got some humus or compost in it, adding peat or hop manure if necessary. Rhododendrons are surface-rooting, and must have some moisture-retaining material in the topsoil. Set the plants 90cm (3ft) apart if for a hedge, and 1.5m (5ft) apart or more for a screen, depending on the thickness of the screen required. Water on planting, and keep watering if the first spring is dry. They need no pruning, apart from any trimming necessary to keep them in shape, which should be done in the winter. Dead-head the flowers to stop the seeds forming, unless they are needed for propagation.

Propagation: Seeds sown in spring in pots or pans of soil-less compost. Alternatively, and much quicker to obtain a flowering sized plant, layer some long shoots any time in the summer.

Pests and diseases: Rhododendron bud blast turns the flower buds brown or black in the autumn. Control is by killing the carrier, the rhododendron leaf hopper, by spraying with fenitrothion in August. Leaf-yellowing caused by chlorosis means that your soil is too alkaline to grow rhododendrons. You can try making it more acid by adding quantities of peat and watering with sequestrene.

RIBES

Flowering currants have graced our gardens for more than a hundred years and are indispensable for spring colour. Best known is *R. sanguineum*, an erect shrub to 2.5m (8½ft) with maple-like leaves which are barely showing when the pendant spikes of deep pink flowers appear in April. The cultivars 'King Edward VII' and 'Pulborough Scarlet' have more intensely hued blossom; 'Tydermann's White' is pure white, while 'Brocklebankii' has golden foliage. *R. aureum* and *odoratum* are much alike and confused in gardens. Known as yellow or buffalo currant they are erect in habit to about 2.2m (7ft) tall with loose spikes of fragrant, tubular yellow flowers with the young leaves in spring.

General care: Ribes grow in all but the wettest soils in sun or partial shade. Light sandy or chalky soils should be enriched with garden compost or peat, etc. Pruning is a matter of expediency. If the shrubs are to be kept under 2m (6½ft) then cut back flowered stems by two-thirds annually as soon as the last blossoms fade. Alternatively, remove only untidy stems or branches.

Propagation: By semi-hardwood cuttings in late summer in a frame, or hardwood cuttings in late autumn in the open ground.

Pests and diseases: Generally trouble-free.

Ribes

ROSES

It is impossible to imagine a flower garden, however small or large, without at least a few roses. There are literally hundreds of roses to choose from, but as their growth and flowering habits vary greatly the first thing to do is to decide on the type of rose plants you want to grow. Bush roses, for example, are divided into two groups, Large-Flowered (Hybrid teas) which produce large individual blooms on single stems, and Cluster-Flowered (Floribundas) whose characteristic of many blooms produced in clusters or trusses has made them very popular for mass colour displays. Both can also be grown as standards, flowering on 75–150cm (2½–5ft) high stems which need staking.

To prune roses, use sharp secateurs to make a clean cut on a slant (left). Climbers and ramblers snould be pruned to a framework of healthy wood (right), and bush roses cut right down in late autumn (bottom).

For covering pergolas, walls or fences, roses with vigorous growth habits are needed. These are classified as climbing or rambling roses, of which the older varieties will flower only once during the summer. Some of the more recent additions, however, provide repeat displays of blooms throughout or later on in the season. Some of the modern shrub roses, too, have the same repeat-flowering qualities and merit consideration, not only as individual plants in a bed or border but also for planting as flowering hedges.

The first golden rule for success with roses will always be the preparation of the soil before planting. A heavy clay soil, which is the best type for growing roses,

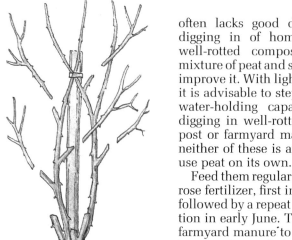

'Just Joey'

often lacks good drainage; digging in of home-made, well-rotted compost or a mixture of peat and sand will improve it. With lighter soils it is advisable to step up the water-holding capacity by digging in well-rotted compost or farmyard manure. If neither of these is available, use peat on its own.

Feed them regularly with a rose fertilizer, first in March, followed by a repeat application in early June. Try to get farmyard manure to use as a top dressing early in March.

Pruning

The pruning of roses is a controversial subject. March is the recommended month, but it can be carried out from late autumn onwards during mild spells. With bush roses remove entirely all very thin growth, then for hybrid teas cut back all the previous season's growth to one third. For floribundas cut back only to two thirds or one half to maintain a bushier plant. Make sure that your secateurs are really sharp so that you achieve a clean sloping cut without crushing the wood. Bush roses should

also be pruned just after their first flowering to encourage a second flush of blooms.

Climbers and ramblers should be pruned back to a framework of healthy wood; with shrub roses it is wise to cut out all the thin, straggly growth and cut back the strong wood by one-third.

Propagation

Nurserymen propagate the Bush roses by bud grafting (budding) on to wild species (usually dog rose) in summer. Strong-growing cultivars can also be raised from cuttings, as can all other roses. Take these in September and October, selecting strong shoots of the current season's growth and cut an 18–20cm (7–8in) length of stem cleanly below a node at the base, and just above a node at the top. Carefully remove all the leaves without damaging the buds, then dip the bottom end of the cutting in a rooting powder or solution. These cuttings are now ready for planting in a prepared position outside. When doing so, make sure that only one third of the cuttings are above ground, otherwise too much drying out will occur. Rooted cuttings will be ready for transplanting to their permanent positions in November the following year.

Pests and diseases: Black spot, rust and powdery mildew are the chief problems. Aphids are always a problem on shoot tips and buds.

HYBRID TEA ROSES

'Alec's Red' has deep red fragrant blooms on erect stems.

'Blessings' is coral salmon and free-flowering on erect stems.

'Fragrant Cloud' has fragrant coral scarlet flowers on strong stems.

'Grandpa Dickson' has lemon-yellow blooms which are lightly scented.

'Josephine Bruce' bears velvety deep crimson flowers but is susceptible to mildew.

'Just Joey' has fragrant coppery orange, red veined blooms on erect stems.

The fully open blooms of 'Maestro' are deep crimson edged with white, making it a very striking rose.

'Mullard Jubilee' bears many large rose-pink blooms.

'National Trust' is deep scarlet with coppery-red young shoots.

The large, creamy-yellow edged and shaded pink blooms of 'Peace' are never produced very freely, but it makes a spectacular show.

'Piccadilly' bears scarlet and gold buds in abundance.

'Pink Favourite' has shapely, fragrant, rose-pink blooms on erect stems.

'Prima Ballerina' bears richly fragrant deep pink blooms.

'Whisky Mac' adds scent to its deep gold, bronze shaded flowers.

For growing as 'standard roses' any of the following are recommended: 'Alec's Red', 'Blessings', Fragrant Cloud', 'Just Joey', 'National Trust' or 'Piccadilly'.

FLORIBUNDAS

'Arthur Bell' produces large bright golden yellow flowers on erect stems.

'Australian Gold' has a colouring akin to ripe peaches and has a long flowering season.

'City of Leeds' has rich salmon flowers over a long period.

'Elizabeth of Glamis' produces coral-salmon and pink blooms of great beauty but is rather disease prone.

'Iceberg' is probably the finest white floribunda of all time and has been popular for almost 30 years.

'Lili Marlene' has semi-double, crimson-scarlet flowers but can suffer from mildew.

'Mary Sumner' produces coppery red flowers and glossy disease-resistant foliage.

'Masquerade' has yellow flowers which flush pink and age to crimson.

'Matangi' bears fragrant blooms of orange, vermilion and silver.

'News' has purple, semi-double flowers from wine red buds.

'Queen Elizabeth' has great vigour and height and plenty of soft clear pink flowers.

'St Boniface' produces its

ABOVE: 'Trumpeter'
BELOW: The free-flowering 'Iceberg'

vermilion blooms on dwarf compact bushes.

'Scarlet Queen Elizabeth' is a strong tall grower with scarlet flowers.

'Trumpeter' produces an abundance of scarlet blooms on compact dwarf bushes.

Some floribundas are very good for growing as standard roses. Of those listed here, 'Iceberg', 'Mary Sumner', 'Matangi' and 'Trumpeter' are recommended.

REPEAT-FLOWERING SHRUB ROSES

These are a real asset to any garden but generally need more space than either hybrid teas or floribundas. In a smaller garden, a single specimen is acceptable, but if the garden is on the large side these shrub roses look well planted in groups of three.

'Ballerina' makes a 1.2m (4ft) shrub which bears great clusters of small single pink flowers with white eyes.

'Dorothy Wheatcroft' grows up to 1.5m (5ft) high producing glowing bright red single blooms in large trusses.

'Louise Odier' grows to 1.8m (6ft) and has rich pink blooms softly shaded with a tinge of lilac and a rich scent. 'Westerland' has bright golden orange semi-double blooms.

SUMMER-FLOWERING SHRUB ROSES

There are many different types of roses that come under this heading; the damask, moss and rosa species being some of them. Only a few can be mentioned here; but any good rose catalogue will give a more extensive list.

'Fritz Nobis' produces long, pointed salmon-pink buds followed by large semi-double blooms of soft creamy pink. It can grow to 1.8m (6ft) or more.

'Madam Hardy', a damask rose, makes a vigorous bush of medium height. The pure white blooms give out a wonderful fragrance.

'Nuits De Young' is a beautiful moss rose with deep blackish-purple small blooms which, when fully open, show yellow stamens. It grows to about 1.2m (4ft).

Rosa x highdownensis can reach 3m (10ft) in height and has deep pink single flowers and large red flask-shaped hips.

Rosa rubrifolia is grown for its dark red stems and purple grey foliage. The small pink flowers are followed by deep red hips.

CLIMBING AND RAMBLING ROSES

Any long stemmed rose can be grown as a climber. Some species of roses climb naturally and go higher than any cultivated roses. Being disease-resistant, they do

'Madam Hardy'

better than modern roses in the close conditions near to walls and fences. R. filipes, with clusters of white single flowers, is a very vigorous climber, up to 12m (40ft), and has a cultivar called 'Kiftsgate' with bigger flowers. R. multiflora (polyantha rose) grows to 4.6m (15ft) in height and width. It is a parent of the modern polyanthus roses, carries white flowers, and has a number of cultivars in different coloured flowers – 'Carnea' (pink), 'Goldfinch' (buff-yellow to white) and 'Platyphylla' (mauve-pink ageing white).

Ramblers are not much planted these days because they produce only one flush of flowers and need a lot of careful pruning. Justifiably more popular are the modern climbers which give repeat flowering, need little pruning, and are more-or-less disease-resistant. Recommended are 'Handel' (white flowers with a pink edge), 'Schoolgirl' (apricot), 'Compassion' (pink and apricot, very fragrant), and 'Danse du Feu' (crimson). All these climb to about 3m (10ft). A Victorian climber which goes to 6m (20ft) is 'Mme Alfred Carrière', which carries a succession of white fragrant flowers right through the summer. It is also suitable for a north wall, and so is 'Mme Grégoire Staechelin', which has only one flush of large fragrant pink blooms in June.

BELOW: *The miniature 'Baby Masquerade'*
BOTTOM: *'Albertine'*

MINIATURE ROSES

While some of the miniature roses are recommended for open ground planting, practically all exceed their catalogue heights even during their first year outdoors. However there is undoubtedly a place for them in containers or pots where root restriction has a considerable effect on the size of the plant.

'Baby Masquerade' is a charming small bush with multi-coloured miniature yellow, pink and red flowers right through the summer.

'Dresden Doll' produces miniature shell-pink moss roses.

In this same category come the 'ground cover roses', so called because their spread is greater than their height.

'Nozomi' is dainty with small pale pink single flowers in large clusters. It will grow to a height of 30–45cm (12–18in) and is very effective when grown in a tall container or where it has the opportunity to trail down. 'Snow Carpet' forms mats of dark green leaves studded with tiny double white flowers. It does not exceed 20cm (8in) in height.

A discreet, yet well-constructed arch support shows the natural attributes climbing roses to good advantage.

ROSMARINUS

Fragrant leaved, lavender-blue flowered rosemary has a variety of roles in the garden; as a hedge, a scented evergreen flowering shrub and as a herb. There are several different sorts. Best for hedges is 'Miss Jessup's Upright', an erect-growing cultivar to 1.8m (6ft). 'Severn Sea' is dwarf and arching with bright blue flowers. 'McConnells Blue' makes a low hummock.

General care: Well-drained, even poor, sandy or chalky soil is ideal, plus a sunny, reasonably sheltered site.

Propagation: Take tip cuttings in late summer in a cold frame, or use longer more woody stems planted *in situ* in autumn.

Pests and diseases: Generally trouble-free.

SALIX

There are no less than 300 species of willows plus many more hybrids and varieties. All are deciduous and produce minute flowers in catkins, the best known being those of the pussy or goat willow *Salix caprea*. Salix contains tiny mat-formers, shrubs of various sizes and quite tall trees. It is the shrubs which are of most value in the garden. *S. caprea* is too large a shrub for the smaller garden and anyway can be enjoyed in the countryside. Its now popular weeping form known as Kilmarnock willow (*S. caprea* 'Pendula') however, makes a nice little weeping tree for a small lawn. Far better to plant this than the common weeping willow (*S. × chrysocoma*, syn. *S. alba* 'Tristis' and *S. a.* 'Vitellina Pendula'), which rapidly outgrows its space in the smaller garden and becomes a lovely nuisance. A willow of quality is *S. fargesii*, a comparatively slow grower for a willow, eventually to 2m (6½ft). It has robust, polished winter twigs set with sealing-wax red buds. The leaves too are large and handsome. Rarely above 120cm (4ft) tall is the dwarf alpine pussy willow, *S.*

Senecio

hastata 'Wehrhahnii'. Erect and compact growing with age it bears a profusion of silvery, then yellow catkins before the leaves in spring. Huge pussy willow catkins are produced by the woolly willow *S. lanata* but they are borne with the large, grey-woolly young leaves in late spring or early summer. In time it forms a spreading bush 90–120cm (3–4ft) tall. Eventually to 2.4m (8½ft) in height is the black pussy willow *S. melanostachys* (syn. *S. gracilistyla* var. *melanostachys*). It has bright green leaves and, before they expand in early spring, almost black catkins set with red anthers which finally turn yellow with pollen. For the rock garden, *S. × boydii* is a must, a gnarled shrublet of slow growth rarely above 30cm (1ft) in height bearing small corrugated grey leaves.

General care: Almost any soil is acceptable, although *S. × boydii* does not like wet conditions. Pruning is not necessary except for removing untidy stems or branchlets.

Propagation: By semi-hardwood cuttings in a cold frame in late summer or hardwood cuttings in the open ground in late autumn to late winter.

Pests and diseases: Generally trouble-free.

SANTOLINA

The grey frothy foliage of cotton lavender or lavender cotton (*S. chamaecyparissus*) has been a garden stand-by for at least 200 years. It is an evergreen shrub to 50cm (2ft) tall or more, but is best cut back close to ground level annually and then rarely exceeds 30–45cm (1–1½ft) in height. In late summer the stem tips produce flower-heads like lemon-yellow buttons. Some people remove them because they spoil the smooth grey outline of the foliage, but they are not without charm.

S. c. insularis (syn. *S. neapolitana*) has looser, taller, more feathery foliage, which in the cultivar 'Sulphurea' is topped by primrose-yellow buttons.

General care: Any well-drained soil is suitable, growth being more compact in the poorer sandy or chalky ones. Full sun is essential. Cut back annually in spring.

Propagation: Take semi-hardwood cuttings in late summer or hardwood in autumn, both in a cold frame.

Pests and diseases: Generally trouble-free.

SENECIO

Grey-leaved plants have a wide appeal and when they are garnished with bright yellow daisy flowers they become desirable garden decoration. *Senecio × 'Sunshine'* (syn. *S. greyi* and *laxifolius* of gardens) is just such a plant, forming a low, compact evergreen shrub to 90cm (3ft) tall. An excellent plant for windswept sites by the sea but suffers damage in severe winters. *S. monroi* has smaller, beautifully crimped-edged leaves which are dark green above and white-felted beneath. Yellow daisy flowers similar to those of *S. × 'Sunshine'* appear in summer.

General care: Any well drained site, preferably in sun is suitable. In cold areas the foot of a south wall is best.

Propagation: Take semi-hardwood cuttings with a heel in late summer and root them in a propagating case.

Pests and diseases: Generally trouble-free.

SKIMMIA

This genus of smallish shrubs is valuable for its fragrant, spring-borne flower clusters, crimson berries and evergreen leaves. The hardiest and best known species, *S. japonica*, unfortunately has male and female flowers on separate plants. To get the

Skimmia

bonus of berries therefore at least two specimens must be planted. Should you have room for only one, then choose *S. j.* 'Rubella', a rounded male plant 90–120cm (3–4ft) in height, with dark foliage and red-budded, white flowers. If red berries are desired then plant *S. j.* 'Foremannii', a large-fruited female, beside it. Less hardy and needing acid soil, *S. reevesiana* is the only species generally available which has hermaphrodite flowers and so can produce fruit without a companion plant.

General care: *S. japonica* will grow in any soil which is not too dry, but chalky and sandy soils should be enriched with peat, leaf mould or garden compost. *S. reevesiana* must have a lime-free rooting medium. Both will grow in sun or partial shade. Pruning is not required.

Propagation: Take cuttings of semi-hardwood in late summer, or hardwood in autumn, placing them in a cold frame.

Pests and diseases: Generally trouble-free.

SPIRAEA
No garden should be without at least one member of this large genus of deciduous trees and shrubs. All those offered at garden centres are hardy and easily grown, producing their frothy clusters of small white, pink or red flowers in abundance. Best known is *S. japonica*, a twiggy shrub to 1.5m (5ft) but only half this if annually pruned. In late summer it produces large flattened clusters of pink to red flowers. *S. j.* 'Anthony Waterer' has a scattering of cream and pink variegated shoots and crimson flowers. *S. j.* 'Bumalda' (syn. *S. × bumalda*) is more compact, bearing carmine flowers above rich green leaves. *S. j.* 'Little Princess' (dark pink) and 'Snowmound' (white) form dense low mounds wider than high and are best not pruned. *S. × vanhouttei* achieves 2m (6½ft) or more in time, and pure white floral pompoms smother its arching stems in early summer. Quite different are the similar *S. douglasii*, *S. salicifolia* and their hybrid × *billiardii*. All are upright in growth to 2.2m (7ft) tall, bearing in late summer erect terminal plumes of pink to rose flowers. The best of the bunch is *S. × billiardii* 'Triumphans' (syn. *S. menziesii* 'Triumphans'), which bears large clusters of rose-purple blossom.

General care: Almost any soil is suitable, even wettish ones, though a moist but well drained site is best. *S. × vanhouttei* will grow in quite dry places. Sun or partial shade is acceptable. Cut all stems of *S. japonica* back to 5cm (2in) every spring if desired.

Propagation: Take semi-hardwood cuttings in late summer or hardwood ones in autumn and insert in a cold frame. *S. × billiardii* and its allies produce suckers which can be severed from late autumn to early spring.

Pests and diseases: Generally trouble-free.

SYMPHORICARPOS
Symphoricarpos, or snowberry, is a useful hedging or screening plant that will grow practically anywhere, producing in the autumn large white berries like marbles, lasting through most of the winter. *S. albus* is an evergreen growing up to 2.1m (7ft) or taller under good soil conditions. Of the cultivars, 'Laevigatus' has even bigger berries and 'White Hedge' (syn. 'White Hedger') is a compact, erect grower which is considered best for the purpose.

General care: Snowberry will grow anywhere – sun or shade, or under trees – and in any soil, no matter how poor. Plant any time in the winter, 45cm (18in) apart for hedging, and 75cm (30in) or more apart for screening, depending on how thick a screen you want. The young plants should then be cut down to within 25cm (10in) or so of the soil, and the growing tip pinched out from time to time to encourage branching. No routine pruning is needed, and hedges and screens can be trimmed as and when required.

Propagation: Take cuttings in the autumn and strike in a 50–50 sand and peat mixture or remove suckers any time from late autumn to early spring.

Pests and diseases: Generally trouble-free.

SYRINGA
Although syringa is sometimes, quite wrongly, used as a common name for philadelphus, it is strictly the botanical name for lilac. *Syringa vulgaris* is common lilac, that deservedly popular deciduous shrub so prodigious of its trusses of fragrant flowers in late spring and early summer. Bluish-purple is the basic colour but there are many cultivars in shades of purple, red, pink and yellow, both single and double. Recommended are: 'Firmament' (almost blue), 'Charles Joly' (rich purple-red, double), 'Esther Staley' (pink), 'Maud Notcutt' (white), 'Primrose' (pale yellow), 'Sensation' (red-purple edged white, very striking). *S. × prestoniae* is a hybrid of *S. reflexa* and makes large vigorous bushes with more plumy flower trusses than those of *S. vulgaris*. Among the best of the named cultivars are 'Bellicent' (clear pink) and 'Elinor' (lilac to violet-pink). If space is at a premium and a really small lilac is desired, go for *S. microphylla* 'Superba'. This small-leaved sort grows to 1.5m (5ft) or more in height and bears fragrant, rosy-pink blossom in early summer. Unlike other lilacs it gives an encore in autumn though the display is on a lesser scale.

General care: All soils that are not too dry or wet are suitable, though light sandy and chalky ones should be enriched with garden compost, leaf mould or peat. Pruning is not necessary except to maintain a shapely outline.

Propagation: Take semi-hardwood cuttings in late summer and root in a propagating case or cold frame.

Pests and diseases: Generally trouble-free.

TROPAEOLUM
This group includes the familiar garden nasturtium and Canary creeper, which

Tropaeolum speciosum

climb like clematis: twisting their leaf stalks round any available support. *T. majus* is the common nasturtium, an annual growing to 2.1m (7ft) or more and flowering from June to September. Dwarf and trailing strains are available. *T. peregrinum*, Canary creeper, is also an annual. It is a rapid climber, up to 3m (10ft) in a season, and produces its bright yellow flowers from June to September. *T. speciosum*, or flame nasturtium, is a perennial growing to about 3.6m (12ft), with flame-red flowers from July to September. It is the only one of the group that does not like full sun, and although it comes from Chile, it seems to prefer cool, damp conditions – a north-facing wall is ideal. *T. tuberosum* is a vigorous climber, up to 3m (10ft), with red and orange flowers. Some strains do not flower until September and are then cut down by frost. Look for the early flowering variety 'Ken Aslet', which blooms in June.
General care: Canary creeper needs average garden soil but the other annuals should be given poor soil or they will produce a lot of vegetation at the expense of the flowers. Most of the perennials will thrive in any good fertile soil, but *T. speciosum* must have an acid soil. Add peat if necessary to achieve this. *T. tuberosum* grows from tubers which will survive the winter only in the mildest areas. If in doubt, lift and store in a frost-free shed, planting out again in May when all danger of frost has passed.
Propagation: The annuals can be grown from seed sown in April into the flowering site, or sown in pots of soil-less compost in March for planting out later after hardening off. The tubers of *T. tuberosum* can be separated when they are lifted for over-winter storage. The other perennials can be propagated by dividing the roots in March.
Pests and diseases: Tropaeolum are attacked by blackfly, cabbage caterpillars and thrips: derris will deal with all these.

VIBURNUM
The viburnum genus includes a very wide variety of evergreen and deciduous shrubs, flowering in winter, spring and summer. Some are grown for their flowers, some for their berries, some for their colourful autumn leaves, and some for all three. Certain species are best grown as bushes, but many make excellent wall shrubs – although most viburnums are hardy, they flower earlier and better on a wall or fence. *V. × burkwoodii* is a spreading semi-evergreen which grows to about 2.1m (7ft) and bears clusters of fragrant white flowers from March to May. *V. farreri*, formerly known as *V. fragrans*, is a deciduous winter-flowering species. It grows to 3m (10ft) or more against a wall, and bears its fragrant white and pink flowers from November to March intermittently, in spells of fine weather. The leaves follow the flowers in spring. *V. × bodnantense* is a useful hybrid of *V. farreri* and *V. grandiflorum*, since it is more vigorous, growing to 3.6m (12ft) and hardier than either. It is deciduous, and carries white-pink fragrant flowers on the bare wood, sometimes from October to February. 'Dawn' is the cultivar usually available, but 'Deben' has a longer winter-flowering period than any, from October to April if the weather is mild. *V. rhytidophyllum* is an upright evergreen species, 3.6m (12ft) tall, with whitish flowers in May and June followed by red berries that turn black when ripe. It is however mainly grown for its large oblong leaves, which have a finely wrinkled glossy surface.
General care: Viburnums grow in most soils, ideally with compost dug in, and a mulch of leaf mould from time to time. Plant deciduous varieties any time in the winter, and evergreens in April. A west-facing wall is ideal. Viburnums do not need regular pruning: any tidying up needed should be done when they have finished flowering.
Propagation: Take cuttings at the end of the summer and root them in a 50–50 sand and peat mixture. Or shoots layered at this time will be ready for separating a year later.
Pests and diseases: Generally trouble-free.

WEIGELA
This is undoubtedly one of the 10 most popular garden shrubs. *W. floribunda* (syn. *Diervilla floribunda*) is a hardy, easy to please, deciduous species growing to 2.2m (7ft) tall which, without fail, produces numerous small trusses of foxglove-shaped flowers in summer.

Viburnum tinus

Several good cultivars are available, the best being 'Bristol Ruby' (ruby-red), 'Abel Carrière' (rosy carmine), 'Avalanche' (white), 'Folliis Purpureis' (rose-pink with purple foliage), 'Variegata' (pale pink with yellow-margined leaves). If you would like to try something different, look out for the smaller growing sulphur-yellow, *W. middendorffiana*.

General care: All but the wettest soils are suitable but light sandy and chalky ones should be enriched with garden compost or peat etc. To maintain a compact bush, cut back flowered stems by two thirds to threequarters as soon as the last blossoms fade.

Propagation: Take semi-hardwood cuttings in late summer in a propagating case, or hardwood cuttings either in a cold frame or in the open ground.

Pests and diseases: Generally trouble-free.

WISTERIA

Wisteria sinensis (Chinese wisteria) is the most popular species: not surprisingly, for it is fragrant and spectacular, the long racemes of mauve flowers appearing in May before the leaves, with a smaller second flowering in warm summers in August. There are several cultivars, including 'Plena' (double flowers) and 'Alba' (white flowers). *W. floribunda* (Japanese wisteria) is similar, but not so vigorous, growing up to 9m (30ft). Since it was introduced to Europe in Victorian times many cultivars have been produced, some with extra-long racemes of flowers, notably 'Macrobotrys', whose purple racemes are 90cm (3ft) long. These look best when they are trained over an arch or pergola so that the racemes of flowers hang down clear of the plant.

General care: All wisterias prefer a sunny site, such as a south-facing wall, except for *W. floribunda*, which will tolerate some shade. They like a rich moist soil with plenty of compost dug into it. The young plants can be put in at any time during the winter, and need support until they can start twining and climbing. Eventually wisteria will grow into a self-supporting tree with a head of new young growth. Prune unwanted climbing shoots back to five basal leaves throughout the summer to promote more flowering spurs.

Propagation: Take cuttings 10cm (4in) long of the current year's growth in August, and strike them in a 50–50 mixture of peat and sand or layer in spring and remove one year later.

Pests and diseases: Generally trouble-free.

BELOW: *The fragrant and spectacular flowers of Wisteria sinensis and (right) one of its cultivars, 'Alba'.*

HOUSE PLANTS

Not only do plants embellish the decor of one's home, but they provide an important link with the natural world. A whole new industry has risen to meet the tremendous demand for house plants from dwellers in crowded cities and suburbia. New plants are continually being tested for their suitability and, indeed, never before has there been such a wide variety of plants for the home.

Where do house plants come from? Most are native to warm countries, some from the shady floors of tropical forests, others, the epiphytes or air plants — eg, orchids and bromeliads — from the branches high above. Many come from the semi-deserts — the succulent plants with fleshy stems and/or leaves. A surprising number come from temperate climates, eg ivy from the forests of Europe and Asia, aspidistra from similar shady places in China and cyclamen from mountain woods in the eastern Mediterranean. As this indicates, house plants come from habitats with extremes of shade or exposure; not surprising when you consider the climate of an average house. In most homes the atmosphere is very dry, the light except near windows is poor and, unless there is central heating, the temperature fluctuates widely between day and night, especially in winter. Despite this there are species suitable for most sites in the house. The best localities are window ledges, tables and shelves nearby and room corners. Plants can be used as dividers in larger rooms, to embellish the harshness of a fireplace in summer or simply to brighten a dull corner.

Light is essential to all plants though some need a lot more than others. The desert dwellers obviously need lots of direct sunlight, while forest or jungle plants tolerate shade. The more shade-tolerant species will also thrive under artificial light, and nowadays there is a variety of custom-made units to take either one plant or a whole shelf or trayful. By such means plants can be grown in the darkest of rooms and even in basements and window-less cellars. Not only is it important to purchase the right plant for the right situation, but the plant itself should be the best available. Shop around before you buy what you want. Look for sturdy specimens with leaves of a good green colour. Do not purchase plants with a lot of bare stem or with yellowish or brown-marked leaves. Check for such pests as aphids (green- and blackfly), white fly, mealy bug and red spider (see pests chart on pp. 166–170). Get the plant home as soon as possible in cold weather because chilling can trigger off premature leaf or flower drop.

Watering

The correct watering of a containerized plant is essential if it is to flourish. Without doubt, most plants perish as a result of too much or not enough water. Frequency of watering depends upon the stage of the plant's development, temperature and time of year. A newly potted plant for example, with unexploited soil around its roots, will need less water than one which is pot bound (the pot container tightly filled with roots). Plants actively growing and producing new leaves and perhaps flower buds also will need more water than those which are dormant. Deciding when a plant needs water is a skill that comes with experience. With most plants the aim is to keep the potting mix moist but not wet. There are a few exceptions. *Cyperus alternifolius* is a waterside plant and is best kept wet. All succulents, including cacti, are best if they are allowed to dry out between waterings and kept dry or almost so during the winter.

The most reliable means of deciding when a plant needs water is to scratch into the soil surface with the tip of the finger. If it feels dry on the surface and dryish for about 1cm (½in) down, watering is necessary. Do the job thoroughly, filling up the space between the soil surface and rim of the container. Rain water is ideal, but tap water is perfectly adequate.

Humidity

Plants whose native homeland is forest or jungle thrive more happily if some sort of humidity can be provided. The easiest way is to stand the pots on gravel-filled trays with water just below the surface. Alternatively, deeper trays or troughs can be filled with moist peat and the pots sunk in this up to their rims. A little water from time to time keeps the peat moist. Another method is to dampen the foliage daily with a small spray adjusted to produce fine droplets.

Feeding

Sooner or later the plants will exhaust the potting mix of its essential nutrients. If feeding, top-dressing or re-potting is not resorted to, the growth of the plant will slow down or cease, leaves will be small and yellowish and flower buds fall or fail to develop. Liquid fertilizer is the best way of feeding containerized plants. All the well known proprietary sorts are suitable, but must be used according to the maker's instructions. It is usual to carry out feeding from spring to autumn, but plants which continue to grow in winter should still be fed, though preferably at half strength.

Select plants with healthy-looking leaves, sturdy stems and, if choosing a flowerer, plenty of buds.

Potting soil

The quality of the rooting medium — potting compost mix or soil — is crucial to the health and vigour of a containerized plant. As the root system is packed into a small space the soil must be richer than that in the garden. For this reason it is best to purchase a properly formulated mixture rather than mess about with garden soil, peat and fertilizers. There are packs of plant food especially formulated to mix with a set amount of peat or peat and perlite, so creating a fairly cheap potting mix. If garden soil is used, mix it with equal parts of peat and apply a liquid feed regularly.

Potting on

If a bigger, finer plant is needed then a larger container and more soil is the answer. Choose a new container which is large enough to allow about 2.5cm (1in) or more space all around the root ball. Make sure the new pot is clean, put a single crock (piece of broken pot or a square of perforated zinc) over the drainage hole followed by a handful of compost. Take the plant to be potted and turn it upside down onto your hand with the stem between the fingers. Holding the pot itself with the other hand, rap the rim against a hard surface, preferably a wooden one. The pot will then lift off. Place the root ball in the new container, adjusting so that when

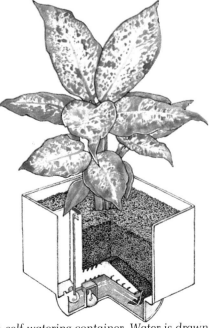

To remove dust or dirt from tough-leaved specimens (eg, Ficus elastica), wipe the leaves gently with a damp pad of cotton wool.

Plants with leaves that are delicate or awkward to clean (eg, Saintpaulia) should be sprayed with tepid water.

A self-watering container. Water is drawn up from a reservoir by a wick, which distributes moisture through the soil.

filled around it will be covered with about 1cm (½in) of new soil and there will be a space for watering. The latter is very important for efficient watering. If in doubt, leave a gap between soil surface and rim equivalent to about one seventh or one eighth of the container depth. After filling in with potting soil, water and return the plant to its original site.

Re-potting

This is a means of giving a long-term pot plant some fresh soil while preventing it from getting much bigger. Turn the plant out of its pot as before, then with a hand fork and, if necessary, a knife reduce the root ball by one third. Return it to the same pot, or preferably a clean one of the same size, and fill in with fresh soil. This re-potting operation should be done in late winter or spring or while the plant is semi-dormant. The top growth should be trimmed at the same time to balance the shoot/root ratio. Re-potting can be carried out annually on a vigorous plant such as bougainvillea or × fatshedera or at intervals of several years as with palms (howeia and phoenix).

Top dressing

This is an alternative to re-potting and is usually done annually or biennially in early spring. Strip away the top layer of compost, removing up to a quarter of the total depth of the root ball. Any fibrous roots in the way can go but avoid damaging the thicker main ones. Replace the old soil with a fresh mix, firm lightly and water using a rose-nozzled can to settle it in.

Supporting

House plants with a climbing mode of growth, eg ivy, stephanotis and bougainvillea must be given a support system. Custom-made structures of plastic or wire are obtainable, or a U-shaped support of galvanized wire can easily be made. Alternatively, several slim green canes or spills can be inserted in a fan-shape to one side of the pot. Sometimes plants splay or collapse, perhaps due to an over-warm or under-lit site. Such plants can be made tidy with a few small twiggy sticks around the base or a green spill carefully secured to each stem with a green tie. All such supporting should be as inconspicuous as possible so as not to detract from the beauty of the plant.

Propagation

Raising new plants for friends, as presents or for a charity sale can be an absorbing and satisfying pastime. Many

BELOW: Propagate from stem tip cuttings by taking a stem with several leaves attached from the top of a mature plant and pot up in a peat and sand mixture.

LEFT: A simple method of repotting, using a pot the same size as the outgrown one as a guide. This enables the new pot to be filled to the correct height with compost, leaving a hollow the right size for the plant's root ball.

house plants root easily from cuttings or can be increased from seed without much skill or knowledge. Some kind of propagating case is necessary to ensure success. This can be improvised from a seed tray covered with plastic sheeting and supported by U-shaped lengths of galvanized wire. Single pots can be placed in polythene bags with or without a support. Best of all are the custom-made structures with a clear rigid top, ideally with a heating element in the bottom. A number of the less easy plants to propagate root as cuttings when provided with bottom heat.

Softwood cuttings: These are leafy stem tips in a state of leafy growth provided in abundance by such plants as beloperone (shrimp plant), coleus (flame nettle), hedera (ivy), impatiens (busy lizzie) and tradescantia (wandering Jew). Any time from early spring to early autumn, sever stem tips 5–7.5cm (2–3in) long. Cut beneath a node (leaf or bud), remove the lowest leaf or two and insert the basal one third into pots of equal parts of moss peat and coarse sand. Water with a rosed can and place in the propagator. For a more sure rooting the cuttings can first be dipped into one of the hormone rooting powders. The actual pot size to use is a matter of choice. Single cuttings can be put into 5–6cm (2–2½in) pots, or several set around the edge of larger containers at 2.5–4cm (1–1½in) apart. At a minimum temperature of 18°C (65°F) rooting takes anything from 10–30 days, depending on the type of plant. Once growth recommences, pot singly into 7.5–9cm (3–3½in) containers of potting soil, water and keep lightly shaded for a few days.

Semi-hardwood cuttings: These are the current season's stems just starting to get

LEFT: *Propagation by leaf cuttings (**top**) and by leaf-bud cuttings (**below**). For leaf cuttings, take a mature healthy leaf with the stalk attached and insert it in a pot of seed compost, ensuring that the base of the leaf is clear of the compost. For leaf-bud cuttings, take a 10cm (4in) cutting with a leaf attached and pot it in a mixture of sand and peat. Support the cutting by means of an elastic band secured to a stake.*

woody at the base. Shrubs and woody climbers such as cissus, codiaeum (croton) and ficus (ornamental fig) often root more successfully when starting to become more woody. Sever whole side shoots, then trim off the soft tip so as to make a cutting 7.5–10cm (3–4in) long. Remove lower leaves and treat as for softwood cuttings.

Hardwood cuttings: These are fully woody stems that have stopped growing. Very few house plants are propagated in this way, the only one mentioned here being bougainvillea. Cut 10–15cm (4–6in) lengths of dormant leafless stems (prunings are often used), treat with a rooting powder and place in a heated propagating case; late winter to early spring is the best time.

Leaf cuttings: Certain plants can regenerate from a single leaf or even a piece of one; begonia, peperomia, saintpaulia, sansevieria and streptocarpus come into this category. Small leaves, eg peperomia and saintpaulia, are usually used whole. Take a mature (fully sized) but not old leaf, remove all but about 2.5cm (1in) of leaf stalk and insert 2cm ($\frac{3}{4}$in) of this into a 50–50 peat and sand mix in the same way as for softwood cuttings. Streptocarpus and sansevieria leaves are cut transversely into 5–7.5cm (2–3in) long sections, which are then inserted obliquely so that the lower one third is buried. Large begonia leaves can be used whole or cut

into 2.5cm (1in) squares. If used whole, only a stub of stalk is left and this is pressed into the surface of the same sandy compost so that the blade lies flat. Take a sharp, pointed knife or razor blade and pierce all the main veins at 2–2.5cm ($\frac{3}{4}$–1in) intervals. The tiny plants that will develop from some of these wounds can be separated from the leaf and potted singly when well rooted. Place the leaf squares on the surface of a container of soil so they are close but not touching. One or more plantlets will arise from most of the squares. Both the squares and whole leaves must be kept warm and humid in a propagating case. If they don't sit flat on the soil, anchor with U-shaped pieces of thin wire or small pebbles.

Leaf-bud cuttings: These are single leaves attached to short sections of stem. *Ficus elastica* is entirely propagated in this way by nurserymen. Cut a mature stem into pieces about 2–2.5cm ($\frac{3}{4}$–1in) long so that each piece has one leaf. Loosely roll each leaf cigar fashion and secure with an elastic band. Apply rooting powder to the stem and insert up to the base of the leaf blade. A short spill of cane through the rolled leaf will hold it erect. A temperature of not less than 24°C (75°F) is necessary for success.

When the lower parts of dieffenbachia and dracaena stems become leafless and unsightly, take the top as a soft or semi-hardwood cutting then cut

up the bare stem into 5cm (2in) lengths. Lie them on their sides and barely cover with soil. In time, each will produce one or more shoots and grow into a young plant. These are in effect leafless leaf-bud cuttings.

Air-layering: For information on basic layering see under Shrubs and Climbing Plants, p. 58. Basic layering is not always easy to carry out in the home, especially if a plant has stiff, erect stems, as have Ficus elastica and dracaena. These two plants frequently become bare and unsightly, and air-layering is a sure way of rooting the top, allowing new shoots to form below. Nick or make a shallow slice in the stem about 15–20cm (6–8in) below the growing tip and dust with rooting powder. If the slicing method is used, wedge it open with a tiny pebble. Cut a piece of 'lay-flat' plastic tubing that opens to a tube diameter of not less than 7.5cm (3in). Bunch the leaves and slip the tubing down to the nicked area of the stem, positioning it so that its middle point is opposite the wound. Secure the base of the tube to the stem with insulating tape. Now, firmly pack the tube with a mixture of equal parts of moist potting or seed sowing soil and moss, ideally sphagnum moss. Secure the top of the tube in the same way as the base. Rooting may take several months. When a good network of roots is visible, sever below the layer, remove the tube and pot up. Keep partially shaded and humid for 1–2 weeks to aid establishment.

Division: Several house plants, notably Asparagus fern, true ferns, Cyperus, fittonia, maranta, saintpaulia, etc can be divided as described under Garden Flowers (p. 20). For the smaller plants in pots, however, two hand forks placed back to back will give the essential leverage; a knife may also be useful. Pot each division as soon as it is made and water carefully until established.

Seeds: Comparatively few plants for the home are regularly raised from seed though many can be when seed is available. For the procedure see the seed-sowing entry under Garden Flowers, p. 20. Most house plant seed germinates best at between 18°C and 24°C (65–75°F).

ADIANTUM

The best-known species grown as a pot plant is *Adiantum raddianum*, commonly known as maidenhair, which is one of the most popular ferns. Its delicate fronds, rosy pink when young, mature to a fresh bright green.

General care: The maidenhair fern requires a humid environment. It will tolerate temperatures as low as 10°C (50°F), but its optimum temperature is 21°C (70°F). It needs a situation well away from direct sunlight. Make sure that the compost never dries out. If this happens, and the plant looks as if dehydration has killed it, don't give up. Provided it has not been allowed to stay dry for too long, it is possible to rejuvenate the plant. Cut off the dead fronds about 0.5cm (¼in) above soil level and carefully water the plant over the next few weeks. Usually the plant will eventually produce fresh growth and regain its former glory.

Propagation: Adiantum can be propagated from spores in the same way as other ferns (see Asplenium qv). However, division in spring is a much easier and quicker method.

Pests and diseases: Generally trouble-free.

AECHMEA FASCIATA

The aechmea or urn plant is a member of the bromeliad or pineapple family. Its large, greenish grey strap-like leaves radiate upwards and outwards. At their centre, where water collects, the large pink bracted flower spike emerges. The spike produces flowers of violet-blue that are relatively short-lived. They are, however, produced in succession and the flower spike can live for as long as 6 months. They normally appear in autumn.

General care: Aechmeas are relatively easy to look after. A semi-shaded position away from direct sunlight is best, with a temperature of about 15–18°C (50–65°F); they will tolerate lower temperatures, however. During the growing period, give the plants rainwater (if possible) in the central funnel

Asplenium (see p. 96), Howeia (see p. 104) and Adiantum

Agave

and in the compost. But though the compost may be allowed to dry out, do not let the funnel run dry. Remove the flower spike when it has faded by gently pulling; if it does not come away easily, do not tug too hard, but wait a little longer. Clean the leaves by rinsing them with tepid water. Never wipe them with a cloth, for this removes the decorative banding.

Propagation: Once the plant has finished flowering, it will usually produce one or more offsets. When these have grown to approximately one-third the size of the parent cut them off and pot singly into 10cm (4in) pots of a sandy lime-free compost. Keep extra humid until rooted, then place in 15cm (6in) pots of an all-peat mix.

Pests and diseases: Aechmeas are sometimes attacked by root mealy bugs and aphids on the flower spike, but generally they are trouble-free.

AGAVE

The agaves are succulent plants which grow wild in Mexico and the warmer parts of the Americas. All members of the genus carry their well-defined succulent sword-shaped leaves in the form of a rosette. One of the most attractive varieties is *Agave americana* 'Marginata', with its variegated green and cream leaves. *Agave victoriae-reginae*, has dark green fleshy leaves with white margins.

General care: Agaves must be given full light and kept on the dry side. Excessively wet conditions spell the rapid demise of the plant. Agaves may eventually flower from the centre of the rosette if grown in tubs or similar large containers. After flowering most agaves will produce offsets around their bases and then die. *Agave victoriae-reginae* does not produce offsets.

Propagation: Carefully remove offsets produced around the base of the plant and pot them singly in 13cm (5in) pots of John Innes No.2 potting compost. Spring is the best time to do this. Propagate from seed by germinating in a mixture of 4 parts seed compost to 1 part fine sand at about 18°C (68°F); prick out the young plants when they are large enough to be handled and pot them up individually in a similar mixture.

Pests and diseases: Mealy bugs and sometimes root mealy bugs attack agaves, but they are troubled by very little else.

AMARYLLIS
See under Hippeastrum

ANTHURIUM
The anthurium, or flamingo flower, is an unusual plant which produces colourful spathes that look like exotic flowers. The two most commonly grown are *Anthurium andreanum*, which has a shield-shaped flowering spathe of white, pink or brilliant red from which a finger-like flower spike protrudes, and *Anthurium scherzerianum* which has an orange-red spathe and a piglet's-tail-like flower spike.

General care: The flamingo flower needs a fair amount of care and attention. It prefers a temperature of 18–21°C (65–70°F) and humid conditions. While it does not like too much direct sunlight, it will not thrive in too much shade. A well-lit position where the temperature is reasonably constant will provide a good growing situation.

Do not let the plant dry out, especially during the growing season. Mist regularly with tepid water. Feed it once a month from April to September with a tomato fertilizer applied at half strength.

The flowers, which appear throughout the year, can be used in cut flower arrangements where they may live 3–4 weeks or more. If they are left on the plant, however, they may last for up to 8 weeks.

Propagation: Sometimes the plant will produce an offset at its side. This can be separated when it is about 15cm (6in) tall and potted up individually in a mixture of equal parts potting compost and moss peat.

Alternatively, anthuriums can be raised from seed produced from the true flowers, which swell up and yield the seed. These should be sown in half pots of seed compost and lightly covered. To germinate, keep the pots at 21°C (70°F) and enclosed in a polythene bag to conserve water and heat. When large enough to handle they can be transplanted and potted up singly.

Pests and diseases: Mealy bugs can sometimes be a nuisance and aphids occasionally attack young leaves and flowers.

APHELANDRA

Zebra plant or *Aphelandra squarrosa* bears cones of bright golden-yellow flowers on a flower spike rising from luxurious leathery green leaves with white veins. The flowers last several weeks before they eventually fade and fall off. Flowering takes place annually in autumn and winter, sometimes later.

General care: The aphelandra likes lots of light. Avoid draughts and aim for a temperature of about 18°C (65°F). It likes water and will suffer if left to dry out. Once the plant has flowered, it tends to produce rather straggly growth. This can be controlled a little by careful pruning and by feeding with half-strength tomato fertilizer. Spring pruning, cutting back after flowering to above the last pair of leaves, will encourage a good shape and improve the chances of it flowering again.

Propagation: When you prune the plant back in spring, use the prunings as cutting material. Cut up the stem, leaving about 5cm (2in) below each pair of leaves. Dip each cutting in hormone rooting power and insert singly in 9cm (3½in) pots of John Innes No.2 potting compost. Cover with polythene bags and keep them at a temperature of 21°C (70°F) until rooted. Grow on and eventually pot up into 13cm (5in) pots to grow to maturity.

Pests and diseases: Scale insects on the undersides of the leaves and on the stems are the worst nuisance. Aphids attack the young leaves and flowers in spring and summer.

ARAUCARIA EXCELSA

Better known as Norfolk Island pine, *Araucaria excelsa* (syn. *A. heterophylla*) is a close relative of the Monkey Puzzle tree – the tall pine-like tree that is often seen in gardens. The Norfolk Island pine is an elegant Christmas-tree-like houseplant that normally grows to between 1.5 and 2m (4 and 6½ft) indoors. It is not a hardy plant and must be grown indoors.

General care: The adaptable araucaria tolerates a wide range of conditions. As an optimum, it prefers a temperature of 15–18°C (60–65°F) and a reasonably well-lit position, even in full sun. The plant can, however, be grown at lower temperatures down to 10°C (50°F) with more shade. Leggy plants can be cut back hard and will grow again.

The one thing araucaria does not like is too much water. Allow the compost to almost dry out between waterings. The soft spine-like foliage collects dust, which is best removed by regularly spraying the plant with tepid water.

Propagation: The easiest way to propagate araucaria is from seed, which should be sown in a half pot filled with seed compost. Lightly cover the seed with compost and keep at 20°C (68°F) until germinated. When the seedlings are large enough to handle – approximately 5cm (2in) tall – gently prick them out and pot up singly in 9cm (3½in) pots filled with potting compost. Shoots from cut-back plants can be taken as cuttings in late summer, inserting them in a 50–50 peat and sand mix in a propagator.

Pests and diseases: Generally trouble-free, but may be attacked by mealy bugs and root mealy bugs.

ASPARAGUS FERN

Not all types of asparagus are grown to be eaten! Of the ornamental varieties suited to pot culture two make excellent houseplants, *Asparagus plumosus* (syn. *A. setaceus*) and *Asparagus* 'Sprengeri'. They produce beautiful bright green feathery foliage which is, incidentally, invaluable in flower arrangements. They are displayed to good advantage in a hanging basket or on a high shelf.

General care: Although asparagus ferns prefer not to be allowed to dry out completely, they can tolerate this condition even in summer. Nevertheless, the compost is best kept relatively moist through the growing season, and drier in winter. A lightly shaded situation is best, although they will tolerate direct light or deeper shade.

During the growing season, provide a temperature of around 13–18°C (55–65°F). A minimum temperature of about 10°C (45°F) is required in winter.

Propagation: Propagate by division in spring. Water the plant well first to ease separation. Gently tease the roots apart using a sharp knife to cut cleanly through any parts that do not separate easily. Pot up each piece into a suitably sized pot containing John Innes No.2 potting compost and grow on. Also easy from seed sown in spring at 18°C (65°F).

Pests and diseases: Generally trouble-free, but look out for scale insects.

ASPIDISTRA

Although not a spectacular plant, aspidistra is extremely reliable. The dark green leaves are held erect by the plant, which needs a striking container to set it off.

General care: Aspidistra does not demand a great deal of attention. A temperature of around 16°C (60°F) is ideal

Anthurium and Aphelandra

and a position away from direct sun is most satisfactory. A dry environment may cause the leaf tips and edges to turn brown; if this occurs, try misting the leaves with tepid water. Clean the leaves, which tend to trap dust, by lightly wiping with a cotton wool pad moistened with water.

Allow the plant almost to dry out in between waterings. Do not overwater, particularly in winter.

Propagation: This is carried out by division of the roots in spring or summer.

Pests and diseases: Watch for spider mites and mealy bugs.

ASPLENIUM

Asplenium nidus or bird's-nest fern has broad, strap-like fronds radiating from a central rosette.

General care: One of the easiest ferns to grow, it is quite happy at relatively low temperatures, down to 10°C (50°F), although it prefers to be kept at around 18°C (65°F). It is also rather more

Azaleas come in a wide range of colours

tolerant than other ferns of a dry atmosphere, although it shares with them a preference for semi-shade, away from direct sunlight. It is less susceptible than many other ferns to over- or underwatering.

Propagation: This fern is propagated from minute dust-like spores produced from dark brown-coloured gill-like objects on the underside of mature fronds. Collect these spores carefully and sprinkle them on to the surface of a half pot filled with a peat-based seed compost. Place the pot in a polythene bag and keep moist at about 21°C (70°F) until the spores germinate. Leave until large enough to handle, then prick out and pot on.

Pests and diseases: Scale insects are the most likely pests.

See p. 93 for illustration

AZALEA

Rhododendron indicum hybrids, the so-called Indian azalea, is a most colourful flowering plant that is seasonal from autumn to spring.

Azaleas are available in a wide range of colours from white, rose-pink and salmon to cerise-red. If looked after reasonably well, they will last in flower for up to 8 weeks.

General care: Keep azaleas reasonably moist but not over-wet. Azaleas that are allowed to get dry seldom recover and rapidly decline.

Temperature and light are equally important. Keep the plant in a light and airy situation – a bedroom windowsill at not above 15°C (60°F) is ideal. Central heating can often be fatal and will certainly reduce the flowering period to as little as 2 weeks.

When the plant has finished flowering it can be placed outdoors from May until September. Plunge the pot in a peat bed and keep it moist throughout the summer. Feeding with a tomato fertilizer at about half strength once a month will assist growth. One or two applications of sequestrene will prevent yellowing of the leaves. When they have been brought back indoors in September, most azaleas will flower reasonably well.

They can be made to flower in greater profusion by a simple technique. In the evening, spray the plant with tepid water and place it in an airing cupboard overnight. Repeat this for a few weeks and you will find that the relatively high temperature and humidity have helped to produce flowers. Do remember to place the plant in full light during daylight hours.

Propagation: Azaleas can be raised from cuttings in summer or seed in spring but the results are usually so disappointing that it is not worth trying.

Pests and diseases: Azaleas suffer from few pests although aphids can sometimes be a problem on the flower buds.

BEGONIA REX

Begonia rex or 'fan plant' is available in a wide range of leaf colours and patterns. The leaves are roughly heart-shaped with prominent fleshy veins on the underside. The small, insignificant flowers may be pale pink or white.

General care: *Begonia rex* must be kept away from direct sun. It is therefore best to place the plant on a shaded windowsill or even up to 1.5m (5ft) away from the window. The plant is fairly tolerant of a warm dry environment and is usually happy at a temperature of about 18°C (65°F). Water regularly but in moderation; reduce the watering to a minimum in winter or the plant may rot.

Propagation: The method of propagation is by leaf cuttings. Select a well-formed mature (not old) leaf, lay it face down and cut into postage-stamp squares using a sharp knife. Gently lay right-side up on the surface of a seed tray or half pot filled with moistened seed compost. Cover with a polythene bag and keep at about 21°C (70°F). Remove any cuttings that wither or rot; about half should 'take'. Remove the

cover when the little plant-lets start to grow from the cut edge of the pieces. When they are large enough to handle, pot up singly in potting compost.

Pests and diseases: Generally trouble-free.

See p. 99 for illustration

BELOPERONE GUTTATA

Beloperone guttata (syn. *Justicia brandegeana*) is known as the shrimp plant because of the oddly shaped shrimplike flower-spikes it produces. They are small and white, enclosed in reddish-brown bracts, and last several weeks before dropping of.

General care: Since the beloperone likes plenty of light, put the pot in a well-lit window. During the winter months, the plants may become straggly. Prune in early spring to encourage more compact growth. Feed once a month with half strength tomato fertilizer rather than a house plant fertilizer in order to induce sturdy growth and plenty of flowers rather than leaves.

In the flowering period, give water freely. In the winter, give just enough to prevent the compost drying out.

Propagation: When you prune the plant in spring, make the trimmings into cuttings 5–7cm (2–3in) in length. Dip into hormone rooting powder and insert in individual pots of equal parts of peat and sand. Cover the pots with polythene bags to conserve moisture, and keep at about 20°C (68°F). Pot on into John Innes No. 2 potting compost when they have rooted well.

Pests and diseases: May be affected by red spider mites or whitefly.

BOUGAINVILLEA

The bougainvillea or 'paper flower' provides a glorious display of colour. It needs the support of canes or a frame. Like poinsettias, the

flowers are insignificant – it is the papery bracts surrounding them that provide colour – pink, red, magenta or orange. The flowering period usually lasts from mid-summer well into the autumn.

General care: Bougainvillea needs as much light as possible during the active growing season. A temperature of about 18–20°C (65–68°F) is ideal and a fairly humid environment is essential. Mist regularly with tepid water during spring and summer

Beloperone guttata (**front**) *and Bougainvillea*

and take care to prevent the compost drying out between waterings. Good drainage is essential, however, and the pot must not sit in a saucer of water for long periods. Weekly feeding with a diluted tomato fertilizer will promote flowering.

Over winter, keep the plant on the dry side at a temperature of around 10–13°C (50–55°F). In spring, prune lightly, reducing the plant by a quarter of its height to encourage bushy, well-shaped growth.

Propagation: To succeed with bougainvillea cuttings you will need a propagator that can provide a constant bottom heat of 21–24°C (70–75°F). Take 7.5–10cm (3–4in) cuttings in summer and insert in 5cm (2in) pots of 4 parts seed compost to 1 part sand. Keep in the case until rooted – about 3 weeks – and allow the young plants to adjust gradually to room conditions.

Pests and diseases: Aphids, mealy bugs or red spider mites may attack.

CALCEOLARIA

The unusual flowers of calceolaria look like half-inflated balloons of bright yellow, orange or red. The flowers are often spotted or streaked and are borne on short stems above a rosette-like cluster of broad leaves.

It lasts fairly well indoors and usually flowers in spring and summer for 2–3 months. They are best disposed of after flowering.

General care: Calceolaria will not give of its best in warm, dry conditions, and prefers a fairly cool, light position such as a north-facing windowsill. A temperature of 10–15°C (50–60°F) is best. Temperatures may well rise during summer, but this will not seriously affect the plant – it is only troubled by constant high temperatures. Always keep the compost just moist but not wet. Occasional feeding with diluted tomato fertilizer will encourage the plant to remain fairly stocky and to carry a good show of flowers.

Propagation: Calceolaria

seed should be germinated from May to July in half pots or seed trays filled with seed compost. Keep it around 18°C (65°F) until germinated and grow on until large enough to handle. At this stage, prick out the seedlings and pot up singly into 9–13cm (3½–5in) pots of potting compost. For sturdy plants grow in a cold frame or greenhouse and only bring indoors when the weather cools in autumn.

Pests and diseases: Often attacked by aphids and whitefly.

CHAMAEDOREA ELEGANS

Also called *Neanthe bella* or parlour palm, this is a compact palm that takes some time to reach 60cm (2ft) in height and grows taller only slowly. It is one of the easiest palms to cultivate.

General care: Parlour palms prefer a semi-shaded position away from direct light which turns the leaves pale. Maintain a minimum temperature of about 18°C (65°F) in spring and summer and spray once or twice a day

*Chamaedorea elegans (**behind**) and Nephrolepis exaltata (see p. 106)*

with a mist of tepid water to increase humidity. In winter it prefers to be kept cooler, at 7–10°C (45–50°F). Let the compost dry out between waterings. Feed about once a month during the growing period (April–September).

Chamaedorea sometimes produces a flower spike, which can be snipped off if you do not like the look of it. The flowers that form look like small yellow blobs. If you are lucky, tiny pea-like fruits may set, and these can be used for propagation. Flowers are unlikely to appear before the plant is 3–4 years old.

Propagation: You can buy seeds or save your own if you have a plant that flowers. Sow in a half pot filled with seed compost and then cover with a polythene bag. The seeds need a temperature of at least 21°C (70°F) to germinate and even then, they may take 3–6 months to grow.

Pests and diseases: Generally trouble free, but red spider mites, mealy bugs, root mealy bugs and scale insects are occasional problems; red spider mites are the most damaging to this plant.

CHLOROPHYTUM

Chlorophytum has long been known as the spider plant. It has green and white striped leaves and reproduces itself by producing plantlets on the flowering stems – seed being seldom or never produced.

General care: Chlorophytum is very easy to keep and adapts well to various household conditions. Lots of light and a temperature of about 15°C (60°F) are best but by no means essential.

In early spring, shade the plant from the first scorching rays of the sun as these can brown the leaves. The plant adapts rapidly, however, and can soon tolerate direct sunlight for periods of the day.

Avoid overwatering and

allow the plant to become almost dry between waterings. If the leaf tips turn brown, simply snip them off with a pair of scissors.

Propagation: The plantlets on the flowering stems can easily be used as a ready means of propagation. Simply look for the start of the first roots which appear even before the plantlet is removed from its parent. When these are evident, cut off the plantlet and pot up in a 9cm (3½in) pot of potting compost. Cut back the flowering stems to the base of the parent to keep the original plant looking tidy.

Pests and diseases: Generally trouble-free.

CISSUS ANTARCTICA

Sometimes referred to as the kangaroo vine, this cissus has a very similar habit to the rhoicissus. The leaf shape is a pointed oval with a serrated but not sharp edge.

General care: An indoor temperature of between 15 and 18°C (60–65°F) is best, although 13°C (55°F) is adequate. A reasonably light position is favoured. Too much direct sunlight will bleach the colour out of the leaves. Do not keep the plant in a dry atmosphere as dehydration causes leaf tips and edges to turn brown.

The cissus is a good climbing plant but it may become a little straggly. If this happens, trim back to keep it in shape.

Propagation: Use stem cuttings produced when pruning the plant. Cut them into sections each with 3–4 leaves, retaining about 4cm (1½in) stem below the bottom leaf. Dip this end into hormone rooting powder and insert into potting compost. Several cuttings can go in one pot – about 5 to a 9cm (3½in) pot is perfectly all right. Cover the cuttings with a polythene bag until they have rooted. Pot on as necessary.

Pests and diseases: Mealy bugs and aphids may attack.

COLEUS

The flame nettle, *Coleus blumei*, together with its numerous cultivars has long been a popular pot plant with its brightly coloured and patterned leaves. Named sorts can be obtained from nurserymen, but seed strains are good and available in varied forms and colours.

General care: A window ledge with half-day or dappled sun is best. Extra humidity is not essential. Use one of the standard all-peat potting composts and apply a standard liquid feed at intervals of 2–3 weeks once the plants are well rooted and growing strongly. Keep the compost just moist but not over-wet. Pinch out the tips of the plants when 10cm (4in) tall to promote bushy plants. The long spikes of blue flowers are attractive but they drop and make rather a mess so it is usually recommended to pinch them out when young.

*Chlorophytum, Cissus antarctica and (**front**) Begonia rex (see p. 96)*

Columnea (right) and Gardenia (see p. 103)

Propagation: Sow seeds in spring at about 18°C (65°F); prick off the seedlings into boxes and then pot the best coloured ones when they have 4–5 pairs of leaves. Take cuttings in late summer or spring in a propagating case at seed sowing temperatures. Each cutting should have two pairs of leaves and will root better if dipped in a hormone rooting powder.

Pests and diseases: Generally trouble-free.

COLUMNEA

Few trailing plants give flowers; of those that do, none is as beautiful as columnea, with its magnificent flame red flowers streaked with yellow, projecting like trumpets from its long stem of tiny paired leaves.

General care: If you have a warm, reasonably well-lit bathroom or kitchen where the temperature is about 20°C (68°F) and there is sufficient ceiling space to hang a columnea, you will be delighted by the colourful display that it will give each year. A bathroom or kitchen is best because the columnea thrives in a relatively humid environment. Although the plant needs light, it should not have prolonged exposure to direct sunlight which will discolour and scorch the leaves.

While columnea likes a relatively moist atmosphere, too much water at the root is harmful. Reduce watering to the bare minimum over winter. In this season they can also tolerate a lower temperature – down to about 13°C (55°F). After this cooler period, columnea will gently break into a massive display of flowers down the lengths of the trails.

If the plant gets unmanageably long, simply trim back the trails to an acceptable length.

Propagation: Take cuttings and divide them into sections of 3–4 pairs of leaves, leaving approximately 1–2cm ($\frac{1}{2}$–$\frac{3}{4}$in) below the bottom pair. Dip the cuttings in hormone rooting powder and insert about 4 cuttings into a 7.5cm (3in) pot of seed compost. Cover with a polythene bag to conserve moisture.

When rooted, remove the bag and grow the cuttings on in the pot. Pot the plants up, still together, into a larger pot the following year.

Pests and diseases: Occasionally mealy bugs, and aphids may attack the flowers during spring and summer.

CYCLAMEN

Cyclamen must be one of the most popular flowering houseplants, producing blooms of white, pink, salmon, mauve, red or lilac over a long period, from early autumn to summer.

General care: Unfortunately, cyclamen is not the easiest plant to care for. Warm, dry, airless conditions spell its rapid demise and induce the all-too-common sight of a plant that has collapsed, its leaves and flowers drooping around the pot. Cyclamen prefers cool, light airy conditions with a temperature of about 13°C (55°F). It does not tolerate central heating. A cool bedroom windowsill or any other light position away from excessive heat is ideal.

Watering is best carried out from below to avoid the risk of botrytis setting in on the corm.

After flowering, the plant will gradually die back to its corm. It can be left for a few weeks to rest; during this period it should be kept on the dry side. After about a month, start to give water again. Once active growth commences, feed every 2 weeks with a tomato fertilizer to encourage flowering.

The silver-leaved cyclamen is probably the best known type. It is, however, the one most likely to suffer from the normal home environment.

The mini-cyclamen is hardier and more tolerant of household conditions. As the name suggests, it is smaller and the leaves are less colourful than the silver-leaved strain, but its flowers are magnificent; some of them even have a slight scent.

Propagation: Cyclamen is relatively easy to propagate from seed. You can either buy seed or collect your own from the plant. When the flowers have been pollinated, their petals fall off, leaving behind a globular seed capsule where the seeds ripen. When the receptacle has matured, it splits open, exposing the seeds.

Sow seed in half pots of seed compost. Cover the seed with about 3mm (⅛in) of compost and keep it at about 18°C (65°F) until germination has occurred – usually about 6–8 weeks. When the seedlings are large enough to handle, carefully prick them out into separate pots and grow on.

Pests and diseases: Cyclamen is prone to botrytis (grey mould fungus).

DIEFFENBACHIA

Best known as dumb-cane, this group of plants is grown for its large paddle-shaped boldly variegated leaves. When mature the plant may produce an insignificant flower spike that looks like an arum lily. The sap of the plant is poisonous and care should therefore be taken when trimming any leaves on the plant. Do not have one if there are children about.

General care: Dieffenbachia likes a warm, humid environment with a temperature of about 20°C (68°F). As it prefers light shade it is happiest in the middle of a room.

Though watering is not so critical, dieffenbachia is best kept relatively moist in summer, somewhat drier in winter. Yellowing leaves should be cut off at the base before they rot. If the plant becomes too tall with a long bare stem, cut it back to about 5cm (2in) above soil level and it will break into growth again.

Propagation: Dieffenbachia sometimes produces offsets which can be removed from the parent plant and potted on. Alternatively, if you cut the plant back, divide the stem into 5cm (2in) sections. Lay them on their sides in a tray of moist seed compost. Cover and keep at 21°C (70°F) until rooted. Remove the cover and allow to grow on until large enough to handle and pot up.

Dracaena marginata

Pests and diseases: Red spider mites and mealy bugs are the worst nuisance; root mealy bugs may inhibit growth.

DRACAENA

Dracaena deremensis is one of the hardier species of this genus. The leaf colour of the plant is attractive and the long, slender, pointed leaves are beautifully patterned in parallel streaks of green, white and cream. *Dracaena marginata* is less spectacular and bears narrow dark green leaves with red edges.

General care: A slightly shaded situation is best, but short periods of exposure to sunlight will be tolerated. Let the compost almost dry out between waterings. Because of their thick leaves, dracaenas can store water for quite a long time and can cope with being kept on the dry side. A temperature of around 18°C (65°F) is best although plants will tolerate cooler conditions.

Propagation: Basal shoots or stem tips can be rooted as cuttings in a propagating case at 21°C (70°F). The leafless stems of cut-back leggy plants can also be used. Cut into pieces 2–3cm (about 1in) long. Lay these sections on their sides in a tray of seed compost. Rooting should take place within 8 weeks. Pot up when the young plants are large enough to handle and grow on.

Pests and diseases: Mealy bugs and root mealy bugs are the major pests; the former may be found tucked in the little niche at the base of the leaf stalk where it joins the main stem.

ECHEVERIA

This genus contains 150 succulent plants, some rosette forming, others of shrubby appearance. They bear tubular flowers of white, yellow-orange or red. *Echeveria glauca*, with blue-grey leaves, is one of the most common varieties,

and can be grown outside in summer.

General care: Echeveria is a tough little plant but it does have certain preferences. In summer it needs plenty of water; in winter it should be kept almost dry. The plant likes to spend summer outdoors in the sun and air. Bring it indoors in autumn and give it plenty of light, with a minimum temperature of 5°C (41°F).

Propagation: Echeveria can be propagated quite easily from cuttings by gently pulling off a leaf and obliquely inserting it in a mixture of equal parts seed compost and sand. Use the same mixture to raise echeveria from seed.

Pests and diseases: Generally trouble-free, but mealy bugs and root mealy bugs may attack.

EPIPHYLLUM

Epiphyllum or orchid cactus is one of the most attractive of the flowering cacti. The beautiful flowers are borne on green, fleshy, flat-sided stems and vary in size from 5–15cm (2–6in) across. They may be single or double, and coloured white, yellow, pink, orange, red, or lilac. Some of the flowers are fragrant.

General care: In winter, keep the plant relatively cool, down to 7°C (45°F), but never let it dry out. In spring and summer, maintain regular watering. Give a liquid feed every 2 weeks once the flower buds are visible in spring. The best position is one where the plant can enjoy plenty of light but not direct sun during mid summer.

Propagation: Epiphyllum can easily be propagated from stem cuttings taken in summer and inserted into pots of seed compost after they have been allowed to dry off for a few days. Alternatively, raise it from seed sown in spring in a mixture

101

of 4 parts seed compost to 1 part sand and germinate at 20°C (68°F). Prick out the seedlings when they are large enough to handle and later pot on.

Pests and diseases: Mealy bugs and root mealy bugs may attack; aphids occasionally infest the flowers.

EUPHORBIA PULCHERRIMA

The 'flowers' of Euphorbia pulcherrima, known as poinsettia, are in fact modified leaves called bracts. The range of colours extends from white or cream, through pink to the colour which everyone knows, bright red.

The flowers of euphorbia are the little pips in the centre of the bracts.

General care: Euphorbia should be kept at about 18°C (65°F), well away from draughts. They like plenty of light but should be moved away from a window at night during winter when they are in colour, for they are very sensitive to low temperatures and temperature fluctuations. As the temperature drops, so do the leaves, followed by the bracts.

Care should also be taken with watering. Although they should not be allowed to dry out, they must not be overwatered, or the roots will rot.

After 'flowering', prune the plant in April or May by removing one third to one half of the growth so that the plant will start to 'break'. As the new shoots grow, feed the plant every week with tomato fertilizer at half strength. If the plant starts to outgrow its pot, transfer it to a larger one.

At the end of September, do not allow the plant to be exposed to any artificial light after the hours of daylight, otherwise it will not form its coloured bracts. Euphorbia by nature responds to the shortening autumn days by initiating flowers and bracts. Artificial light during the hours of darkness makes the plant behave as if it were still summer!

Propagation: Euphorbia can be propagated by taking basal shoots from cut-back plants as cuttings consisting of a shoot with 2 or 3 mature leaves. Dip this into hormone rooting powder and then into a small pot of equal parts peat and sand. Cover with a polythene bag and keep at around 21°C (70°F) until rooted. This normally takes 3–4 weeks. When the roots are established, pot the plant on into a larger container of potting compost.

Pests and diseases: Whitefly are more unsightly than harmful, but should not be left to get out of hand.

FATSIA JAPONICA

Also known as *Aralia sieboldii*, this Japanese shrub makes a very handsome and desirable foliage house plant for a cool or unheated room. Eventually growing to 1m (3¼ft) or more, it bears large, hand-shaped leathery leaves with a bright gloss.

General care: Dappled or partial shade provides the best conditions. Extra humidity is not essential. Use any of the approved potting omposts and repot or top-dress annually. Keep the compost moist but not overwet.

Propagation: Stem tips or sucker shoots can be taken as cuttings in a propagating case in late summer, but purchased seed is easiest. Sow fatsia japonica in spring and pot the seedlings singly once the first true leaf is well developed.

Pests and diseases: Generally trouble-free.

Ficus elastica

X FATSHEDERA

This useful foliage pot plant arose from the mating of *Fatsia japonica* with the Irish ivy *Hedera helix* var. *hibernica*. All the comments for Fatsia apply here, but the leaves are smaller. If allowed to grow naturally it becomes a loose, thin shrub which needs support. Frequent pinching out of the stem tip will make it bushy and self-supporting.

Propagation is by cuttings or layering.

FICUS BENJAMINA

Ficus benjamina, weeping fig, is an elegant plant with cascading foliage that makes it particularly suitable as a single specimen plant rather than as part of a group display.

General care: Not as hardy as its sturdy relative, the rubber plant, *Ficus benjamina* needs a stable temperature of around 20°C (68°F), although a steady 15°C (60°F) is adequate. The plant must be kept free from draughts. If it is subject to sudden 'chilling', premature leaf drop rapidly ensues, leaving the plant looking like a skeleton. Give weeping figs a situation of semi-shade 1m (3ft) or so away from a window; direct sunlight may bleach the leaves. Allow the plant almost to dry out between waterings. A humid environment is beneficial but not essential.

Propagation: *Ficus benjamina* is very tricky to propagate. Those who are keen, however, should take tip cuttings about 7.5–10cm (3–4in) in length, dip them in hormone rooting powder and insert individually in a 6cm (2½in) pot filled with seed compost. Keep at 21°C (70°F) and cover with a polythene bag to conserve moisture. When rooted, pot on into John Innes No. 2 compost.

Pests and diseases: Mealy bugs and scale insects are the most likely problems.

FICUS ELASTICA

The rubber plant, as it is familiarly known, has become amazingly popular. Its thick glossy green leaves grow alternately up the stem of the plant, borne erect when young, drooping as they get older. Variegated forms are available with pink or cream tints on the margin. New leaves form inside a rosy-pink protective sheath, which is discarded when the young leaf unfurls.

General care: The rubber plant's reputation for durability has probably been overstated. Ideally, it should be grown in light shade at a temperature of about 18°C (65°F) away from draughts. Allow the compost almost to dry out between waterings; if it is kept too moist, the lower leaves may fall, giving you 1m (3ft) of bare stem with 2–3 leaves at the top! To remove dust, clean the leaves with a cotton wool pad or soft cloth moistened with tepid water.

Propagation: Take stem-tip cuttings in spring, making them 10-15cm (4–6in) long. Insert in pots of equal parts peat and sand and maintain a temperature of 21–24°C (70–75°F) until rooted.

Leaf bud cuttings are used commercially for propagation, but results for the amateur are not always successful, so you are better off using stem cuttings.

Pests and diseases: Mealy bugs and scale insects are the main pests to watch for, though aphids may disfigure young leaves.

FITTONIA ARGYRONEURA

Perhaps better known as the snakeskin plant, this pretty species is delicately patterned in green with white veins. It is a low-growing plant, good for ground cover in mixed plantings or bottle gardens.

General care: If there is one thing the fittonia dislikes, apart from the cold, it is to be allowed to dry out. Keep it moist most of the time, at a temperature of about 18°C (65°F) in a well-lit situation away from direct sunlight. Avoid draughts and a dry environment. Trim as necessary to maintain a compact plant during growth.

Propagation: The method of propagation is easy and usually successful. When the plant becomes rather leggy, cut off the straggling shoots, and insert 5 of them in a 9cm (3½in) pot of seed compost. Cover with a polythene bag until they have rooted. Remove the bag and let the plants grow on.

Pests and diseases: Generally trouble-free.

GARDENIA

Gardenia is one of the most highly scented flowering plants, with magnificent creamy-white flowers and glossy dark leaves. A compact, bushy plant, it is lovely if you can master its rather demanding requirements.

General care: Gardenia likes a semi-shaded position away from direct sunlight and a temperature of about 20°C (68°F). It also requires humid conditions and a fairly acid compost. Watering with rainwater is beneficial, but if you cannot collect any, use boiled, cooled tap water. Boiling removes some of the calcium salts from hard water, which gardenias dislike.

Throughout spring and summer, water every two weeks with a half strength solution of tomato fertilizer, to help it produce good quality flowers in profusion. An application or two of sequestrene during the flowering period will prevent chlorosis, a condition typified by yellow patches between the leaf veins. This is caused by an iron deficiency due to too much lime.

Propagation: It is difficult to propagate gardenia from cuttings, but worth a try. Take tip cuttings with 3–4 leaves and dip the base of the stems into hormone rooting powder. Insert the cuttings in individual pots containing 50–50 parts peat and sand. Cover each pot with a polythene bag and keep at about 21°C (70°F) until rooted. Reduce the temperature to 18°C (64°F) and keep the pots away from direct sunlight.

Pests and diseases: Red spider mites and mealy bugs occasionally attack. Aphids attack the flower buds and young growth.

See p. 100 for illustration

HEDERA CANARIENSIS

The Canary Island ivy is a magnificent species with large, deep green glossy leaves of triangular outline. *H. c.* 'Gloire de Marengo' has the leaves irregularly bordered with cream.

General care: It likes sun or shade but dislikes being kept too warm. Keep it where the temperature will not exceed 20°C (68°F). In rooms warmer than this, the atmosphere is likely to be too dry and the leaf tips and edges will turn brown. In winter, the variegation tends to fade a little, but once light intensities increase in spring, the brighter pigments return.

Like all ivies, *Hedera canariensis* is a good climber or trailer. It is a useful plant for a porch or unheated conservatory. Take care not to overwater this ivy, but let the compost become somewhat dry between waterings.

Propagation: Simply trim off any unwanted stems and cut them into pieces with 2–3 leaves on each. Leave about 2.5cm (1in) of stem below the bottom leaf. Dip the cuttings in hormone rooting

Hedera canariensis

powder and insert them 5 per 9cm (3½in) pot of seed compost. Cover with a polythene bag to conserve moisture during rooting and remove the bag as soon as the plants start to grow.

Pests and diseases: Scale insects can cause severe damage by mottling the leaves. Aphids, mealy bugs and root mealy bugs can also be a problem.

HEDERA HELIX

The small-leaved English ivy produces an attractive climbing or trailing plant that can be grown outdoors as well as indoors. There are many variations with leaves of different shape, size and colour.

General care: None of the ivies likes to be too warm. They prefer cool, even cold, light airy conditions, and are particularly happy in an unheated porch or conservatory. In a warm, dry environment the leaves will dehydrate and eventually die. A temperature between 7–10°C (45–50°F) is adequate. Take care with watering, and allow compost to become almost dry before rewatering. Most ivies that die have been overwatered.

Don't worry if any variegation fades in winter; in the spring, as light intensities increase, it will return. Trimming of wayward growth can be done at any time. If the plant begins to outgrow its home, you can always plant it outside, preferably in spring or early summer.

Propagation: When you trim the ivy, cut the stems into pieces with 2–3 leaves, leaving about 2.5cm (1in) of stem below the bottom leaf. Dip the bottom piece of stem in hormone rooting powder and insert about 5 cuttings in a 7.5cm (3in) pot of seed compost. Cover with a polythene bag until the cuttings have rooted. Remove the bag and grow on in the same pot.

Pests and diseases: Watch for aphids, red spider mites or mealy bugs.

HIPPEASTRUM

For most of the year hippeastrum has little to show other than its broad straplike leaves. When it flowers, however, the display is dramatic. Each bulb produces one or more magnificent blooms that are especially welcome in the drab months of late winter when prepared bulbs are usually brought into flower. The natural flowering time is spring. The flowers produced on 60cm (2ft) stems can be more than 15cm (6in) across and vary in colour from white to pink and deep red.

General care: Plant the bulb in a 13–18cm (5–7in) pot of John Innes No. 2 potting compost, leaving about one half of the bulb proud of the compost. In winter, give the plant as much light as possible and water moderately, but regularly. Give a weekly liquid feed and keep the plant warm, at around 18–20°C (65–68°F). Increase watering as the plant grows and eventually flowers.

After flowering, the leaves will grow more actively and the plant should continue to be fed at reduced strength. This will help to promote flower production for the following year. As the leaves start to wither, reduce watering and allow the plant to rest in a dry state for its dormant period during the autumn and early winter before starting into growth again in about early spring.

Propagation: Either offsets or seed can be used. Separate offsets from the main plant when starting it into growth and pot up singly into 9cm (3½in) pots, transferring them to the final pot as the bulb expands.

Sow seed in half pots of seed compost in spring, cover and keep at about 21°C (70°F). When they have

Hippeastrum

germinated and are large enough to handle, prick them out, pot up separately and treat in the same way as offsets, although they will take at least 2 years to flower. Bulb offsets are produced less freely than seeds but will flower sooner.

Pests and diseases: Mealy bugs may attack.

HOWEIA (syn. *Howea*)

Howeia forsteriana, commonly called the kentia palm, is one of the most elegant palms, with leathery leaves and a height of 2m (6ft) or more.

General care: The kentia palm prefers a shady position away from draughts in a temperature of 13–18°C (55–65°F). Humidity and ventilation are important; in a stuffy, dry environment the fronds will dehydrate and the edges turn brown. Although these can be trimmed off this is only a cosmetic treatment. Some move must be made to increase the humidity, such as spraying the plant with a mist of tepid water twice a day. Do not be tempted to treat the fronds with a leaf-shine cleaning material as this can often cause serious damage. Wipe dust from the fronds with a cotton wool pad or soft cloth moistened with tepid water.

Propagation: It is not easy to propagate palms from seed but possible – with patience. Germination is slow and erratic and may take 3–6 months. Sow the seeds in a half pot of seed compost. Lightly cover and keep in a polythene bag at about 24–26°C (75–80°F). When the seeds have germinated, pot them on singly.

Pests and diseases: Generally trouble-free.

See p. 93 for illustration

IMPATIENS

Impatiens, popularly known as busy lizzie, is still one of the best-loved flowering house plants. While the familiar plain green-leaved type with pale-pink or rose-pink flowers holds its own, variegated varieties are now freely available.

General care: Easily maintained, impatiens needs little special treatment. Place the plant in a light situation, but not in direct sunlight behind glass. Do not allow the soil to dry out. During the main growing period, April–September, feed the plant once every 2–3 weeks with half strength tomato fertilizer.

To prevent the plant becoming straggly, trim it occasionally or pinch out the growing points. This helps to keep it compact and well-shaped. A more drastic pruning in early spring will ensure that the plant retains its good shape.

Propagation: Busy lizzies are very easy to propagate. Simply take a 7.5–10cm (3–4in) cutting from a top shoot and root it in a pot of sandy compost or in a jar of water. In either case, pot up as soon as rooted.

Pests and diseases: Aphids and whitefly are the most likely troublemakers; it may also be attacked by red spider mites.

MAMMILLARIA

Mammillaria is one of the most commonly grown genera of cacti. No less than 200 different species are known. They are covered with nipple-like tubercules that give the plant its name. These are arranged in whorls that spiral around the plant. *Mammillaria hahniana* and *Mammillaria zeilmanniana* are among the most popular spices, both of which bear red flowers in a ring at the top of the plant. Other species have white, yellow or pink flowers.

General care: Mammillaria needs to be in full sun in order to flower. In summer, water generously without soaking; in winter, let the compost dry out and do not

let the temperature drop below 7°C (45°F).

Propagation: In May and August offsets are produced which can be removed from the parent. Let them dry for a day and pot up in a mixture of 50–50 compost and coarse sand.

Alternatively, in spring they can be raised from seed sown in a similar compost, lightly covered with sand and kept at 20°C (68°F) until germinated. When seedlings are large enough to handle, prick them out and pot up.

Pests and diseases: Mealy bugs and root mealy bugs may be a problem.

MARANTA LEUCONEURA

Maranta is sometimes known as prayer plant because of its nightly habit of raising its leaves together like praying hands. Maranta produces tiny, violet-pink flowers on a long slender stalk but is entirely grown for its decorative paddle-shaped leaves. *M. l.* 'Kerchoveana' is additionally called 'rabbit tracks', owing to the shape and positioning of the bronze-brown blotches. *M. l.* 'Erythrophylla' has leaves with a red herring-bone pattern.

General care: Maranta is not difficult to grow. It likes warm, humid conditions in semi-shade with a steady temperature of about 20°C (68°F). Give maranta a liquid feed every 2 weeks, April–September.

Propagation: Division of the main plant is recommended. Alternatively, take tip cuttings, inserting them in pots of equal parts peat and sand in a propagating case at 21°C (70°F). When rooted pot on

into larger pots of John Innes No. 2 potting compost.

Pests and diseases: Red spider mites, mealy bugs and root mealy bugs may occasionally cause trouble.

See p. 107 for illustration

MONSTERA DELICIOSA

Sometimes called Swiss cheese plant or Mexican breadfruit plant, monstera is an unusual species with slits and holes in its large glossy green leaves. It may reach 2m (6ft) or more in height. Its tentacle-like aerial roots are an unusual feature.

General care: Monstera adapts to most environments with little trouble. To get the best out of the plant, ensure that it enjoys a semi-shaded position where the atmosphere is relatively humid, as these two factors are important if the plant is to produce leaves of characteristic shape. In a bright, dry position it will revert to a small leaf without slits or holes. To remove dust, clean leaves occasionally with a cotton wool pad moistened with tepid water.

If the aerial roots become too rampant, wind them around the plant to encourage them to grow back into the compost, or put them into damp sphagnum moss or moss peat. Plants over 60cm (2ft) need support; a 'moss pole' is ideal.

Propagation: Monstera may produce a side shoot that can be separated when it is 15cm (6in) tall and potted in one of the all-peat potting mixes.

Pests and diseases: Generally trouble-free.

See p. 107 for illustration

NEOREGELIA

Neoregelia is a magnificent bromeliad with glossy green strap-like leaves in rosettes with the bases forming a cup. In the form generally seen as a house plant, *Neoregelia*

Plain and variegated Impatiens

Neoregelia carolinae 'Tricolor'

carolinae 'Tricolor', the leaves are bright rose-pink at their base and white-striped above. At flowering time, which tends to be spring, this colour may radiate outwards from the centre. Lilac-pink flowers appear just above the red leaf bases.

General care: Neoregelia is easy to keep because it is so adaptable. A lightly shaded situation away from direct sunlight is best with a temperature around 15–18°C (60–65°F) although temperatures down to 10°C (50°F) can be tolerated. The funnel should always be kept topped up with water, rainwater if you can provide it. In summer, water frequently without soaking; in winter keep the compost just moist. After flowering, the plant will devote all of its energy to producing offsets and the old parent plant will gradually die.

Propagation: Let the offsets make roots while still attached to the parent plant. Sever them in June/July and put them in individual 13cm (5in) pots of equal parts sand and medium loam. Provide each plantlet with a supporting stake and do not plant too deeply. Water sparingly but keep the atmosphere relatively humid until a sound root formation has been made.

Pests and diseases: Generally trouble-free but root mealy bugs may occasionally attack.

NEPHROLEPIS EXALTATA

Nephrolepis or ladder fern is one of the more common ferns grown as house plants. It has long, stately fronds of pale or bright green depending on variety and looks attractive on a plant stand or in a hanging basket.

General care: Nephrolepis prefers a semi-lit situation away from direct sunlight. A temperature of about 18°C (65°F) is ideal provided that the atmosphere is not too dry, for its thin fronds are susceptible to dehydration. It will, however, tolerate a minimum winter temperature of 10°C (50°F). Do not let the compost dry out as this can at worst cause the plant to die back, at the least exacerbate the problem of drying fronds. An acid compost is required and feeding every 2 weeks from mid-summer will give a good growth of fronds.

Propagation: Nephrolepis can be propagated from spores but it is easier to increase by division or removing plantlets that form on the stolons (runners). The plant-lets should be potted in a moist peaty compost in late spring or summer. They will establish quickly if kept moist and warm.

Pests and diseases: Generally trouble-free.

See p. 98 for illustration

NOTOCACTUS

The most commonly grown species of notocactus is *N. leninghausii*, also sometimes

known as goldfinger cactus. It grows slowly to a magnificent thick column and produces yellow trumpet-shaped flowers at its top that may reach about 5cm (2in) in diameter.

General care: Like most cacti, notocactus like full light. In winter keep them cool at a temperature of about 13°C (55°F) and let the compost dry. Summer temperatures of about 18°C (65°F) are best, and allow the compost to dry out between waterings.

Propagation: Seed is the only sure means of increase. Sow in spring at a temperature of at least 21°C (70°F). Large plants can be decapitated, the top being used as a cutting after several days of drying out. Mature plants sometimes produce basal shoots which can be treated as cuttings.

Pests and diseases: Mealy bugs and root mealy bugs.

ABOVE LEFT: *Notocactus*
BELOW: *Pellaea rotundifolia* (*back*) *and Platycerium bifurcatum* (see p. 109)

OPUNTIA

Opuntia is better known as prickly pear or bunny ears. Its stems are like round or oval pads which are covered with fine bristles and require careful handling. There are many different species with flowers which vary in colour from yellow to orange and red. One of the most suitable species for the home is *Opuntia microdasys*. It is a plant to 60cm (2ft) or more which produces numerous pads dotted with tiny white or yellow spines.

General care: Opuntia is quite easy to grow. It requires a well-drained growing medium and, unlike many cacti, needs some water the whole year round – plenty in summer, enough to prevent the compost drying out in winter. If it becomes dry, brown spots appear on the pads. A minimum winter temperature of 7°C (45°F) is necessary. Repot opuntia annually or biennially in spring.

Propagation: The easiest way is to propagate from the pads taken in June/July. Wear garden gloves and wrap a piece of coarse cloth or paper round the plant to protect your hands from the spines. Simply pull off a pad, let it dry out for 2–3 days and insert in a pot of equal parts peat and gritty sand. Keep the compost moist but not waterlogged, otherwise the roots will rot.

Pests and diseases: Mealy bugs and root mealy bugs may attack.

PELLAEA ROTUNDIFOLIA

The fronds of the diminutive pellaea or button fern are composed of small circular leaflets or pinnae. Fronds up to 50cm (20in) long form a low spreading mat as the fern grows.

General care: Unlike most ferns, pellaea is happy in a light environment, though not direct sunlight. It will grow well under the low in-

tensity of fluorescent lighting. Pellaea ideally likes a temperature of about 18°C (65°F) and needs to be kept reasonably moist. It will not tolerate temperatures below 7°C (45°F).

Propagation: Like other ferns, propagation from spores is possible (see Asplenium) but division is easier and quicker.

Pests and diseases: Generally trouble-free.

PEPEROMIA MAGNOLIIFOLIA

Commonly known as desert privet, *Peperomia magnoliifolia* is a most attractive plant with oval waxy leaves. *P. m.* 'Variegata' has green and cream variegated leaves.

General care: Desert privet is exceptionally adaptable and is ideal for a beginner's collection. It will continue to thrive in a wide temperature range of 10–18°C (50–65°F). Light is important as it keeps the variegated colours bright. In a shady position the leaves will become dull and the variegation will be less bold.

As the thick fleshy leaves act as water storage reservoirs, it is advisable to keep the compost rather dry. Too much water will drown the roots and the plant will rot. Let the compost almost dry out between waterings.

Propagation: This is best achieved by rooting stem cuttings. When the plant becomes rather leggy and top-heavy, cut it back to a more

Peperomia (**front right**). Also shown – Maranta 'Erythrophylla' (**left background**), M. l. 'Kerchoveana' (**left foreground**) and Monstera (**right background**); see p. 105

compact shape. Trim each cutting to a section about 5–7.5cm (2–3in) long and insert cuttings into a 9cm (3½in) pot of moist seed compost. Do not cover with polythene, as the leaves can store enough water to stop the plant wilting and could rot if kept in a humid environment.

Pests and diseases: Aphids and red spider mites sometimes attack in spring and summer. Take prompt action to stop any damage.

Philodendron scandens,
Rhoicissus rhomboidea and
(**front**) *Tradescantia (see p. 111)*

PHOENIX CANARIENSIS

Better known as the Canary Island date palm, *P. canariensis* is a plant of superb geometric form with gently cascading fronds radiating from the centre. It tends to grow about 2m (6ft) high in the home, but can well exceed this in time.

General care: The leathery fronds of the date palm make it adaptable to the warm, dry environment of the home. Watering should be carried out when the compost is almost dry. Do not over-water. A temperature of about 18°C (65°F) is ideal, but the date palm will tolerate 10°C (50°F). Place the palm where it gets as much sun as possible as in its homeland it grows in desert oasis and needs full light.

Propagation: Phoenix palms can be propagated from seed (date stones) germinated in a half pot filled with seed compost, enclosed in a polythene bag and kept at about 21°C (70°F). They will take up to 3 months to germinate. Each seedling can then be potted up in John Innes No. 1 potting compost.

Pests and diseases: Red spider mites, mealy bugs, root mealy bugs and scale insects may occasionally attack stems and leaves.

PILEA CADIEREI

Sometimes known as aluminium plant, this pilea is naturally variegated in the wild, its oval leaves always being patterned with silver. It is an evergreen, shrubby perennial to 45cm (1½ft) tall, much wider when mature.

General care: Provided the temperature does not fall below 10°C (50°F) this is one of the easiest and most good-tempered of house plants. The leaf colouring is best in partial shade.

Propagation: Very easy from

PHILODENDRON SCANDENS

The heart-shaped leaves of *Philodendron scandens* have given it the appropriate popular name of sweetheart plant. These handsome plain green leaves and a climbing habit make it a good-looking specimen plant or background feature in mixed arrangements. It normally requires some form of support, but can be treated as a trailer.

General care: A semi-shaded position away from direct sunlight is ideal with a temperature of about 18°C (65°F). The plant should be allowed almost to dry out between waterings; keep watering to a minimum during the winter months.

As the plant grows, it may become untidy. If so, cut back to maintain its shape, and use the trimmings to provide cuttings.

Propagation: Take stem cuttings with one leaf each and about 2.5cm (1in) of stem below. If the tip of the shoot is used, make sure it has one mature leaf and about 2.5cm (1in) of stem below it. Dip the cuttings into hormone rooting powder and insert 3–5 in a 9cm (3½in) pot of peat-based seed compost. Cover tightly with a polythene bag. When rooted, remove the bag and leave to grow on, potting on the plants together as they mature.

Pests and diseases: Generally trouble-free.

7.5cm (3in) long tip cuttings inserted in equal parts peat and sand and put in a propagating case in summer.
Pests and diseases: Generally trouble-free.

PLATYCERIUM BIFURCATUM

The common stag's horn fern is a most extraordinary plant. It produces two totally different frond shapes: the spore-bearing antler-like green frond that gives the plant its name and the simple basal sterile frond which helps to secure the plant to its location.
General care: Platycerium is fairly tough and quite content at a temperature of about 15°C (60°F), although happiest at about 18°C (65°F). Allow the compost to almost, but not quite, dry out between waterings. Take care not to overwater. Give the plant a lightly shaded situation away from direct sunlight. It can be grown in a mixture of sphagnum moss and potting compost in equal proportions.
Propagation: Stag's horn fern can be propagated from spores produced from velvety brown patches that appear on the underside of the frond tips. Collect the spores carefully and sprinkle lightly on the surface of a half pot filled with a mixture of equal parts peat and loam-based seed compost, or in a peat-based seed compost. Enclose the pot within a polythene bag and keep moist at a temperature of about 21°C (70°F). When the spores have germinated and are large enough to handle, pot up singly. Mature plants produce offsets which can be detached when they have 2–3 fronds and grown on more quickly than sporlings.
Pests and diseases: Watch for scale insects.
See p. 106 for illustration

POINSETTIA
See under Euphorbia

PTERIS ENSIFORMIS 'VICTORIAE'

This fern makes a most attractive pot plant for the home. Well grown plants can exceed 30cm (1ft) in height and have a very erect habit. The leaflets (pinnae) are narrowly strap-shaped with a broad median stripe of silvery-white.
General care: Pteris is susceptible to dehydration. It must be kept in at least moderately humid conditions; occasional spraying with a fine mist of tepid water helps. It prefers a temperature of around 20°C (68°F) and, in common with other ferns, prefers a semi-shaded position away from direct sunlight. The minimum temperature it will tolerate is 10°C (50°F).
Propagation: Pteris spores can be germinated in the same way as other ferns, but mature plants can be divided in spring, a quicker and more satisfactory method.

Pests and diseases: Generally trouble free – which makes up for its rather exacting cultural requirements.

REBUTIA

Rebutia is a small cactus that regularly produces an amazing number of flowers for its size. The low, flattened, globular stems seldom exceed 6cm (2½in) in height, but in summer produce a mass of trumpet-like flowers from white to yellow-orange and brilliant red, all round the base of the stem. Recommended are: *R. deminuta* and *R. krainziana*, both of which are red-flowered, and *R. aureiflora* which is orange-yellow.
General care: Rebutia is one of the easiest cacti to cultivate and is an ideal plant with which to start a collection. It is happy growing on windowsills in full light and is tolerant of varying conditions. A cool dry winter followed by a warmer and more moist spring and summer are the ideal conditions. The flowers close during the evening but reopen with the next day's light.
Propagation: Rebutia is easy to raise from seed, germinated in the usual way for cacti.
Pests and diseases: Mealy bugs and root mealy bugs are the main problems.

RHOICISSUS RHOMBOIDEA

Rhoicissus rhomboidea or grape ivy is an accommodating climbing plant with shiny green leaves composed of 3 leaflets of roughly diamond shape, the top half with well spaced teeth. The slender stems climb by using tendrils.

The grape ivy can be trained up a single trellis or support to grow about 1m (3ft) tall.
General care: Rhoicissus prefers a slightly shaded position away from sunlight – indeed, it is an ideal plant for a shady corner. If the plant receives too much sunlight the leaves may take on a yellowish suffusion.

Rhoicissus will happily grow at temperatures between 15–18°C (60–65°F). Allow the compost to become almost dry before rewatering; do not overwater. Prune to tidy the shape of the plant if necessary in late winter.
Propagation: Use prunings as stem and tip cuttings. Trim these 7.5–10cm (3–4in) in length. Remove the lower 1–2 leaves and dip the end into hormone rooting powder. Insert 5–7 cuttings in a 9cm (3½in) pot, using a peat-based potting compost or John Innes No. 1 potting compost. Cover with a polythene bag to keep them moist. Once they have rooted, remove the bag and allow the plants to grow on, potting singly later.
Pests and diseases: Generally trouble-free.

Phoenix canariensis

SAINTPAULIA

Saintpaulia or African violet is a very attractive little plant that forms a close rosette of fleshy, heart-shaped leaves and produces flowers in a wide range of colours. Most commonly known for its deep purple/blue flowers, it is also available in white, pink, wine-red, light blue, dark blue and even bi-coloured and frilled forms.

General care: It prefers a temperature of about 20°C (68°F), away from draughts and direct sunlight. Humidity is also important; many people grow them well in kitchens or bathrooms. Humidity can also be increased by plunging the plant, still in its pot, into another larger pot filled with moist peat.

It is best watered from below. Place the plant in a saucer of water and allow it to soak up what it requires within about 20 minutes before pouring away the surplus. Dust can be removed from the hairy leaves by spraying the plant with tepid water. This should always be done at room temperature and away from direct sunlight. Cold or direct sunlight are equally bad for saintpaulia, the leaves of which will disfigure if water is left on them in either of these conditions.

A stubborn African violet can be coaxed into flower by a very simple technique. Keep the plant on the dry side for 6–8 weeks, watering only if it looks like drying out and dying. Gradually increase the water, and feed every 2 weeks with tomato fertilizer at half strength.

Propagation: It is very simple to propagate African violets from leaf cuttings. Select a semi-mature leaf, and cut it off cleanly at the base of the leaf stalk close to the centre of the plant. Cut back the leaf stalk to about 3–4cm (1½in) and insert the stalk into a 5cm (2in) pot of seed compost, leaving a small space between the base of the leaf and the compost surface. Cover the leaf with a polythene bag and be patient. Rooting may take 6–8 weeks and it may be as long again before a plantlet emerges from the base. Pot on the new plant into a 9cm (3½in) pot of potting compost.

Pests and diseases: Aphids and mildew sometimes attack during spring and summer; the latter is more difficult to control.

SANSEVIERIA

The sansevieria commonly known as mother-in-law's tongue is *S. trifasciata* 'Laurentii'. Its familiar upright green and yellow edged leaves grow up to 1m (3ft).

Various shades of Saintpaulia

General care: Mother-in-law's tongue prefers a well-lit situation at a temperature of about 18°C (65°F); in winter the temperature should not drop below 10°C (50°F) and the compost should then be kept on the dry side. Allow the compost to dry out between waterings. Wet soil conditions lead to rotting.

Propagation: Sansevieria is easily propagated by cuttings. Cut a leaf into 5cm (2in) sections and put 4–5 sections into a pot of moist potting compost. Make sure the cuttings are the right way up. A propagating case is not required. When rooted, pot each plantlet into a 7.5cm (3in) pot of John Innes No. 1 potting compost.

Propagation by division is relatively easy and is the only way to increase *S. t.* 'Laurentii'; leaf cuttings only produce the common species without the yellow margins. Water the plant very sparingly after separation.

Pests and diseases: Generally trouble-free.

SOLANUM

What makes winter cherry *Solanum pseudocapsicum* ornamental is not its flowers but a display of round, bright orange cherry-like fruits in winter. The small white flowers of summer are insignificant. The plant may reach 45cm (18in) in height and is fairly compact. Deep green foliage sets off the berries well. Although solanum is from the same family as the tomato and the potato, its fruits are poisonous.

General care: Solanum can be grown for more than one season, although most people dispose of them once the fruits have dropped. They are very easy to grow provided there is plenty of light and the plants are not allowed to dry right out, particularly when in flower or after fruit has set. During spring and summer, a temperature of about 15–18°C (60–65°F) is ideal; they may even be kept outside from the end of May to the end of August. Feeding with diluted tomato fertilizer throughout the growing season will help to encourage stocky growth and a good covering of flowers – hopefully followed by berries. Fruit set can be increased indoors by lightly misting the plant with tepid water or by tickling the flowers with an artist's paintbrush to pollinate them. During the winter months solanum will tolerate a temperature down to around 10°C (50°F).

Propagation: Sow seed in early spring in a half pot or seed tray of seed compost, cover and keep at 18–20°C (65–68°F). When the seedlings are large enough to handle, prick out and pot up singly in 13cm (5in) pots of potting compost.

Pests and diseases: Aphids and whitefly may attack.

STEPHANOTIS

Stephanotis is a climbing plant with thick, fleshy green leaves and is usually grown on a hoop so that its scented, waxy white flowers can be displayed to best advantage.

General care: A temperature of 20°C (68°F) is ideal. A reasonably well-lit situation, away from direct sun will provide ideal conditions.

Keep the plants on the dry side over the dormant winter period. During the active growing and flowering period, do not allow it to dry out. A monthly feed with half strength tomato fertilizer promotes stocky growth.

Propagation: Propagate from stem cuttings taken from non-flowering side shoots in early summer. Dip 10cm (4in) cuttings in hormone rooting powder and insert in a 7.5cm (3in) pot of seed compost. If you keep at about 18°C (65°F), they should root in a few weeks. Pot on as necessary.

Pests and diseases: Generally trouble-free.

STREPTOCARPUS

Popularly known as the Cape primrose, this plant bears pink, red, purple or lilac flowers. The mid-green leaves are broadly strap-shaped, thick-textured and rich green, providing a perfect background to the lovely summer blooms.

General care: While flowering in spring and summer, streptocarpus prefers a temperature of around 15–18°C (60–65°F) in a lightly shaded situation, away from direct sunlight. Do not allow the plants to dry out between May and October, but keep them fairly dry for the winter, maintaining a temperature of 10–13°C (50–55°F). From March onwards, as temperatures gradually rise again, water more frequently.

Propagation: Streptocarpus is easily propagated from seed or leaf cuttings. During spring and summer, sow seed in half pots or seed trays filled with seed compost and keep covered at about 21°C (70°F) until germinated. When the seedlings are large enough to handle, prick them out and pot them up individually in 13cm (5in) pots of John Innes No. 2 potting compost.

Streptocarpus cuttings are worth trying for fun. Select a semi-mature leaf and cut it off cleanly. Using a sharp knife and a chopping board, lay the leaf flat on the board and cut it in half down the middle of the vein. Cut each half into pieces about 2.5cm (1in) wide, cutting outwards from the main vein to the leaf edge. Insert at an oblique angle, barely covering the lower third, in half pots or seed trays filled with seed compost. Mist with tepid water several times a day, or cover with a polythene bag, to reduce water loss. When the cuttings have rooted, pot up singly in 7.5cm (3in) pots of growing compost and grow on.

Pests and diseases: Generally trouble-free.

TRADESCANTIA

Wandering Jew, *Tradescantia fluminensis*, is one of the commonest and easiest of all house plants. An attractive trailing foliage plant, it looks best in small hanging baskets, high on a shelf or in a pot fixed to the wall. The best forms are those with variegated leaves.

General care: Tradescantia is a most adaptable plant. It grows well in various environments, but is best in a well-lit position at a temperature between 10–15°C (50–60°F). Allow the compost almost to dry out between waterings. Apply any of the proprietary liquid feeds at 2-week intervals from spring to autumn. Trim the plant back when it looks straggly and bare stems are visible.

Propagation: Take cuttings from leading shoots, reducing them to about 5cm (2in) in length. Insert 3–5 cuttings in a 7.5cm (3in) pot filled with potting compost and keep moist, but not wet. Rooting is rapid; during spring and summer it may take 2–3 weeks. Once rooted, grow on in the same pot.

Pests and diseases: Generally trouble-free.

See p. 108 for illustration

VRIESIA SPLENDENS

Vriesia splendens is a bromeliad similar in shape to the aechmea, but its leaves are more slender. Banded dark green and strap-like in shape, they form a funnel-shaped rosette that collects water at its base. When mature, the plant produces a long orange-red bracted flat-sided flower spike; from this the yellow, short-lived, flowers emerge.

General care: Vriesia adapts to a variety of indoor conditions. Although it will tolerate temperatures down to 10°C (50°F), around 18°C (65°F) is best, in a semi-shaded position away from direct sunlight. Use rainwater if possible, although tap water is perfectly adequate. Try to keep the compost just moist most of the time. When the flower spike dies, gently remove it from the funnel.

Vriesia splendens is an epiphytic or tree-living bromeliad, using its host for support. Adventurous indoor gardeners will find that it adapts well to being grown attached to a branch bound with sphagnum moss in a plant arrangement like a miniature jungle.

Propagation: Usually propagated from offsets in the same way as Aechmea (q v). Pot the offsets singly in 13cm (5in) pots of lime-free compost.

Pests and diseases: Root mealy bugs are the most likely pests.

ZEBRINA

Also known as wandering Jew and additionally as inch plant, *Zebrina pendula* is frequently mistaken for *Tradescantia fluminensis*. The two are similar in appearance and closely allied botanically, but the flowers of zebrina have the bases of the petals united into a tube. The leaves are always purple beneath and on the upper surface are 2 silvery longitudinal bands.

General care, Propagation and Pests and diseases are as for Tradescantia (q v).

Vriesia splendens

VEGETABLES

With very few exceptions, good vegetables can only be produced under good conditions. They need to be grown in an open position with plenty of light and sunshine, and will never flourish tucked away in dark corners, under the shadow of buildings or in the shade of trees. Nor will they do well in an exposed or draughty position (the wind funnels created between high buildings and gaps in garden fences are particularly lethal), and in such situations some kind of windbreak or shelter must be erected to protect the plants.

The ideal garden windbreak is about 50 per cent permeable, so that it filters wind rather than stops it in its tracks. Lath and wattle fences are good, as are netted windbreaks made from special nylon windbreak materials. These have to be battened to posts, making sure the posts are well anchored as they take a tremendous strain in high winds. A windbreak is effective for a distance two to six times its height — the further from the windbreak the less the effect.

By far the most important factor, however, is the soil. Vegetables *must* have fertile soil, and the key to successful vegetable growing lies in building up soil fertility. There are many ways in which poor soil can be improved. (See Back to Basics, p. 8.)

Most vegetables do best on slightly acid soils, at a pH of around 6.5.

Garden planning
A vegetable garden can be almost any shape. Traditionally vegetables were grown in large plots in rigid rows, with plenty of space between the rows (see photograph on p. 114). Today it is realized that vegetables can be grown much closer together, and very often, instead of being in rows, they are planted in 'blocks' or patches with equidistant spacing between them. This has the additional advantage that the plants form a 'canopy' over the ground, which helps to suppress the weeds.

Growing vegetables at equidistant spacing lends itself to much smaller beds, which can be accommodated more easily in small modern gardens. Beds 1–1.2m (3–4ft) wide are very convenient, not least because they can be worked from the edge without treading on the soil — and the less the soil is compacted, the better its structure.

In small gardens where it is hard to find space for vegetables, a few can be grown in flower beds. Runner beans look very decorative growing up a trellis or wigwam at the back of a border, while beetroot, chards, carrots and the 'Salad Bowl' types of lettuce look pretty growing among flowers. But the soil must be rich enough to support them.

The choice of vegetable crops has to be determined largely by family requirements and available space. Few people aim to be self-sufficient, so where space is limited, it is probably not worth growing maincrop potatoes, or vegetables like cauliflowers, which require a large amount of space for long periods. Concentrate instead on salad crops, which are so much better picked fresh from the garden.

A big headache is arranging for a continuous supply without gluts and shortages. With the wide range of varieties available today, continuity is much easier to achieve. Wherever possible in the text, suggestions are made for successive sowings of suitable varieties with this in mind. With some vegetables, root crops such as parsnips for example, the whole year's supply can be obtained from one sowing. With others, such as lettuces, carrots, beetroot and cabbages, it is necessary to make several small sowings for a constant supply throughout the season.

Any keen vegetable grower would be well advised to invest in a cold greenhouse or an inexpensive 'walk in' polythene tunnel. This increases the scope enormously, by making earlier sowings and later harvesting possible. On a smaller scale, cloches and frames can be put to excellent use to extend the season.

A well-planned vegetable garden will provide produce throughout the year.

Rotation
It is sound gardening practice to avoid growing the same type of vegetable in the same piece of ground several years running. This is because certain soil pests and diseases, which attack members of the same botanical family, will build up if they have constant access to their host plants.

In practice rotation is a problem in small gardens, but is easier when vegetables are grown in several small or narrow beds rather than a few large ones: there are more permutations and allows greater flexibility.

Wherever possible, try to rotate over at least a 3-year cycle. The main family groups which should be grown together in one area then moved on another year are legumes (all the peas and beans), brassicas (all the cabbage family, including swedes, radishes, and turnips); onions and leeks. Important crops like lettuces, potatoes, and carrots should also be rotated. (See the simple rotation system illustrated on p. 114).

Seed selection
Most vegetables are raised from seed, either bought over the counter or from mail order seed houses , whose cata-

ABOVE: *The traditional method of organizing a vegetable plot. The drawbacks are that space is wasted between the plants and the soil structure is damaged by constant treading.*

	Year 1	Year 2	Year 3
Plot 1	A	B	C
Plot 2	B	C	A
Plot 3	C	A	B

A simple rotation system: The garden is divided into three plots or areas, and the main vegetables grown are divided into three groups. Each group is grown in turn on each plot.
Group A: Legumes, onions and salad crops
Group B: Brassicas (plus radishes, swedes and turnips)
Group C: Root crops such as potatoes, carrots, beetroots and parsnips

logues are a mine of information. Several developments in seed technology have been of particular help to gardeners, and these include:

F_1 **hybrids:** These are specially bred varieties that produce exceptionally vigorous and uniform crops. The seeds are more expensive than ordinary 'open pollinated' varieties, but are usually worth the extra cost.

Disease resistance: Several varieties (of tomatoes and cucumbers for example), have been bred with resistance, or at least tolerance, to serious diseases. These can be very useful.

Treated and dressed seed: Seed can be treated by the seedsman to kill diseases that are normally carried on the seed (celery, for instance, can be treated against celery leaf spot). Seed can also be dressed with chemicals to combat soil diseases likely to attack after sowing. Corn-on-the-cob and pea seeds are often dressed to increase the chances of success with early out-door sowings.

Pelleted seed: The seed is made into tiny balls with a protective coating, which breaks down in the soil. The individual seeds can be handled very easily and spaced out accurately so that thinning is not required. The ground *must* be kept moist until the seeds germinate.

Foil packaging: Seeds packed in air-sealed foil packs keep fresh much longer than seeds in ordinary packets. Once the packets are opened, however, the seeds deteriorate normally.

Choosing a cultivar (variety)

With so many cultivars to choose from today, there's bound to be some trial and error before deciding which ones are best for your conditions and requirements. A few outstanding varieties are mentioned in this book, but there are many others worth growing. Varieties with the Royal Horticultural Society awards can always be relied upon to be of good quality. In order of merit these are FCC (First Class Certificate), AM (Award of Merit) and HC (Highly Commended).

Keeping seeds

Seeds gradually lose their viability, or ability to germinate. In some cases (parsnips, for instance), this happens much faster than in others (radishes, for example). Seeds will remain viable much longer if kept in cool, dry conditions, preferably in air-tight tins or jars. Never keep seeds in a damp shed or hot kitchen.

Sowing outdoors

Outdoor sowings are either made directly into the ground where the plant is to grow (generally described as *in situ*) or into a 'seed bed', which is an area set aside for raising plants; from there they are later transplanted into permanent positions. The main reason for sowing in a seed bed is to save space. While the seedling is developing in the seed bed the ground it will eventually occupy can be used for another crop.

Preparing the ground

Whether sowing in a seed bed or *in situ*, the ground has to be prepared for sowing, a process known in both cases, as 'making a seed bed'.

A seed bed can only be made satisfactorily when the soil is in the right condition, neither so wet that the soil sticks to your feet, nor so dry that it is unworkable. In spring, especially on heavy soil, it is often a question of waiting until it dries out sufficiently. Putting cloches on the soil can help to dry it out. In very dry conditions the soil may need to be watered before a seed bed can be made.

The purpose of a seed bed is to create a surface tilth where the soil is fine enough for seeds to germinate. The underlying soil needs to be firm, but not so consolidated that roots cannot penetrate.

Some soils can simply be raked down in spring and a fine tilth is created with no difficulty. More compacted soils may need to be forked over first, then raked, breaking down large clods with the back of the rake and raking off large stones and persistent earth lumps. Tread the soil lightly so that it is reasonably firm, and continue raking backwards and forwards until a good tilth is formed.

Seeds are normally sown in drills. In a seed bed the drills are close together, about 10–13cm (4–5in) apart. Having prepared the seed bed, mark the position of the row with a garden line and make the drill, which is really just a slit in the soil, with the point of a trowel or corner of a hoe. The depth of the drill varies with the seed: most seeds are sown at a depth roughly two or three times their width. Place the seeds in the bottom of the drill, and use a rake to cover them with soil.

The golden rule of gardening is to sow seed as thinly as possible. There is always a temptation to sow thickly in case germination is poor. In practice either soil conditions and seed are right and there will be very high germination (and the resulting seedlings may be of poor quality because they are so crowded) or virtually none will germinate and one will have to sow again.

Either space the seed evenly along the drill, or, to save on thinning, sow 2–3 seeds together at 'stations' several centimetres (3–4in) apart. Thin to one seedling at each station after germination. If your plants will eventually be grown, say, 15cm (6in) apart, station sow about 7.5cm (3in) apart. Quick growing seedlings like radishes can be intersown between the stations.

Thinning
Seedlings grow very rapidly and must never be allowed to become overcrowded. Thin them in stages, so that each just stands clear of its neighbour, until they are the required final distance apart. To avoid disturbing the remaining plants in the row, seedlings can be nipped off at ground level, though in some cases, with lettuce for example, they can be eased out carefully and replanted elsewhere.

Sowing single seeds
Large seeds such as beans, peas, corn-on-the-cob, cucumbers, and marrows, can be sown by making individual holes with the point of a dibber.

Broadcasting
This is a rapid method of sowing used principally for seeding crops such as

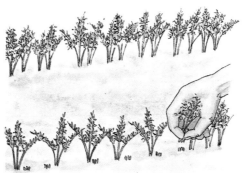

Thin by nipping off unwanted seedlings just above soil level; this method leaves the remaining seedlings undisturbed.

cress. Make the seed bed, then scatter the seeds thinly over the surface. Rake it over first in one direction, then at right angles. Cover the seed bed with a sheet of polythene or newspaper until the seeds have germinated.

Never sow broadcast on soil known to be full of weed seed; it will be an impossible task separating the weed and vegetable seedlings. In such cases prepare the seed bed, then leave it for a couple of weeks so that the main flush of weed seeds can germinate, hoe them off and then sow broadcast as described.

Sowing indoors
Half-hardy vegetables like tomatoes and peppers have to be started indoors, otherwise they would never mature in our short summers. With other vegetables, such as celery and lettuces, early crops or larger specimens can be obtained by sowing indoors. 'Indoors' implies sowing in a protected environment such as a greenhouse, in frames, under cloches, or even on a windowsill. These early sowings are often made in an electric propagator which provides gentle 'bottom heat'.

Raising seedlings indoors is simplified by using commercially prepared sowing and potting composts, which are either soil- or peat-based. It is also possible to mix suitable composts.

Seeds are generally sown in seed trays or pots, but any container with drainage holes made in the bottom can be used. Fill it to within 2cm (¾in) of the top with damp seed compost, firm it with the fingers, and level the surface with a block of wood. Sow the seeds thinly on the surface, spacing them out carefully if only a few plants are required. Cover them by sieving a little more compost over the top, and level the surface once again. If the compost is dry, stand the seed tray in water to absorb moisture. Finally, cover it with a sheet of glass, or pop it into a plastic bag, to keep the surface moist until the seedlings germi-

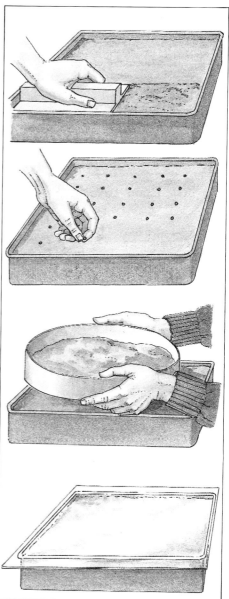

Sowing indoors, **top to bottom:** Level the compost in the seed tray. Ensure that the seeds are well spaced out. Sift more compost over the seeds. Cover the seed tray with a pane of glass to germinate.

nate. Remove the glass or plastic for about half an hour a day for ventilation.

Once germinated, the seedlings must be in full light, but not direct sunlight. When they are large enough to handle, generally with about three true leaves, they need more room and richer compost. At this stage prick them out into seed trays, or individually into small 6–8cm (2½–3in) pots, filled with potting compost. Water the seedlings beforehand, then uproot them one by one with a small dibber, taking care not to damage the fine roots. Always hold them by

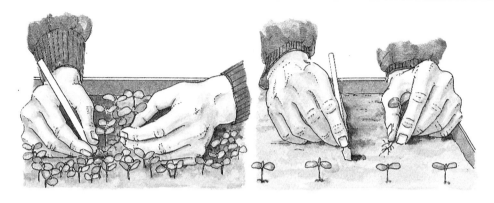

*Individually prick out crowded seedlings, (**left**) and transfer them to richer compost to*

*develop (**right**), holding them by their leaves to avoid damaging the root hairs.*

their leaves. Make a hole in the compost large enough for the roots, put in the seedling, and firm the soil around it with a dibber. The seed leaves, the first tiny pair of leaves to develop on the stem, should be just above soil level. Space the seedlings 4–5cm (1½–2in) apart, and shield them from bright sunlight until established.

Hardening off
Before plants are moved into their final position outdoors, whether raised in pots or in seed trays, they must be gradually acclimatized to lower temperatures by 'hardening off'. This takes about 10 days. Start by increasing the ventilation, then move them outdoors during the day for increasingly longer periods, bringing them in at night, and finally leave them out at night. They are then ready for planting.

Planting
Planting is inevitably something of a shock and everything has to be done to minimize the set-back and damage to the plant, especially to the root and delicate root hairs. In most cases the ground is prepared beforehand by forking it over (brassicas, however, can be put straight into un-dug ground). Remove any weeds and rake the surface smooth. The soil should be moist but not saturated; water lightly if it is dry. It is best to plant in the evening, or in overcast conditions.

It is most important that the plants being moved are watered well several hours beforehand, whether they are in a seed bed, in seed trays or in blocks. Then dig them up carefully with a trowel. Make a hole in the ground large enough to accommodate the roots, and holding the plant in one hand, fill in the soil around the roots, pressing it down with the fingers. Firm the soil around the stem, then give the leaves a tug. If the

plant wobbles, it is not firm enough. If it seems necessary, water the plant afterwards.

Watering
Vegetables need moisture throughout their growth, but there are certain times when it is more important than others. Soil must be moist for seeds to germinate, for planting, and when fertilizers are being applied. For different groups of vegetables there are also 'critical periods', when shortage of water is very damaging. Wherever possible, try to ensure that plants are watered at these times.

The leafy vegetables — spinach, lettuces, brassicas, celery and so on, are thirsty plants, and benefit from heavy watering throughout their growing season, especially in dry summer months. A weekly rate of 11–16lt/sq m (2–3gal/sq yd) is sufficient. Their critical period is 10–20 days before maturity. If regular watering is impossible, concentrate on giving one very heavy watering, at twice the rate recommended above, during this period.

The so-called 'fruiting' vegetables include peas, beans, tomatoes, cucumbers, marrows, and corn-on-the-cob. These are less demanding in the early stages, but once the flowers appear and the fruits start to form, they need heavy watering. Water them then at a weekly rate of 22lt/sq m (4gal/sq yd).

Root vegetables have less of a critical period, but if the soil dries out root quality will be poor. When the plants are small, light watering may be needed in dry weather, at the rate of 5lt/sq m (1gal/sq yd) of row. Later in the season, when the roots are swelling, heavier watering at a fortnightly rate of 16–22lt/sq m (3–4gal/sq yd) is recommended in dry weather.

Water penetrates the soil slowly, layer by layer, and it is much more useful to

water occasionally, but heavily, rather than frequently but lightly. Surface watering simply evaporates before it reaches the plant's roots. Always water gently but thoroughly. Large droplets damage the soil surface and young plants, and splash mud up onto the leaves. Use a watering-can with a fine rose when watering seedlings and young plants.

Mulching
Mulching means covering the soil with a protective layer. This is generally some type of organic material, which will slowly rot into the soil, but over shorter periods plastic sheeting can be used. Mulching conserves moisture by preventing evaporation and prevents weeds from germinating. It also protects the soil surface from the damaging effect of heavy rain, and from compaction.

Many materials can be used for mulching. Their texture is important: they need to be fairly compact but not so compact that moisture and air cannot filter through to the soil. Home-made compost, leaf mould, lawn mowings which have been allowed to dry out first, well-rotted manure, straw and bracken, are all suitable. Provided the plants are not completely swamped, the mulch can be anything up to 10cm (4in) thick.

Ideally you should mulch when the soil is moist and warm. Never mulch when the soil is very dry, very wet, or very cold; it will simply remain that way, providing poor conditions for the plants. The best time to mulch is after planting, or when plants sown *in situ* are several inches high.

Plastic mulches are useful in the short term, especially for summer crops, such as tomatoes and cucumbers. Either lay the film on the ground and cut cross-like slits through which the plants are planted, or plant first then roll the film gradually over them, making slits and pulling the plants through. Anchor the edges of the film in vertical slits in the soil. Plants can be watered, when necessary, in the gaps around the stem.

Black plastic sheeting is most effective for preventing weed germination, while transparent and white sorts warm up the soil, the latter reflecting light up onto the plant.

Protected cropping
Cloches, frames, greenhouses, and low and 'walk in' polythene tunnels are all devices that can be used to give vegetables extra protection – 'protected cropping', to use the modern term. (Also, see The Greenhouse. p. 140–1.)

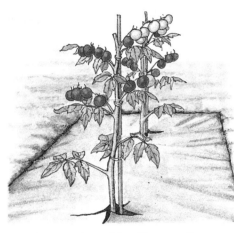

TOP: *An organic mulch will generally improve the soil structure because it encourages worms. When applying the mulch, care should be taken not to swamp the plant.*
BOTTOM: *A mulch of black polythene is particularly effective for preventing weed germination.*

Cloches are small units made in a variety of materials ranging from glass to plastic. Glass cloches are the most expensive, but breakages apart, are the most durable and give the best light transmission. They are, however, heavy to handle and a little awkward to erect. Of the many plastic materials, the double layered corrugated propylene, sold as Correx, provides excellent growing conditions, plants doing well in the somewhat diffuse light they create.

Cloches are easily moved from one crop to another and are often placed end to end to cover a row. Their disadvantages are the labour involved in lifting them for watering, weeding, harvesting and ventilation, and that tall plants outgrow all but the largest cloches.

Ventilation is essential in warm and close weather; if there is no built-in ventilation method, move cloches a few centimetres (3–4in) apart.

Low polythene tunnels are cheaper than cloches and used in much the same way. They consist of polythene film stretched over a series of low, galvan-ized wire hoops. The film is held in place with fine wire or string stretched from side to side. The ends are anchored in the soil or tied to a stake (see illustration). The sides can be rolled up for watering and ventilation. The film usually needs replacement after two years.

Frames: Traditional frames were usually permanent fixtures, with brick sides and glass 'lights' or lids. Modern frames tend to be portable, and constructed of wood, plastic material, or aluminium and glass. They are fairly expensive for the amount of ground covered, and are best used for raising and hardening off plants, for summer crops of half-hardy vegetables such as cucumbers, tomatoes, and peppers, and for winter salad crops.

Weed control

Weeds have to be controlled because they compete for nutrients in the soil, for moisture, and for light. There are two types: perennials and annuals.

The perennials last from one year to the next by means of very deep roots, or by creeping stems and roots. Common examples are ground elder, bindweed, docks, couch grass and creeping thistle. Once a garden is well established they pose little problem, but in the early stages they have to be dug out manually, making sure that no little pieces of root or stem are left in the soil, as they are very likely to regenerate. Chemical weedkillers may prove useful in clearing a weed-infested site initially. Suitable weedkillers include glyphosate, and dalapon (which is very effective against grasses). They can be applied with a watering-can, using either a rose or a dribble bar. Always follow the manufacturer's instructions implicitly. In some cases it is necessary to leave the ground for several weeks or months before it is safe to sow or plant.

Annuals germinate, flower and die at least once, maybe two or three times in a season, and are far more of a problem. Chickweed, groundsel, shepherd's purse, and annual meadow grass are most common. They seed prolifically, and because weed seeds often remain viable for many years, the proverbial one year's seeding really can mean 7 years of weeding. It is essential to prevent them going to seed.

They are also best controlled by hand weeding or hoeing. Always hoe as shallowly as possible, to prevent damage to surface roots, and to cut down on the loss of moisture from the soil. In wet weather small weeds may re-root, so should be removed. In dry weather they can be left on the surface to wilt. Weeds that have gone to seed should be burnt.

It is now known that the most competitive weeds in a vegetable garden are those between rather than within the rows — so concentrate on removing them first. For a crop sown directly in the ground, competitition starts to become really serious 2–3 weeks after the crop germinates. Start weeding then, if not before. Raising plants indoors gives them a head start over weeds. Also, relatively close, equidistant spacing reduces the light reaching the soil, and is therefore an effective means of keeping down weeds — as is mulching.

Using chemical weedkillers in an established vegetable garden is liable to damage plants, and is not generally recommended.

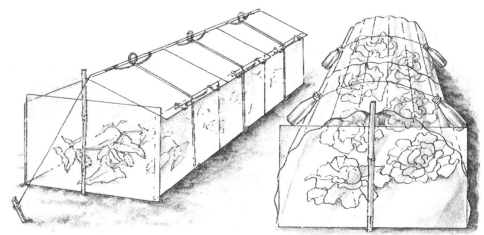

*Glass cloches (**left**) can be anchored by a system of string, 'eyes' and pegs, while plastic cloches (**right**) can be held down by* *water-filled plastic bottles attached to strings. The open ends of cloches must be covered to avoid draughts.*

ARTICHOKE, GLOBE

The globe artichoke is a gourmet's vegetable, and also strikingly handsome with its beautiful silver foliage and thistle-like flowers. The edible parts are the fleshy bases of the scaly bracts enclosing the bud and the 'choke' beneath.

Artichokes are perennial, but they start to deteriorate after their third season, so it is wise to replace a few with new plants each year.

Cultivation: They need fertile, well-drained soil. Prepare the ground by digging in plenty of well-rotted manure or compost. A general fertilizer can be given before planting, or feed them with a seaweed-based fertilizer during growth. Choose an open but not too exposed position, as artichokes cannot withstand severe winters, particularly if growing on heavy soil. A recommended variety for this country is 'Vert de Laon'.

Plants are raised either by planting rooted suckers, known as offsets, or by seed. The former is the more reliable method of obtaining quality artichoke plants.

Either buy offsets between February and April, or take them from the outside edge of a mature established plant. Slice them off cleanly with a spade, making sure you have plenty of root attached to the shoot. Plant them 75cm (2½ft) apart each way.

If using seed, sow indoors in February or outdoors in March, planting in May. The quality will be variable, so build up the stock by taking offsets from the strongest plants in future years.

During the growing season keep the plants weeded, mulched, and watered so that they do not dry out. The first heads should appear towards the end of the summer period.

In cold parts of the country, artichokes need some winter protection. Earth up the base of the stems in late autumn and protect the crowns with bracken, dead leaves, or straw. Remove the protective covering gradually in April.

Pests and diseases: Greenfly and blackfly sometimes attack the developing flowerheads.

Harvesting: The artichokes are ready when the buds are nicely plump and the scales still soft.

ARTICHOKE, JERUSALEM

Jerusalem artichokes are tasty, nutritious tubers, which can be baked or boiled like potatoes, or used to make an excellent winter soup. They are easily grown, and one of the most suitable crops with which to break in heavy, previously uncultivated soil. They will, however, tolerate a wide range of soils.

Jerusalem artichokes grow very tall, up to 3m (10ft), so can usefully be planted 2–3 deep around the outside of a vegetable patch as a windbreak. Or you can use them to screen off an unsightly feature.

Cultivation: The knobbly tubers can be planted any time between February and May, about 10–15cm (4–6in) deep and 30cm (1ft) apart. They are not always available in garden shops, but you can always buy a few from a greengrocer. Tubers the size of a hen's egg are best, but larger tubers can be cut into several pieces, provided each has a shoot.

Globe artichokes; the top head is ready for cutting

Once planted they require very little attention. In exposed gardens earth up the stems when the plants are about 30cm (1ft) high, so that they are not rocked by winds. When the foliage dies off in autumn, cut the stems back to a few centimetres (2–3in) from the ground.

Pests and diseases: Slugs may be a problem in some soils.

Harvesting: The tubers are extremely hardy and can be left in the ground all winter and lifted as required. Always keep back a few tubers for planting the following year, but to prevent them spreading be sure you lift even the tiniest tubers and broken pieces.

ASPARAGUS

An asparagus bed is a luxury, permanently occupying a fair amount of ground in return for a short, but glorious, season.

Cultivation: A bed should last up to 20 years. Make it on an open site (not where asparagus has previously been grown), avoiding frost pockets. Asparagus will grow on a wide range of soils, but the site must be well drained. Traditionally it was grown on raised beds or ridges to ensure good drainage and long white stalks, but today it is usually grown on the flat. The variety 'Giant Mammoth' is recommended for heavy soils; 'Connover's Colossal' for light soils.

To prepare the bed, eliminate annual and perennial weeds, using weedkillers if necessary. Then dig in plenty of well-rotted manure or compost the autumn before planting. Very acid soils should be limed.

Asparagus can be raised from seed or purchased as 'crowns'. The quality from seed is more variable, and it takes a year longer to mature, but it can be quite satisfactory. Sow the seed several inches apart 2.5cm (1in) deep in a seed bed in spring. Leave the plants until the next spring, when the largest

should be planted in the bed in the same way as bought crowns.

If starting with asparagus crowns, which look rather like a cross between a spider and octopus, buy one-year, rather than two- or three-year crowns. They become established much better. Dig a trench 30cm (1ft) wide and 20cm (8in) deep, and for each plant make a mound a few centimetres (2–3in) high in the bottom of the trench. Spread the crown on the mound, cover it with 5cm (2in) of soil, and fill in the trench as the shoots grow. Asparagus can be grown in single rows, or in beds 2–3 rows wide. Average spacing is 45cm (1½ft) between plants.

Contrary to popular belief, there is no need to mulch or apply salt to the beds during the winter. However, they can be given a general fertilizer in spring (preferably high in nitrogen and potash) or a seaweed-based fertilizer during growth.

Pests and diseases: Slugs can be a major problem in some gardens. The grubs and adults of the asparagus beetle — which has orange marks on a black body — attack stems and foliages. Spray with derris.

Harvesting: Asparagus should not be cut until its third season — 2 years after planting. Using a sharp knife cut the spears, 13–18cm (5–7in) long, about 2.5cm (1in) below ground. Once the bed is established, start cutting the asparagus in April and continue for about 8 weeks;

Long-podded broad bean plants (see p. 120 for entry)

but stop after 6 weeks in the first cutting season.

AUBERGINE

Aubergines are among the most striking looking vegetables. The large pendulous fruits are normally a deep purple-black, but there are white forms such as the variety 'Easter Egg', which look uncommonly like hens' eggs, and presumably gave rise to the alternative name for aubergines — eggplant.

Cultivation: Aubergines are demanding, so avoid poor, shallow soils. Dig in plenty of well-rotted manure or compost before planting, and make sure the plants have

119

Dwarf French beans

plenty of moisture throughout their growing season.

Sow seed in a greenhouse in gentle heat in March or early April, provided that a minimum night temperature of 16°C (60°F) and day temperature of 18°C (65°F) can be maintained. When the seedlings are about 5cm (2in) high, pot them up in 8cm (3in) pots. Plant them in their permanent positions when the first flower truss is visible, generally April/May. Do not plant them outdoors until there is no risk of frost, in late May or early June depending on the region. Harden them off well beforehand.

Plant them about 43cm (17in) apart. Aubergines can grow very large and top-heavy, so should either be staked or tied to some kind of support. To encourage bushy growth, nip out the growing point when the plant is about 38cm (15in) high.

It is best to allow only four fruits to develop on each plant. From then on the plants can be fed with a tomato fertilizer approximately every 10 days.

Pests and diseases: Red spider mites, greenfly and whitefly are liable to attack plants grown indoors.

Harvesting: Aubergines need a long season to mature, and are not normally ready until late summer. Pick them when they look plump and glossy. If frost threatens, uproot the plants and hang them indoors; fruits will keep for a few weeks on the plant.

BEAN, BROAD

Broad beans are relatively easy to grow and hardy enough to over-winter to provide an early crop in all but the coldest areas.

Cultivation: Prepare the ground by digging and working in plenty of organic matter. The summer crops require an open site, though the autumn-sown, over-wintered plants will benefit from a more sheltered position.

The first sowings can be made in the open in February with further sowings until May. The seeds are large, and should be sown 4–5cm (1½–2in) deep, either in drills, or in single holes with a blunt-

tipped dibber. Space them about 23cm (9in) apart each way, either in staggered rows, or in blocks 4–5 plants wide — which makes economical use of the ground.

For the earliest spring sowings, use the tall, long, podded varieties, such as 'Imperial Green Longpod' and 'Exhibition Longpod', which are very hardy. For the later sowings use the broader, shorter-podded 'White Windsor' and 'Green Windsor' varieties.

Except in the coldest parts of the country, broad beans can also be sown in October and November to provide the first spring pickings. Use the variety 'Aquadulce' or the dwarf variety 'The Sutton'. These sowings can be protected with cloches. 'The Sutton', can also be sown in spring, and is a very useful variety for small gardens.

The taller varieties of broad beans can become rather top-heavy and may need support. Put canes at the corners and midway along the blocks or rows, and run strings between them. Wire-netting can also be used as support.

Pests and diseases: The commonest pest is blackfly or black aphid, which colonizes the growing points. The best remedy is to nip off the tips of the plants once they are flowering well. This discourages the aphids and encourages the beans.

Harvesting: Beans are ready from about May onwards. Pick the pods before the beans have toughened; they are much better when young. *Illustration on p. 119*

BEAN, FRENCH

There are many shapes of French bean, ranging from the flat-podded ones, which become stringy when old, to the round, pencil-like varieties such as 'Loch Ness' and 'Tendergreen', which are less stringy and excellent for freezing. If it's flavour you are after, try the Waxpods, such as 'Kinghorn Wax', or the purple varieties, such as 'Royal Burgundy'. Both dwarf (bush) and climbing varieties are available; the latter require supports during growth, just like runner beans.

Cultivation: French beans love warmth and hate an exposed, windy position or cold, wet soil. They do best on rich, light, well-drained soil.

Space the plants 15cm (6in) apart in each direction, or 5–8cm (2–3in) apart in rows 30cm (1ft) apart. Take precautions against slugs in the early stages, keep the ground mulched to conserve moisture, and keep down weeds. Push small twigs between the plants to give some support and to help keep the pods off the ground.

The sowing plan opposite is recommended for a continuous supply of French beans from June to October.

Pests and diseases: Aphids are the most likely pest, but watch for slugs in the early stages.

Harvesting: Keep picking the beans regularly while still tender. This also encourages further cropping.

FRENCH BEANS

When and how to sow	Suitable varieties	When to harvest
Sow in a cold greenhouse in mid April, harden off and plant out early June	Dwarf: 'The Prince', 'Tendergreen'	late June and July
Sow under cloches in mid April, keep plants covered until June	Dwarf: 'The Prince', 'Tendergreen'	July and August
Sow outdoors in mid May and mid June	Climbing: 'Loch Ness' Dwarf: 'Tendergreen'	late July to September
Sow outdoors in mid July	Dwarf: 'The Prince'	mid September to mid October.

BEAN, RUNNER

Runner beans are a very popular, decorative and heavily yielding vegetable, many people preferring the flavour to that of French beans.

Most of the varieties are vigorous climbers, reaching up to 3m (10ft). If dwarfer beans are required, grow the variety 'Kelvedon Marvel' or 'Bokki', nipping out the growing point when the plant starts to flower. Runner beans cannot stand frost and need a fairly long season. Good varieties are 'Achievement', 'Enorma', 'Mergoles', 'Scarlet Emperor' and 'Streamline'.

Cultivation: Runner beans need fertile soil. If possible prepare it the previous autumn by making a trench about one spade deep and 60cm (2ft) wide. Put in a really thick layer of manure or garden compost and mix it in well with the soil from the trench. The flowers are pollinated by insects and it is not true that syringing the flowers helps them to set.

Sow the seeds outdoors in late May in the south, early June in the north. Sow 5cm (2in) deep, about 15cm (6in) apart, in double rows about 60cm (2ft) apart.

The beans must have really sturdy supports as the weight of the mature crop is enormous. Traditional supports were stout crossed poles at least 2m (6½ft) high, with a cross-member along the top. Ideally, use one pole for each plant, or allow intermediate plants to climb up strings. Bamboo canes can also be used. These are often roped together at the top to make a 'wigwam'. Alternatively, supports can be made utilizing string, or patented supports with nylon netting.

Keep the plants well mulched, and water as generally suggested for 'fruiting' vegetables, see p. 116.

Pests and diseases: Blackfly can be troublesome.

Harvesting: See French beans.

BEETROOT

Beetroot can be pulled fresh from the garden from about the end of May until late autumn, and then either pickled, or lifted and stored, for the winter. There are flat, round and long, tapered varieties in red, yellow and white forms.

Many varieties are liable to bolt (run to seed) rather than form roots if sown early in the year and/or subjected to spells of cold weather. Fortunately newer varieties such as 'Avonearly' and 'Boltardy' are bolt resistant and suitable for these early sowings.

Cultivation: Beetroot needs rich, light soil. Very acid soils should be limed. If possible use ground manured for the previous crop.

The roots are best used when young and tender, before they become tough. So for a continuous supply of good quality beet it is advisable to make several sowings.

The first sowings can be made in March under cloches, followed by unprotected sowings outdoors in late March and April, in both cases using bolt-resistant varieties. Make further sowings at monthly intervals until July using any variety. For winter storage sow any of the round varieties, or 'Cheltenham Greentop', one of the long varieties, in late May or June.

Beetroot should never be sown thickly, because the so-called seed is in fact a fruit containing several seeds, all of which may germinate. Single seeded, monogerm beet is sometimes available, and if so, is worth using. Sow seed 1–1½cm ($\frac{1}{2}$–$\frac{3}{4}$in) deep, about 2.5cm (1in) apart, thinning later to the required distance. Rather surprisingly early crops need the widest spacing. They can be as far apart as 8cm (3¼in) between plants, in rows 20cm (8in) apart. Main summer supplies and beet for winter storage can be 2.5cm (1in) apart in rows 30cm (1ft) apart.

Beet needs to grow steadily, so the aim with any watering should be to prevent the soil drying out. If possible you should water at the rate of 11lt/sq m (about 2 gal/sq yd) every 2–3 weeks in a dry season. A top-dressing of a general fertilizer might be necessary during the growing season if growth is poor.

Pests and diseases: Blackfly can sometimes be troublesome.

Harvesting: Summer beet are pulled as required. For winter storage lift the roots

Young summer beetroot

carefully in late autumn and twist off the stems. Store them in a frost-free place in layers, in boxes of moist peat or sand, or in clamps outdoors. If you are unable to provide any of these conditions, you can try to stimulate them by using perforated polythene sacks.

BEET, LEAF

Both perpetual spinach and Swiss chard are useful crops, being productive, reasonably hardy, and much less prone to bolt than spinach. Perpetual spinach is more widely grown than Swiss chard, but has less pronounced midribs, smaller stems, and crops less heavily.

There are several coloured varieties of Swiss chard, the best known being rhubarb chard, which has bright red leaves and stems. Besides its culinary value, it is decorative — as are all the chards.

Cultivation: For the main summer crop of leaf beet, sow in March or April in rows 38–45cm (15–18in) apart, thinning to 30cm (1ft) apart in the rows. Give cloche protection during the winter. These plants may well crop from early summer until the following spring. A second sowing can be made in July.

Pests and diseases: Aphids (green- and blackfly) are occasionally a problem.

Harvesting: Cut the leaves 2.5cm (1in) or so above ground level. The plants will continue to throw out more leaves over a long period.

BROCCOLI, SPROUTING

Purple-sprouting broccoli is one of the major standbys of the late winter to spring period. It is very hardy and prolific. Three or four plants are quite sufficient for the average household. The slightly less common white form of sprouting broccoli is somewhat less hardy and less productive. There are early and late selections of both types, but no named varieties. See also Calabrese.

Cultivation: Seed should be sown in a seed bed or in soil or peat blocks from mid April to mid May, starting with the early varieties. Plant out firmly from early June until mid July, spacing the plants 60cm (2ft) apart each way. In good soil purple-sprouting plants can grow tall so it is advisable to earth up the stems and stake the plants.

Pests and diseases: Sprouting broccoli is less prone to pests and diseases than most brassicas, the worst enemy being pigeons in winter. Clubroot, cabbage root fly and caterpillars can be problems.

Harvesting: Snap off the flowering shoots when they are about 15cm (6in) long, before the flowers open. Keep picking regularly.

Sprouting broccoli is very suitable for freezing.

BRUSSELS SPROUTS

We associate Brussels sprouts with Christmas, but by sowing a succession of the modern F_1 varieties, the season can now be extended from September to March. Like purple-sprouting broccoli, brussels sprouts are among our hardiest vegetables, although they do suffer damage in the most severe winters.

Cultivation: All varieties should be sown between mid March and mid April. They can either be sown under cloches or in a garden frame (this will produce the earliest crops), or in a seed bed outdoors.

From mid March to mid April sowing under cover, the following F_1 varieties should provide a continuous supply over a six-month period: 'Peer Gynt' (September to October); 'Valiant' (October to November); 'Perfect Line' or 'Achilles' (November to December); 'Rampart (December to January); 'Fortress' (January to March).

Of course you may only want to select one or two

varieties from this to meet the household's requirements.

Plant between mid May and early June in firm ground that has not been freshly manured. The standard spacing is 60cm (2ft) apart in each direction, a distance that encourages small, uniform sprouts to be ready over a relatively short period. However, if you prefer larger sprouts, maturing over a longer period, plant them up to 90cm (3ft) apart.

Apart from watering soon after transplanting to help the seedlings to become established, further watering is rarely required, except under drought conditions. This is because the wide spacing between plants means there is less competition for moisture.

Sprouts sometimes become loose or 'blown'. This may be caused by loose soil, by planting in freshly manured ground, or by giving too much nitrogen in the early stages of growth. Make sure the stems are earthed up or the plants staked, and if any extra feeding is done, late summer is the most suitable time.

Early varieties of Brussels sprouts, such as 'Peer Gynt', can be 'stopped', which means cutting out the top of the stem. This encourages the sprouts to button up sooner and to be more uniform in size, so giving earlier picking over a shorter season. It is particularly useful if you want all the sprouts to mature together and to be of an even size for freezing. Stop the plants when the lowest sprouts on the stem are about 1cm (⅜in) in diameter. To be effective it must be done before the first week in October — and it is only successful with early varieties.

Pests and diseases: Brussels sprouts are vulnerable to all the brassica problems, such as clubroot, caterpillars and cabbage root fly.

A full stem of Brussels sprouts

Harvesting: Pick the sprouts from the bottom of the stem upwards, and do not neglect the sprout 'top' — which can develop almost into a miniature cabbage in spring and is a lovely vegetable in itself.

CABBAGE
There are many excellent modern cabbage varieties, which unlike the old-fashioned sorts stand in good condition for several months once they have matured. This makes it feasible to cut fresh cabbages from your garden all year round. Follow the sowing plan shown in the table for a continuous all year round supply of cabbages.

Cultivation: All cabbages can either be sown on seed beds outdoors and transplanted, or sown in small pots. You can even sow them direct in the ground and thin them out to the correct spacing. For

A neat patch of summer cabbages with uniform, firm heads

soil conditions, planting, watering, and feeding, treat them as recommended for typical brassicas (see p. 116). For practical purposes, cabbages are divided into spring (including 'spring greens'), summer, and winter types.

Spring cabbages are sown in late summer and planted in autumn. They can be allowed to form small heads in spring or can be harvested as looser, unhearted plants — spring greens. For headed cabbages space the plants 30cm (12in) apart each way. For spring greens arrange them closer, say 15cm (6in) apart each way, or 10cm (4in) apart in rows 30cm (1ft) apart. In this latter case you can use the second and third, fifth and sixth cabbages in the row first (and so on), leaving the remaining plants 30cm, (1ft) apart to heart up. Varieties such as 'Durham Early' and 'Avon Crest' are particularly suitable for use as spring greens.

Spring cabbages should be earthed up during the winter, and given a feed in March or April. Don't, however, feed them when they are planted out, otherwise they will be too 'soft' to withstand the winter. They will survive all but the most severe winters.

Summer cabbages are sown in spring. They are larger, and should be spaced 30–35cm (12–14in) apart each way if you want cabbages with smallish heads, and up to 45cm (1½ft) apart for larger heads.

Winter cabbages come in several distinct types. The Dutch winter white types are excellent fresh or in coleslaw, though they are not very hardy. They can, however, be lifted in November and stored in an airy, frost-free shed, or even in a garden frame — in which case place them on wooden slats, and cover them with a thick layer of loose bracken or straw. Inspect them from time to time and gently rub off any outer leaves which show signs of rotting.

CABBAGES

When and how to sow	Suitable varieties	When to harvest
Spring cabbages Sow directly into the ground in early August, or into a seed bed for planting out in September	'Harbinger', 'Avon Crest', 'Offenham' selections	March to May
Early summer cabbages Sow in heat in late February in blocks or pots, planting out in mid April	'Hispi', 'Marner Allfruh'	May to June
Mid-summer cabbages Sow in a garden frame in late March, planting out in late May	in order of maturity: 'Hispi', 'Marner Allfruh', 'Stonehead', 'Market Topper', 'Minicole'	July to September
Late summer cabbages Sow outside early May, planting June	'Stonehead'	September to November
Early winter and/or storage Sow outside late April, planting in early June	'Hidena', 'Jupiter'	November to December
Hardy winter cabbages Sow outside mid May, planting towards the end of June	'Avon Coronet', 'Celtic', 'Celsa', 'Aquarius'	December to February

The hardier types, which can be left in the ground all winter, include the crinkly-leaved savoys, the flat, reddish 'January King' type, and newer hybrids between savoys and winter whites. Plant winter cabbage about 20cm (16in) apart if you want small heads, 45cm (1½ft) apart for medium sized and 50cm (20in) apart for large heads.

Red cabbages are sown in March and April, planting out 60cm (2ft) apart in May and June. Lift and store any remaining heads in November. Good varieties are 'Langendijker Red' and 'Ruby Ball'.

Pests and diseases: Cabbage root fly, mealy aphids and cabbage white butterfly caterpillars are frequent pests. Clubroot is a disease that will seriously affect cabbage yields on infected land.

Harvesting: With the exception of a few modern varieties, spring and summer cabbages will stand for only a few weeks once mature, before they start to 'bolt' or otherwise deteriorate. They should be eaten in their prime. If the ground is not required for another crop, cut off the heads, leaving a few inches of stalk in the ground. Make a shallow cross, about 5mm (¼in) deep, in the top of the stalk. Provided the ground is fertile and moist, a second crop of small leafy cabbages may be obtained.

Non-hardy winter cabbages must be cut before frost, or, with appropriate varieties, lifted and stored before hard frost. Hardy varieties can be left in the ground until required.

CALABRESE

Calabrese, also known as green or Italian sprouting broccoli, is something of a gourmet vegetable, attractive looking with a beautiful flavour. Moreover it is an

Fine heads of calabrese, also known as green broccoli

excellent vegetable for freezing. It has several other merits: it grows fast, sometimes being ready less than 3 months from sowing; it can be planted very closely; and it requires a less fertile soil than most brassicas.

The best spears (heads) are obtained if calabrese can be sown directly in the ground, to avoid the check of transplanting. Sow 2–3 seeds together at the required distance apart, thinning to one in each position when the seedlings have germinated. Otherwise sow in pots or peat blocks, or if there is no alternative, in a seed bed, transplanting very carefully while the plants are small.

The calabrese season lasts roughly from July to October, if several sowings are made, but the plants are killed off by frost. Make the earliest sowings in late March or early April with the variety 'Express Corona'. Sowing can continue in May, June and early July, using the varieties 'Express Corona', 'Green Comet', 'Green Duke', or 'Premium Crop'. These varieties all take different lengths of time to mature, so

it is quite feasible to sow several of them at the same time to obtain continuity.

Cultivation: Unlike cabbage, calabrese is very insensitive to planting distances, although the heaviest yields of good quality spears are obtained by planting 15cm (6in) apart in rows 30cm (1ft) apart. If the crop is grown for freezing it can be planted closer, say 20cm (8in) apart in each direction. This has the effect of suppressing the sideshoots and making smaller terminal spears, all of which are ready at much the same time.

Calabrese does poorly if checked, so make sure there is plenty of moisture, watering as suggested earlier for brassicas (p. 116). It is beneficial to keep the soil mulched.

A somewhat different type of calabrese is the variety 'Romanesco'. It has large spears with a purplish tinge — and an outstanding flavour. Sow it in April/May, planting out 60cm (2ft) apart in June/July. Harvest from July onwards.

Pests and diseases: As far as pests are concerned cala-

brese is susceptible to the normal run of brassica pests and diseases, but caterpillars are particularly troublesome. They conceal themselves in the crevices of the spears. Soak the vegetable in salted water for an hour or so before cooking to force them out.

Harvesting: Always cut the main, terminal spear of calabrese first, while it is still firm and compact. Smaller lateral spears will then develop so that picking can often continue over a fairly long period.

CARROT

Carrots are fussy about soil. They will always do far better on rich, light sandy soils, where the roots can expand without difficulty, than on heavy clay or stony soils. If you have heavy soil, work in as much organic matter as possible to improve.

There are several different types of carrots. For early crops use the smaller finger-shaped carrots of the Amsterdam and Nantes types (try 'Amsterdam Colora' and 'Nantes Express'), or the little round carrots such as 'Early French Frame' and the selection 'Early French Frame — Rondo'.

For the main summer supply and winter storage use the larger 'Chantenay', 'Berlicum' or 'Autumn King' types. Good varieties are 'Chantenay Red Cored', 'Berlicum-Berjo', and 'Autumn King-Vita Longa'.

Cultivation: For a continuous supply several sowings have to be made. Provided the soil is warm enough (carrots need a minimum soil temperature of 7°C (45°F) to germinate), make the first sowings in frames or under cloches in late February or in March. Follow this with unprotected outdoor sowings in March or April. For both these sowings use early varieties; they will be ready in June and July.

For later summer use and winter storage, sow maincrop varieties from May until

Early carrots pulled ready for use

mid July at roughly 4-week intervals. Finally, for a very late crop of small roots in November and December, sow an early variety in August, clothing in September/ October.

Carrots should be sown very thinly (to minimize thinning), about 1cm (½in) deep. The highest yields are obtained by growing them in rows about 15cm (6in) apart. Early carrots, which should be encouraged to grow very fast, can be thinned to 8–10cm (3–4in) apart. Maincrop carrots can be thinned to 3.5cm (1½in) apart. Weed between the rows in the early stages; subsequently the natural canopy of leaves will help to prevent further weed growth.

Carrots will not grow well if the soil is allowed to dry out, and the roots are likely to split if there is heavy rain, or heavy watering, after a dry spell. Watering at the rate of about 22lt/sq m (3–4gal/sq yd), every 2–3 weeks will usually ensure steady growth.

Pests and diseases: Carrot fly is an almost universal problem with carrots, sometimes causing very poor crops. The flies are attracted by the smell of carrot foliage, and lay eggs which hatch into tiny grubs visible on the roots. There are no completely effective and harmless chemical remedies, but the following measures can be taken to minimize attacks where the problem is serious.

Concentrate on early sowings (February and March), and on late sowings (June and July), which escape the worst attacks.

Sow very thinly, and thin on calm, still evenings, nipping off surplus seedlings rather than pulling them out. Remove and burn the thinnings, or bury them deep in the compost heap to help put the flies off the scent.

Grow carrots in raised beds about 15cm (6in) high, or in boxes, or under cloches, or in beds surrounded by wooden boards. These measures deter the flies because they only fly low.

Use the less leafy varieties such as the Amsterdam and Nantes types.

Lift maincrop varieties by October to prevent the late brood hatching.

Harvesting: Pull the carrots during the summer months as required. In mild areas on well-drained soils, carrots can be left in the ground in winter, covered with about 15cm (6in) of leaves or straw. Otherwise lift them carefully in autumn and twist off the stems. Store them in layers, in boxes of moist peat or sand, in a frost-free place.

CAULIFLOWER

There are cauliflower varieties for every season of the year, but as the winter and spring types (both previously known as 'winter broccoli') require a lot of space over a long period, people with smallish gardens are probably best to restrict themselves to early and mid summer cauliflowers, and/or mini-cauliflowers.

Cultivation: There is no escaping the fact that good quality cauliflowers can only be produced under good conditions. They must have rich soil, preferably on the slightly alkaline side. Very acid soil should be limed. The secret of success with cauliflowers is to try to encourage steady growth without checks of any kind. Plenty of water is a most important factor.

To minimize the transplanting check, cauliflowers are best raised in small pots, or sown directly in the ground and thinned to the appropriate distance apart. If they have to be sown in a seed bed, plant them out as young as possible.

Cauliflower curds are very delicate and easily damaged by exposure to the elements. Summer cauliflowers can be protected from the sun, when nearing maturity, by half snapping a leaf over the head, and can be kept fresh for a few days until you are ready to pull them up. Winter and spring cauliflowers suffer most if they thaw out rapidly, due to exposure to the sun, after frost. This can be avoided by bending the stem over to the north and earthing it up on the south side.

Sowing times, correct planting distances and suit-

A large robust cauliflower with firm white curds

able varieties for the different seasons, are given below.

Early summer cauliflowers: These are ready between mid June and mid July. Either sow them in a garden frame in early October, planting them outdoors in March, or sow them in heat in mid January, harden them off, and plant them out in March, 53cm (21in) apart each way. Suitable varieties, in order of maturing, are 'Alpha', 'Mechelse Classic', and 'Dominant'.

Mid and late summer cauliflowers: The mid-summer ones mature between mid July and mid August. They can be sown under cold glass in March, planting out in mid May. Late summer cauliflowers, ready for use in late August and September, are sown in late April and are planted out in mid June. Varieties 'Nevada' and 'Dok — Elgon' are suitable for both these crops, planted 53cm (21in) apart each way.

Autumn cauliflowers: These mature between September and November, and are sown in mid May, planting out in early July about 60cm (2ft) apart each way. Suitable

varieties, in order of maturity, are 'Flora Blanca' and 'Barrier Reef'.

Winter cauliflowers: This type can only be grown in very mild, south-west coastal areas, for use in winter and early spring. Sow them in early May, planting out in late July, 68cm (27in) apart each way. Suitable varieties are 'St Agnes' (maturing late December to January), 'St Buryan' (February and March) and 'St Keverne' (late March and April).

Spring cauliflowers: These over-wintering cauliflowers, maturing between March and late May, need hard conditions and are therefore unsuitable for south-west coastal areas. Sow them in late May, planting them out in late July. Suitable varieties, in order of maturity, are 'Angers No. 2 – Westmarsh Early', the 'Walcheren Winter' varieties 'Armado April', 'Markanta' and 'Birchington', and 'Angers No. 5'.

Mini-cauliflowers: Mini-cauliflowers are tiny curds, 4–9cm (1½–3½in) in diameter, which make handy single portions and are good

Self-blanching celery

for freezing whole. They are obtained by growing early summer cauliflower varieties very close together, planted in square formation 15cm (6in) apart in each direction. Sow in succession from the third week in March until early July, for supplies from the end of June until the end of October. These, of course, take up far less ground space, and mature much faster, than normal-sized cauliflowers.

Pests and diseases: Clubroot is the most serious disease, and cauliflowers are vulnerable to the same pests as other brassicas. Caterpillars can hide in the curd.

Harvesting: Cut the curds as they are ready. If you have to store them, cover the curds with tissue paper and hang them upside down in a cool place.

CELERIAC

Celeriac is a member of the celery family and forms a large, rather knobbly swollen bulb at the base of the stem. Although a little tricky to scrub clean, this makes an excellent winter vegetable. The leaves have a strong celery flavour and can be used, sparingly, as a celery substitute.

Cultivation: Celeriac, being a marshland plant, must have fertile, moisture-retentive soil, rich in organic matter. It also needs a long growing season if it is to reach a reasonable size. It is best sown indoors, in gentle heat, in February/March. Germination is often erratic, but once seedlings have germinated, prick them out and harden them off, ready for planting in the open in late April, May/June.

Plant about 35cm (14in) apart each way, taking care not to bury the crowns. The key to success is plenty of moisture. So water generously in dry weather, and keep the ground between the plants mulched to con-

serve moisture. Celeriac responds well to feeding with a seaweed-based fertilizer during the growing season. Towards the end of July the outer leaves can be removed, which exposes the crowns and is said to encourage them to swell. A promising new cultivar is Suttons 'Tellus'.

Pests and diseases: Celeriac is unlikely to be troubled by many pests, but leaf miners can tunnel and blister the leaves.

Harvesting: The crowns are ready for use from about October onwards. They are very hardy so can be left in the soil all winter. However, tuck a thick layer of straw or bracken between the plants to protect them from frost, and to make it easier to dig them out when the ground is frozen. They will normally remain in good condition until April or May, when they will run to seed.

CELERY

There are two types of celery. The traditional blanched, trench celery produces long, crunchy, white or coloured stalks between October and February. The more recently introduced 'self-blanching' types have shorter, greenish stems, which nevertheless have a good flavour. They are not hardy, but are ready between mid July and October. They are easier to grow and require less space than traditional celery, which demands time, space and skill.

Good varieties of trench celery are 'Giant Pink', 'Giant White' and 'Giant Red' (reflecting the stalk colour); reliable self-blanching varieties are 'Golden Self Blanching' and 'Lothom Self Blanching'. All of these are good both raw and cooked.

Cultivation: Celery requires moisture-retentive but well-drained rich soil, with plenty of organic matter dug in beforehand. Very acid soils should be limed. For trench celery prepare a trench the previous autumn if possible. Dig it 30cm (1ft) deep, and about 38cm (15in) wide for a single row, 50cm (20in) wide for a double row. Work a thick layer of well-rotted manure into the trench, then replace the bulk of the removed soil to within 10cm (4in) of the top.

Celery has a high nitrogen requirement, so a nitrogenous fertilizer can be applied before planting and during growth; use a seaweed-based fertilizer during growth.

Sow seed in gentle heat indoors in late March/early April. Do not sow any earlier, as the seedlings may 'bolt' (run to seed) if subjected to a cold spell, or indeed any 'shocks'. For this reason it is worth sowing in small pots, thinning to one seedling in each. Sow very shallowly as the seed requires a certain amount of light to germinate.

Plant out in late May or early June after hardening off. Plant trench celery in single rows 23cm (9in) apart, or in staggered double rows 25cm (10in) apart. Plant self-blanching celery in block formation about 23cm (9in) apart each way.

In dry weather when celery is growing, water it heavily at a weekly rate up to 22lt/sq m (4gal/sq yd).

Trench celery is earthed up in three stages, starting when the plants are about 30cm (1ft) high and repeating at three-weekly intervals until only the tips are visible. First tie the stems together just below the leaves, then pull earth up around the stalks to a depth of about 8cm (3¼in). Trench celery can also be grown on the flat and blanched by tying dark paper or black polythene around the stems.

Pests and diseases: Slugs and celery fly are the worst pests.
Harvesting: Cut the stems at ground level when required. Self-blanching celery is destroyed by hard frost. Trench celery may need protection with straw during the winter to keep it in good condition.

CHICORY, WITLOOF
Witloof or Belgian chicory is becoming increasingly popular; the bud-like, pale chicons make a pleasant winter salad and an equally good cooked vegetable. They are not difficult to grow, although the roots have to be forced in the dark to obtain the chicons. Very tight heads are obtained with the new varieties 'Crispa' and 'Normato', though the older 'Witloof' is still worth growing.

Cultivation: Chicory requires reasonably fertile, but not freshly manured soil, in an open position. Sow the seed thinly outdoors in May/early June in rows 30cm (1ft) apart. Thin in stages to 15cm (6in) apart. The plants look like large dandelions. Keep them weeded but otherwise leave until autumn.

In late October/November dig up the roots and cut off the leaves about 2.5cm (1in) above the crown. Reject any roots that are very fanged or very thin. To keep a household supplied throughout the winter it is best to force a few roots at a time, say every fortnight. Store the bulk of the roots until required for forcing in layers in a box of moist peat or sand, in an outdoor shed.

Forcing requires complete darkness and a little warmth. A simple method is to pot up 3 roots, closely together, in any soil in a 23cm (9in) plant pot. Cover this with an up-turned pot of the same size, with aluminium foil over the drainage holes to exclude the light. Keep at a temperature of about 10°C (50°F) or a little higher. Provided the soil does not dry out, the chicons will develop in about 3 weeks.

Chicory roots can also be forced by planting them in greenhouse soil, and excluding light. This can be done by covering them with black polythene stretched over wire hoops, and anchored into the soil on either side.
Pests and diseases: Generally trouble-free.
Harvesting: Once the chicons are ready keep them in the dark until they are used,

as they become green and bitter on exposure to light. Cut them about 2.5cm (1in) above the crown. If left in the pot or ground they often re-sprout to yield a second, smaller crop.

CORN-ON-THE-COB
Corn-on-the-cob or sweet corn is an increasingly popular vegetable, but it is tender and needs a long, warm summer, so becomes progressively harder to grow the farther north one is. Early-maturing hybrid varieties such as 'Ear-liking', 'Kelvedon Sweet-heart' and 'Northern Belle' are to be recommended.
Cultivation: Avoid exposed sites and very heavy or very dry soil. Sweet corn does best on well-drained, reasonably fertile soil, preferably manured for the previous crop.

It cannot be planted outside until there is no risk of frost (in late May or early June, depending on the area) so is normally sown indoors for transplanting. However, the young plants dislike root disturbance, so where possible sow seed in pots of potting compost rather than in seed trays.

Sow about 2.5cm (1in) deep in April in gentle heat, sowing 2–3 seeds to each pot, thinning later to one seedling. Plant out, under cloches if possible, after hardening off. Sweet corn should be grown in blocks rather than single rows, to assist with wind pollination – so space them 35cm (14in) apart each way, several plants deep.

In the south seeds can be sown *in situ*, preferably warming the soil first with cloches, or sowing 2–3 seeds at each 'station' under a jam-jar or cloche, thinning to one seedling after germination. Seeds will not germinate until the soil temperature reaches 10°C (50°F), so it is generally unwise to sow outside until early May.

Corn-on-the-cob is 'rocked'

Corn with the cob ready for cutting

by wind, so when the plants are 30–45cm (1–1½ft) high, earth up the stems, much as one earths up potatoes, to a height of several centimetres (2–3in). Weed by hand if necessary, taking care not to disturb the shallow roots. Once the plants are flowering, water, if the weather is dry, at the rate of 22lt/sq m (4gal/sq yd) every few days. This increases the yield and improves the quality.

Pests and diseases: Generally trouble-free.

Harvesting: Expect only one or two cobs on each plant. They are ripe when the tassels are turning brown and the cobs are at a 45 degree angle to the stem and snap off easily. Press a finger nail into the kernel to see whether the juice is watery (under-ripe), 'doughy' (over-ripe), or milky (ripe). Harvest immediately, otherwise the sweetness is lost.

COURGETTE AND MARROW

Marrows are old English favourites, but courgettes, which are nothing more than marrows picked small, young and immature, are a relatively new 'discovery'. (The word courgette is the French for 'little marrow'.) There are many different types of marrow: green, white, yellow, striped, and long, round, cylindrical, or fluted in shape. In the United States, various unusual types of marrows are known as summer squash.

The plants can either be trailing, in which case they can grow several metres long, spreading over the ground, or a compact bush. Although bushes can be a metre (yard) across, they are the most suitable form for small gardens. Recommended varieties for marrows are 'Long Green Trailing', and the bush types 'Green Bush-Smallpak'. For courgettes, the F₁ hybrid bushes 'Burpeed Golden Zucchini', 'Chefini', 'Early Gem' and 'Zucchini' are good varieties.

Cultivation: All marrows need an open site, well-drained and very fertile soil, and plenty of moisture throughout growth. Prepare the ground beforehand by digging holes, about 30cm (1ft) deep and the same width. Fill them with well-rotted strawy manure and then cover with about 15cm (6in) of soil.

Marrows grow very rapidly but cannot be planted outdoors until the risk of frost is over, so there is little advantage in sowing very early. For planting in frames, under cloches or in a cold greenhouse, sow single seeds, 2cm (¾in) deep, on their sides in small pots, or soil or peat blocks, in early April. Plant them in late April/early May. For the main outdoor crop, sow in the same way in late April/early May, planting in late May/early June, after hardening off.

Marrows can also be sown outdoors *in situ* in late May under jars or cloches. Sow 2–3 seeds together about 2cm (¾in) deep, edgeways down, and cover with a jam jar to assist germination. Alternatively use cloches for protection. Remove the jars when the seeds have germinated; take the cloches away when they are outgrown.

Bush varieties should be grown 90cm (3ft) apart); trailing varieties 1.2m (4ft) apart. Keep the plants well watered at all times.

The plants bear separate male and female flowers, which are distinguished by the tiny, embryonic marrows behind the flower. Male flowers often appear long before the female. Marrows are insect pollinated and in cold summers, when insects lie low, it may be necessary to hand pollinate by picking off a male flower and rubbing the pollen in to the female flower.

Pests and diseases: Powdery mildew is a very disfiguring disease in some seasons. Slugs may also be troublesome.

Harvesting: Start picking courgettes when about 10cm (4in) long; keep picking regularly to encourage further fruiting. The season lasts from mid June until October.

Start picking marrows when they are about 20cm (8in) long. If marrows are required for storage, leave a few on the plant so that they grow larger and their skins harden, then hang them in nets in a dry, frost-free shed. They may keep until about Christmas.

CRESS, MUSTARD AND RAPE

Mustard and cress are traditionally grown on blotting paper indoors, but are also useful and very productive salad crops when grown in an unheated greenhouse or in the open ground, particularly in early spring and autumn. Rape, which has a milder flavour than mustard, is often used commercially as a mustard substitute. It makes an excellent salad crop and, if allowed to grow taller, can be cooked and used as 'greens'.

Cultivation: Very small patches, say 30–60cm (1–2ft) square, of these seedling crops will provide large quantities of salad material over several weeks. Sowings can be made in February and March, and again in October, in unheated greenhouses, frames, or under cloches. The October sowings will provide pickings late in the year and again the following spring.

Sow outdoors from March to early May, and in September. Mid summer sowings may succeed, but are likely to run to seed rapidly in hot weather.

Prepare the soil, broadcast the seeds on the surface and cover with newspaper or plastic film to keep the soil moist until the seeds germinate.

Pests and diseases: Generally trouble-free, although 'damping off' (which prevents seeds from germinating or causes seedlings to wilt) may occur. Avoid by sowing in warm conditions in clean soil or by using seed dusted with a fungicide.

Harvesting: Start cutting the seedlings 1cm (½in) above soil level when they are 5–8cm (2–3in) high. If they are allowed to grow too high they can become very hot-flavoured.

CUCUMBER

There are two types of cucumber. The best quality are the greenhouse or frame cucumbers, which are long and smooth. The plants climb to considerable heights, and require warm, humid conditions and careful attention. Much more rugged are the outdoor 'ridge' cucumbers. These are generally short and have prickly skins, though the improved varieties such as 'Burpless Tasty Green' and 'Burpee Hybrid' are longer and smoother. 'Perfection' is one of the best of the old ridge varieties. Good greenhouse varieties are 'Telegraph Improved', 'Butcher's Disease Resisting', and the all-female 'Femspot' and 'Landora'.

Gherkins are grown in exactly the same way as outdoor ridge cucumbers. Suitable varieties for gherkins are 'Venlo' and 'Condor'.

Cultivation: Cucumber roots appreciate very humus rich soil. Prepare the ground beforehand by making a trench, or digging individual holes, about 30cm (1ft) deep and the same width, filling them with well-rotted strawy manure, covered with about 15cm (6in) of soil.

Cucumber plants dislike transplanting, so they should either be sown *in situ*, or in individual pots to minimize the shock.

Outdoor cucumbers, which sprawl rather than climb, can either be grown on the flat, spaced 60–75cm (2–2½ft) apart, or trained up trellises or supports spaced

Ridge cucumbers

about 45cm (1½ft) apart. Sow cucumbers in mid May in the south, the end of May in the north. Sow 2–3 seeds together about 2cm (¾in) deep, on their sides, and cover with a jam-jar to assist germination. They can also be sown indoors in mid April, hardening off before planting out. Cloche protection in the early stages is beneficial.

To encourage fruiting the old types of ridge cucumber are 'stopped' (the growing point nipped out), above the fifth leaf. The strongest 2–3 laterals are then selected and also stopped beyond the fifth leaf, others being removed. The Japanese varieties bear fruit on the main stem and only need to be stopped when they reach the top of the support.

Keep the cucumbers well watered and mulched, and feed occasionally with a general fertilizer during growth.

Sow greenhouse or frame cucumbers in February, March or April in a propagator at soil temperatures of at least 20°C (68°F). For early crops the greenhouse or frame must be heated, with night temperatures of at least 16°C (60°F).

Plant 45cm (1½ft) apart, when the soil temperature reaches at least 16°C (60°F) and only in warm conditions; keep the greenhouse well ventilated in hot weather, but close it as soon as the temperature drops in the evening.

Cucumbers need to be tied to horizontal wire supports. Train them to the top of the wire then nip out the growing point; stop the laterals 2 leaves beyond a fruit.

With the older varieties it is necessary to remove the male flowers, as pollinated fruit is swollen and bitter. The female flowers are distinguished by a miniature cucumber visible behind the flower. With more recent 'all female' varieties this is no longer necessary.

Pests and diseases: Red spider mites can be a problem; keeping the greenhouse atmosphere moist by syringing daily with water in hot weather will help to control them. Greenhouse cucumbers are subject to a number of diseases, so use disease-resistant varieties where possible.

Harvesting: Pick regularly to encourage further cropping.

ENDIVE

Endives are very useful salad plants all the year round, but especially in autumn, winter and spring. They are slightly bitter compared to lettuce, but this can be remedied by partial or complete blanching, or by shredding them fairly finely in salads. There are two distinct types: the broad-leaved or Batavian, and the curly-leaved, which has finely divided, attractive leaves.

Cultivation: Endives need an open situation and fertile, moisture-retentive soil. Sow in March and April for the summer crop, and from June to August for the winter crop. Sow either *in situ*, or in a seed bed or in seed trays for transplanting. Sow about 1cm (½in) deep in rows about 30cm (1ft) apart, thinning to 30cm (1ft) apart. The thinnings can be transplanted carefully to provide a succession.

Plants from the August sowing can be transplanted into an unheated greenhouse or, alternatively, covered with cloches, for winter use.

The plants are blanched when they are mature. The simplest method of partial blanching is to bunch up the leaves and tie them towards the top of the plant with raffia or an elastic band. This makes the central leaves whiter, and alleviates the bitterness. For complete blanching tie up the leaves when the plant is dry, then cover the plant with a box or plant pot with the drainage holes blocked to exclude light. Alternatively, plants can be lifted and planted in a darkened garden frame. They will be ready for use within 10–15 days. Use immediately otherwise they will start to rot.

Pests and diseases: Generally trouble-free.

Harvesting: Pick individual leaves as required or cut the whole head 2.5cm (1in) above the stem. Leave the stump in the ground as endives will usually resprout over several months, which is most useful in winter and early spring.

FENNEL

Florence or sweet fennel is a beautiful, feathery-leaved plant grown for the swollen

Florence fennel

bulb at the base of the stem – though it may be admitted that in our climate it is sometimes reluctant to form the much-prized bulb. Fennel can be used cooked or raw, but the delicate aniseed flavour is most marked when eaten raw. Florence fennel should not be confused with the hardier, perennial fennel, which is grown as a herb.

Cultivation: Fennel likes much the same conditions as celery and, like celery, is liable to 'bolt' if subjected to spells of very cold or very dry weather, or, because of its susceptibility to different day lengths, if sown too early in the year. Varieties least likely to 'bolt' are 'Perfection' and 'Zefa Fino'.

Although fennel can be grown on heavy soil, it does best on fertile, light, well-drained soil, requiring plenty of moisture throughout its growth. Work in plenty of well-rotted manure or compost before planting.

Seed can be sown 1cm ($\frac{1}{2}$in) deep, *in situ* outdoors, or in small pots or peat blocks indoors, for planting out after hardening off. Make several sowings if a succession is required. The earliest sowings can be made in April and May, but because of the likelihood of bolting, these are something of a gamble. The main sowings are made in June and early July, and a late sowing from mid July until early August. These last can be planted into a cold greenhouse or frames to give a late autumn crop.

Plant out when seedlings are about 10–13cm (4–5in) high, spacing the plants about 30cm (1ft) apart each way. Early plantings will benefit from cloche protection if the weather is cold or windy. Take precautions against slugs in the early stages, and keep the plants well watered and mulched. Feed them from time to time with a seaweed-based fertilizer.

Although by no means

essential, the bulb is traditionally blanched by earthing it up when it starts to swell. Pull earth up a few centimetres (2–3in) around the base.

Pests and diseases: Generally trouble-free.

Harvesting: Depending on sowing times, the season can last from July to November. Cut the bulb about 2cm ($\frac{3}{4}$in) above the ground rather than uproot the plant. It will often throw out further small leafy shoots which are pleasant in salads or for flavouring cooked dishes.

KALE

The kales are especially valuable in the colder parts of the country because they are exceptionally hardy – though it must be said that most people find them rather too coarse.

There are broad-leaved and curly-leaved kales – the latter also known as Scotch kale and borecole. With the broad leaved kales it is the young shoots, produced in spring, that are eaten. With the curly types, the leaves are eaten in winter and the shoots in spring. Kales tend to be rather large plants, but the dwarf varieties of curly kale, such as 'Dwarf Green Curled' and 'Frosty', are suitable for small gardens. The multi-coloured 'ornamental' kales are beautiful plants, and add a wonderful touch of colour to the winter garden. Contrary to general belief, they are edible — though not highly productive.

Cultivation: Kales tolerate poorer soils than most brassicas, though give of their best in fertile soils. Sow them in April and May in a seed bed, planting out firmly in June and July, dwarf forms 38cm (15in) apart, taller varieties 60–75cm (2–2$\frac{1}{2}$ft) apart. These may need staking. Kales can be fed in spring to encourage the production of fresh shoots.

Pests and diseases: Kales are

susceptible to the same problems as other brassicas, although they are less prone to clubroot. Caterpillars are usually the main problem.

Harvesting: Take only a few leaves at a time from any one plant, rather than stripping it. In spring snap off the shoots when they are 10–12cm (4–5in) long; the plants will continue to grow and crop over several weeks.

KOHLRABI

Kohlrabi is an extraordinary looking vegetable – a ball-shaped, leafy swelling on a

Curly-leaved kale

stem. Provided it is used young, kohlrabi has an unusual, delicate flavour, which is much appreciated on the Continent, where it is more widely grown.

Being one of the brassicas, it should be rotated with them in the garden. It does best in fertile, light, sandy soil, and is fast growing, being ready 6–8 weeks after sowing.

There are green- and purple-skinned forms of

Purple variety of kohlrabi

Leeks planted in rows; they are ready for lifting in autumn

under cloches from March (provided the soil has warmed up) to May. Sow in drills 2cm (¾in) deep.

The main plantings are made in June, continuing into July and early August. The ideal size for transplanting is about 20cm (8in) tall; the larger the seedling, the sooner it will mature, so plant in order of size along a row to make lifting convenient.

Water the seed bed thoroughly before lifting the seedlings, and trim off the tips of the leaves to prevent them dragging on the soil. Then make holes about 15cm (6in) deep with the dibber and drop the leek into the hole. The earth will fall back in naturally, so blanching the stem. Leeks can also be planted in a V-shaped drill about 8cm (3¼in) deep. Fill in the drill as the plants grow to blanch the stem. The rows can be 25–30cm (10–12in)

apart, spacing the leeks 15cm (6in) apart, or closer if you want smaller leeks.

Make sure the ground is moist after planting, watering daily (about a cupful for each plant) if necessary. Except in very dry weather no further watering is required, unless you want very large leeks.

Pests and diseases: Generally trouble-free although downy mildew can be a problem in cool, damp seasons.

Harvesting: Lift leeks as required during autumn and winter, starting with the earlier varieties.

LETTUCE

With careful use of different varieties, lettuces can be available most of the year in much of the country, though it is not easy to produce good quality lettuces in winter.

There are four main types: *Butterheads*, such as 'Unrivalled', have delicate leaves.

Early lettuce crop under cloches

kohlrabi. As a general rule the more tender green varieties are sown until about June, and the somewhat tougher purple varieties in July and August.

Cultivation: Kohlrabi can be sown in succession from late February, in mild areas, until August. Either sow in seed trays and plant out when the seedlings are no more than 5cm (2in) tall, or sow thinly in rows 30cm, (1ft) apart, thinning as early as possible to about 23cm (9in) between plants.

Pests and diseases: Seedlings may be attacked by flea beetle.

Harvesting: Use kohlrabi when it is between golf ball and tennis ball size: once they are larger they become tough and flavourless. Cook them without peeling, as much of the flavour lies just below the skin. They are excellent stuffed.

LEEK

The leek season can be spread from September to early May by selecting suitable vari-

eties. Early varieties are long with pale foliage, while the later, hardier varieties are stockier and darker-leaved. The following are recommended varieties:

Earlies: 'Autumn Mammoth-Walton'.
Mid season: 'Autumn Mammoth-Argenta'.
Late: 'Autumn Mammoth-Herwina', and 'Giant Winter-Catalina'.

Because leeks belong to the onion family they should be rotated with onions. They require an open position and rich, well-prepared soil, with plenty of organic matter worked into it. This can be done shortly before planting. They also have a high nitrogen requirement, so apply a nitrogenous fertilizer before planting, or feed with a seaweed-based fertilizer during growth.

Cultivation: Leeks need a long growing season. The first sowings can be made indoors in gentle heat in February for planting out, after hardening off, in May. Make the first outdoor sowings in a seed bed or

LETTUCE

When and how to sow	Suitable varieties	When to harvest
Early spring sowing (under glass) Sow in cold greenhouses, in frames, or under cloches from mid February in the south, early March in the north. Plant out in early April into frames, under cloches, or in a sheltered position outdoors.	*Loose-leaved:* 'Salad Bowl' *Butterheads:* 'Avondefiance', 'Unrivalled', 'Hilde II' *Cos:* 'Little Gem'	late May and June
Summer sowing Make regular sowings between March and October. To ensure a continuous supply, make the next sowing as soon as the seedlings from the previous sowing have emerged.	*Loose-leaved:* 'Salad Bowl' *Butterheads:* 'Avondefiance', 'Continuity', 'Tom Thumb' *Crispheads:* 'Avoncrisp', 'Great Lakes', 'Minetto', 'Windermere' *Cos:* 'Little Gem'	mid June to mid October
Autumn sowing (with winter protection or warmth) These need transplanting into frames, cold, or slightly heated greenhouses for a winter crop. Sow outdoors initially, and later under cover, from late August until October. Provide ventilation in winter to help prevent disease.	*Winter-maturing varieties:* 'Dandie', 'Kwiek', 'Ravel', 'Unrivalled'	November and December; February and March, depending on temperature

Autumn sowing (to over-winter)
These hardy varieties can be over-wintered outdoors, or in frames or under cloches, as seedlings.
    Sow end August or early September, in the open, or under cloches, or in frames, thinning to about 8cm (3in) apart in October, and to the final distance apart in spring.
    Alternatively, sow in soil or peat blocks. Over-winter in the blocks for planting out in spring.
	Butterheads: 'Imperial Winter', 'Valdor'
	Cos: 'Lobjoits Green', 'Winter Density', 'Little Gem'
		about May

Crispheads, such as 'Webbs Wonderful' and 'Iceberg', have larger crispier leaves but take about 3 weeks longer to mature.

Cos lettuce have conical heads and long, sweet, crisp leaves.

Loose-leaved ('Salad Bowl' type) lettuce are decorative and non-hearting, but can be picked over a long period.

A particularly sweet, crisp lettuce is 'Little Gem', usually described as a semi-cos. New lettuce varieties are continually appearing, many with useful resistance to diseases.

Lettuces must have fertile soil, an open position, and plenty of moisture throughout the growing season. Being a leafy crop they also need plenty of nitrogen. Prepare the soil by working in plenty of well-rotted manure or compost. A base dressing of a general fertilizer can be given before planting. Lettuces should be rotated to avoid the build up of soil pests and diseases.

Cultivation: Apart from the 'Salad Bowl' type, most lettuces only stand for a short time once they are mature, so frequent sowings must be made. You can sow them *in situ* and thin to the correct distance apart, or in seed trays or a seed bed and transplant. Mid summer sowings, roughly between mid May and mid August, are generally made *in situ* as lettuces transplant badly in hot weather. If the soil is dry at the time of sowing, water the drill first, sow the seed, then cover it with dry soil. This slows evaporation and lowers the soil temperature, which assists germination in summer. If lettuces are raised in individual pots or peat blocks, which produce excellent plants, they can be transplanted at any time. Seedlings should be planted when they have about 5 leaves, with the seed leaves just above soil level. Small varieties such as 'Little Gem' can be 25cm (9in) apart; butterheads about 30cm (1ft) apart, and crispheads and cos up to 35cm (14in) apart.

For a reasonably constant supply of lettuce, follow the sowing plan (left).

Pests and diseases: Soil pests such as cutworms, leatherjackets, slugs and lettuce root aphid can cause serious losses, as can greenfly. The most serious diseases are botrytis and downy mildew, which are worst in cold damp weather.

Harvesting: Headed lettuces tend to bolt soon after they mature, especially in hot weather. Wherever possible they should be used in their prime. Make smaller, but successive sowings, if you have too many together.

Some types of lettuce will re-sprout if the heads are cut leaving the stalks in the ground. This is particularly successful in spring with over-wintered varieties.

The 'Salad Bowl' types stand for several months without running to seed. The leaves can either be picked off individually as required, or harvested in one by cutting across the head, leaving about 2cm ($\frac{3}{4}$in) of leaf above the stalk. The stalk will throw out further leaves, so allowing a second harvesting a few weeks later, depending on the time of year.

ONION

There are two main types of onion – bulb onions and salad onions. With bulb onions the large, swollen bulbs are used fresh, or stored for winter. With spring or salad onions, the young green leaf and shank, and sometimes the slightly swollen little white bulbs, are eaten – in salads or chopped for flavouring.

Bulb onions: These need a long growing season, and are either raised from sets, which are specially prepared miniature bulbs, or from seed. Sets give them a head start in life and are easier to grow, especially in poorer soils, but they have a tendency to bolt, and only certain varieties are available, for example 'Ailsa Craig', 'Sturon' and 'Stuttgarter Giant', the last two being good keepers. Seed, although a little trickier to grow, works out cheaper and offers a far greater choice of variety. Here recommended modern varieties are 'Rijnsburger Wijbo', and for storing 'Rijnsburger Balstora' and 'Hygro'. Good Japanese varieties for autumn sowing are 'Express Yellow', 'Imai Early Yellow' and 'Senshyu Semi-Globe Yellow'. 'Brunswick Blood Red' is a good red onion variety to choose.

Cultivation: Sets are planted from February until April. Select small rather than large sets as they are less likely to bolt. Sets that have been 'heat treated' to discourage bolting are sometimes available: do not plant these until late March or April.

Make drills about 2.5cm (1in) deep, and plant the sets so that their tips just appear above ground. They can be from 5–10cm (2–4in) apart, the wider spacing giving larger bulbs, in rows about 23cm (9in) apart. Birds sometimes tweak out the sets: if so dig the sets out completely and replant, rather than push them back in. The rows can be protected with black cotton.

When using seed, prepare a seed bed with a finely raked surface about 10 days before sowing to allow it to 'settle'.

For a continuous year-round supply, two sowings should be made, the first with standard varieties from February to April, starting as soon as soil conditions allow. They can also be started indoors in gentle heat in January or February and planted out in March. These will mature in August and September, and the best 'keepers' will last until the following April.

For supplies in the gap that follows in June and July use the Japanese varieties. Sow them in early August in the north of the British Isles, in mid August in the Midlands, and the end of August in the south. Although these cannot be stored for long, they are hardier and more reliable than the old autumn-sown varieties.

Sow onions very thinly about 1cm ($\frac{1}{2}$in) deep, in rows about 25cm (10in) apart. They should be thinned in stages, starting as early as possible, until they are 4–10cm (1$\frac{1}{2}$–4in) apart, the wider spacing producing the largest onions. Use the thinnings as spring onions.

Salad or spring onions: For a regular supply of these, start sowing under cloches in February, and continue sowing at roughly fortnightly intervals until June, using the variety 'White Lisbon'. For very early supplies the following year sow 'White Lisbon-Winter Hardy' in July in the north, August in the south. Prepare seed bed as for other onions but sow thinly, and 'thin' simply by pulling as required.

Pickling onions: Good varieties are 'Paris Silverskin', 'Barletta' and 'The Queen'. Sow the seed less than 2cm ($\frac{3}{4}$in) apart in rows 25cm (10in) apart or in bands about 23cm (9in) wide. No thinning is required as the competition will keep the bulbs small. They will succeed in poorer soils than bulb onions.

Pests and diseases: Onion fly is the most likely pest.

Harvesting: Onions to use fresh are pulled as required during the season. Onions for storage and pickling are lifted once the foliage has died back naturally. Don't bend them over, as this increases the chances of the onions sprouting in store. Bulbs for storage should be lifted and handled gently,

Bulb onions

and if possible dried off in the sun and wind outdoors, off the ground on upturned boxes. Dry them indoors if it is very wet. Store them for winter in a dry, frost-free place, either plaited in ropes or hung in nets. Never store thick-necked or diseased bulbs.

PARSNIP

Parsnips do best on deep, light, rich, stone-free soil, rather than on heavy soil. Improve the soil by working in plenty of well-rotted organic manure beforehand. It has always been suggested that manure causes parsnip roots to fork, but research has indicated that this is not so.

Cultivation: Grow parsnips in an open position. They need a long growing season, but will not germinate in cold soil. Sow outside from early March (provided the soil has warmed up) until early May. Only sow new seed, as parsnip seed loses viability very rapidly. Sow the large, flat seeds 1–2cm ($\frac{1}{2}$–$\frac{3}{4}$in) deep, in rows about 25cm (10in) apart. To minimize thinning, sow 2–3 seeds in groups at 'stations' 13cm (5in) apart, thinning to one per station once the seedlings start to show. Germination is often slow, so it is a good idea to sow a few radish seeds between the stations to mark the rows.

Parsnips can also be started off indoors. Sow seed in peat blocks or small pots in February or early March. Transplant the seedlings outdoors, after hardening off, when they are no more than 5cm (2in) high.

Keep the plants weeded, and water in dry weather at the rates suggested for beetroot (p. 121).

Pests and diseases: Perhaps the most serious disease of parsnips is canker, especially on rich, organic soils. The tops of the roots blacken and crack, and eventually rot. If this is a problem on

Parsnips – best pulled as required

your soil, grow canker resistant varieties 'White Gem' and 'Avonresister'.

Harvesting: The roots are ready from October onwards, and should be left in the soil until required, just pulling a little soil over the crowns to protect them. In low temperatures some of the starch in the roots is converted into sugar, making them sweeter. The foliage dies down completely so mark the end of the rows with sticks so that they can be found in snow.

PEA

Ordinary garden peas are shelled and the green peas eaten. With the sugar or mange-tout peas, which are deservedly becoming increasingly popular, the whole pod is eaten while the peas are still immature. The dual-purpose mange-tout variety 'Sugar Snap' can be eaten early as pods, or allowed to mature and shelled for peas.

In seed catalogues peas are divided into 'earlies', 'second earlies', and 'maincrop' varieties, the difference between them being the time they take to mature. Earlies are ready in a minimum of 11 weeks, while maincrop varieties take up to 14 weeks. There are also round- and wrinkle-seeded types, the round being hardier and useful for very late and very early sowings, the wrinkle-seeded less hardy but sweeter and better flavoured. Peas vary in height from about 45cm (1½ft) to 1.5m (5ft), the taller types being less convenient but heavier yielding.

Good first early varieties are 'Feltham First', 'Early Onward', 'Hurst Beagle', 'Kelvedon Wonder', 'Little Marvel', and 'Meteor'. Good second earlies are 'Hurst Green Shaft', 'Onward', and 'Victory Freezer', while good maincrop varieties are 'Senator' and 'Lord Chancellor'.

Cultivation: Peas need an open site and well-worked, well-manured soil. If possible prepare a trench the previous autumn as suggested for runner beans; otherwise dig plenty of manure into the ground several months before sowing. Peas like coolish weather, so in mid summer they can be grown in light shade.

Like French beans, they will not germinate in cold soil. Early sowings should be made under cloches. Alternatively take out the drills and cover them with cloches to warm the soil, or simply expose them to the sun, for a few hours before sowing. Peas can also be sown indoors in pots or blocks as suggested for French beans.

There are several methods of sowing peas outdoors:–
1. Make a flat-bottomed drill about 23cm (9in) wide and 4cm (1½in) deep, spacing the seeds 5cm (2in) apart.
2. Sow in bands of three rows, each row 12cm (4½in) apart, the seeds also 12cm (4½in) apart. Allow 45cm (1½ft) between the bands.
3. Sow in blocks or patches up to 90cm (3ft) wide, making the holes with the dibber about 4cm (1½in) deep, spacing the seeds 5–8cm (2–3¼in) apart.

Make the earliest sowings outdoors under cloches in late February or early March in a sheltered position, using an early variety.

Make the main summer sowings from April until early July, using second early and maincrop varieties. It is also worth trying to get a late autumn crop by sowing an early variety in July. In good summers this will pay off.

In mild parts of the country hardy, overwintering peas can be sown in October and November to produce very early crops the follow-

Regular picking promotes further cropping of peas

ing spring. Protect the plants with cloches in severe weather.

It is important to support the peas as soon as any tendrils are visible. Small twigs are adequate for dwarf varieties, but taller varieties need longer twigs or some kind of pea netting. Water and mulch peas as suggested on p. 116.

Pests and diseases: Mice can be a serious problem with early and date pea sowings. Birds also attack peas at all stages. Maggoty peas are caused by the pea moth. Spray with fenitrothion one week after the flowers have opened.

Harvesting: As with beans, pick regularly to encourage further cropping. Mangetout peas are ready when the immature peas can just be seen as bumps inside the pod.

POTATO

Potatoes take up a lot of space and are relatively cheap to buy, so if your garden is small, it is probably only worth growing 'earlies', which are so superb when dug straight from the ground and are ready when shop prices are still high. They also escape some of the pests and diseases that affect maincrop potatoes.

Potatoes should always be rotated over at least a 3 year cycle to avoid the build up of soil pests and diseases, especially eelworm.

There is a confusing number of potato varieties to choose from, all with different characteristics. The following are particularly good:
Earlies: 'Maris Bard', 'Suttons Foremost'.
Second earlies: these take a little longer to mature – 'Red Craig's Royal', 'Wilja'.
Maincrop: these take longest to mature but give the heaviest yields – 'Desiree', 'King Edward', 'Pentland Squire'.

Potatoes need fertile soil with plenty of manure or compost in it, a good supply of nitrogen, and most important of all, plenty of moisture

throughout growth. They will tolerate fairly acid soil.

Cultivation: Buy seed potatoes in February and start them into growth by 'chitting' or sprouting them. Stand them upright (the eyes uppermost), in shallow boxes or trays (egg trays are ideal) in a cool room on a north-facing windowsill. Within about 6 weeks the potatoes will sprout: when the shoots are about 2cm (¾in) long they can be planted, provided the soil and weather permit.

Earlies can be planted outdoors from about mid March onwards, followed by second earlies and maincrops in April and May. Make a drill or individual holes 10–13cm (4–5in) deep, and plant the tubers upright. Both earlies and second earlies should be planted about 38cm (15in) apart in rows 38–45cm (15–18in) apart; maincrop potatoes should be spaced the same distance apart in rows 75cm (2½ft) apart.

Early potatoes may need protection from frost. Either cover the leaves with newspaper if frost is forecast, or draw the earth up around the young growths.

As the plants grow, tubers near the surface are pushed upwards and become greened – and therefore uneatable. To prevent this the plants should be earthed up when they are about 23cm (9in) high. Pull earth up around the stems to a height of about 10–13cm (4–5in).

Potatoes are sometimes grown under black plastic film, to cut down weeding and avoid earthing up. If you try this, plant the tubers shallowly and anchor the plastic over them afterwards. When the leaves bulge up beneath the plastic, cut a slit and pull them through. Harvest the tubers by rolling back the plastic: they will be found virtually on the surface of the soil.

Potatoes are heavy feeders and drinkers. Unless the soil is very fertile, work a general fertilizer into the soil before

planting, and apply a nitrogenous top-dressing, or a liquid feed with a seaweed-based fertilizer, during the growing season.

In dry weather the yields of early potatoes will be increased by watering roughly every fortnight at the rate of 16–22lt/sq m (3–4gal/sq yd). With maincrop potatoes the critical point is when the potatoes are the size of marbles. Give them one, very heavy watering at 22–27lt/sq m (4–5gal/sq yd) at this stage.

Pests and diseases: In humid areas maincrop potatoes are often affected by blight, causing brown patches on the leaves. Eelworm causes weak and stunted plants. Where it is a problem, grow the new varieties that have resistance to the commonest types of eelworm: these include 'Pentland Javelin', 'Pentland Lustre', 'Pentland Meteor' and 'Maris Piper' (maincrop).

Harvesting: Lift early potatoes as required. Maincrop potatoes can be lifted for storage once the leaves have died down. Choose a warm

day, spread them on the ground for an hour or so to dry, then store them in hessian sacks, or double-thickness paper sacks, in a frost-free room or shed. They must be kept dark. Cover the sacks with extra matting or blankets if freezing conditions are expected.

PUMPKIN

The term pumpkin embraces those gourds which can be used fresh or stored for winter, known in the United States as winter squash. Most popular in this country is the giant, orange pumpkin – but there are many other types.

Cultivation: Grow pumpkins like outdoor marrows, planting them about 1.2m (4ft) apart. Mark the plants with canes when planting, otherwise it is hard to find the roots for watering when the stems spread. If large pump-

Potatoes may look robust, but harvest them carefully to avoid damaging their tubers

kins are required, limit the fruits to 1–2 per plant, picking off surplus flowers.

Pests and diseases: Powdery mildew and slugs are likely to be the main problems.

Harvesting: Pumpkins earmarked for storage should be left on the plant as long as possible, removing any leaves that are shading them. Cut them off in the autumn before night frosts are expected, and leave them in a sunny spot against a wall for several days for the skins to colour up and harden. Store them on shelves, or if not too heavy, suspended in nets in a frost-free, dry shed or cellar. They should keep in good condition until the following spring.

RADISH

There are two sorts of radish: the familiar small summer radishes and the giant winter radishes which are used raw, sliced, or grated, or cooked like turnips. The pods formed when radishes run to seed are also edible and very tasty.

Radishes do best in rich, light, well-drained, sandy soils, with adequate mois-

Summer radishes

ture during growth. Use soil manured for a previous crop and, if possible, rotate them with brassicas. The faster they are grown the better; slow-growing radishes become woody and unpleasantly hot.

Good summer varieties are 'Saxa', 'Saxerre', 'Robino', 'Ribella' and 'Cherry Belle' (all these can also be used for early sowings under cloches); and 'French Breakfast', 'Long White Icicle' and 'Red Prince' (which stands very well in summer). Good winter varieties are 'Black Spanish Round', 'China Rose' and 'Mino Early'.

Cultivation: Radishes develop so fast that they are frequently intersown in the same rows as slow-growing crops such as parsnips, or used for intercropping. Summer sowings can be made in light shade. For a continuous supply make small, frequent sowings.

Earliest sowings of summer radishes can be made from February onwards under cloches or in frames, followed by outdoor sowings at roughly 10-day intervals. Make final sowings under cloches or in a cold greenhouse in September and October.

Sow seed about 2cm (¾in)

deep in rows 15cm (6in) apart, spacing the seeds about 4cm (1½in) apart. This avoids the need to thin for, unless radishes are thinned very early, they fail to develop. If the soil is dry when sowing, water the drill heavily beforehand. After sowing, cover the seed with dry soil.

During growth, water sufficiently to prevent the soil drying out, but do not overwater, as this encourages leaf growth at the expense of root.

Winter radishes are sown in July and early August in rows 25cm (10in) apart. Sow very thinly spacing the seeds 5cm (2in) apart, thinning in stages to about 13cm (5in) apart.

Pests and diseases: Radish seedlings are often attacked by flea beetles.

Harvesting: Pull summer radishes as required. Winter radishes can be left in the soil, protected with straw or bracken. On very heavy soils they may be damaged by slugs: if so, store them in a

Seakale is well worth growing for its, delicate nutty flavour

shed in boxes of moist peat or sand. If you want radish pods, leave a plant in the ground to run to seed in spring. Pick the pods when green and crisp.

SEAKALE

Although considered an old-fashioned vegetable, the subtle, nutty flavour and crisp texture of blanched seakale stalks in spring is a treat. Seakale is perennial, and once established is productive for 8–10 years.

Cultivation: Prepare an open site by working in plenty of well-rotted manure or compost. Buy plants or rooted cuttings (thongs); alternatively, raise plants from seed or from your own thongs.

Sow fresh seed (old seed germinates poorly) in a seedbed in spring. Keep the ground moist until the seed germinates. Plant seedlings into their permanent position in autumn, 30cm (1ft) apart each way. Alternatively sow *in situ* in rows 30cm (1ft) apart, thinning to the same distance.

Thongs are obtained by lifting plants that are at least three years old in the autumn. Select roots of finger thickness, and cut them into pieces 10–15cm (4–6in) long. Trim them flat across the top and with a slanting cut across the bottom, so that you know which end is which! Store these upright in a box of moist sand until early March, when buds will have formed. Rub out weak buds leaving one strong central bud, and plant the thongs outdoors in spring.

Water so that the ground does not dry out in the summer. Allow the plants to grow undisturbed for their first two seasons, feeding them occasionally with a seaweed-based fertilizer. If they have many feeble shoots thin them out to encourage stronger shoots. In late autumn remove dead leaves from the base of the plant and cover the crowns with a little soil.

Pests and diseases: If clubroot is in the ground, seakale is likely to be affected.

Harvesting: Plants are ready for blanching in their third season. The simplest method is to cover the plants with 30cm (1ft) high buckets or plant pots, with the drainage hole blocked to exclude light, in January. The whitened shoots can be cut in late March and April. Stop cutting in May and remove the buckets or pots, so that they can continue to grow naturally.

Plants can be forced indoors for winter. Wait until the first frost, then lift and pot up the crowns in peat, covering them with a flower pot to exclude the light. Bring them into a temperature of 16–21°C (60–70°F). After forcing, the crown is exhausted, and if planted out again will take several years to recover.

SHALLOT

Shallots are a chunky-shaped type of onion, very much prized for pickling. They also make an excellent substitute for onions in early summer, as they keep better than any other onions, remaining in good condition until June. Single sets can multiply into clumps of up to 20 bulbs. There are both red- and yellow-skinned varieties.

Cultivation: Buy small, good quality, virus-free sets: the ideal size is 2cm ($\frac{3}{4}$in) diameter (larger sets may 'bolt'). They can be planted in December or January in mild areas on well-drained soil, but elsewhere plant them as early in the year as soil conditions permit. Plant them like onion sets 15cm (6in) apart, in rows 25cm (10in) apart.

Pests and diseases: Generally trouble-free.

Harvesting: Lift, dry and store as suggested for onions. Provided the stock remains

ABOVE: *Spinach*
BELOW LEFT: *Shallots suspended above the ground to dry*

healthy, keep back a few of your own bulbs for planting the following year, though it is probably wise to start afresh with bought sets every three years.

SPINACH

Spinach is very sensitive to day length, which is why it is apt to 'bolt' in the long days of summer. It does best in autumn, winter and early spring, when steadier growth allows several pickings.

Cultivation: For a summer supply betwen May and October, frequent small sowings are advisable, as in general only one cut can be made before it runs to seed. In warm parts of the country, the first sowing can be made under cloches in February, followed by outdoor sowings in March. Make further sowings at 2–3 week intervals

until July. For these summer sowings use varieties such as 'Longstanding Round' and 'Sigmaleaf'. Sow 1–1½cm (½–¾in) deep, in rows 30cm (1ft) apart, thinning to 15cm (6in) apart.

Winter spinach, which can be cropped between October and May, is sown in August and September. Suitable varieties are 'Greenmarket', 'Sigmaleaf', and 'Broad Leaved Prickly'. In this case thin to 23cm (9in) apart. The plants will be of a much better quality if they can be protected from the weather by covering them with cloches in October or November. For spinach beet, see leaf beet.

Pests and diseases: Generally trouble-free, but downy mildew can be a problem. Blackfly or greenfly may also attack.

Harvesting: Leaves can be eaten very small or allowed to grow larger. Pick them individually off the plant as required. The plants will make further growth, unless conditions cause them to 'bolt' instead.

SPINACH, NEW ZEALAND

This is a useful vegetable for dry soils, and can be cropped regularly over a long period.

Cultivation: New Zealand spinach is a half-hardy vegetable. It must either be sown indoors in April, hardened off and planted out in May after risk of frost, or sown directly outdoors in mid May – or a little earlier under cloches. To assist germination soak the seed in water overnight before sowing. Space plants about 45cm (1½ft) apart in each direction, allowing them room to sprawl over the ground. Although useful for dry, sunny corners, New Zealand does equally well under normal conditions. It will continue growing until frost kills it, and will often seed itself, reappearing the following year.

Pests and diseases: Generally trouble-free.

Harvesting: New Zealand spinach must be picked regularly, otherwise it becomes tough, and knobbly seedheads are formed. Pick leaves as required or cut whole, young shoots from the base of the plant and strip off the leaves.

SWEDE

The large, rounded, usually yellow-fleshed roots of swedes are extremely hardy, very sweet-flavoured and invaluable for winter. They belong to the brassica family, and therefore should be carefully rotated in the garden.

Swedes do badly in very dry and very wet soils. They require light, fertile soil, limed if acid, and preferably manured for a previous crop.

Cultivation: It is only necessary to make one sowing of swedes, in late April or early May in the north, or late May and early June in the south.

Sow seed 2cm (¾in) deep, in rows 38–45cm (15–18in) apart, thinning as early as possible to about 25cm (10in) apart.

In dry weather water to prevent the soil drying out, but don't over-water, otherwise flavour will be lost.

Pests and diseases: Watch out for flea beetle attacks at the seedling stage. Mildew and clubroot can be real problems. If you've had these troubles, try the excellent, new variety 'Marian', which has considerable resistance to both diseases.

Harvesting: Roots can be ready from September onwards in the south, October onwards in the north. Leave them in the ground until Christmas, when they should be lifted before they become woody. They can be stored in clamps outdoors, or layered in boxes of moist peat or sand and kept in a frost-free place.

TOMATO

Tomatoes need a long season and warm conditions to do well. They can only be grown successfully outdoors in the south of England; elsewhere they are best grown in frames or an unheated greenhouse. A heated greenhouse is only necessary for an exceptionally early crop.

There are numerous varieties, divided into tall, cordon types and dwarf, bush types. The former have to be 'sideshooted' and 'stopped' and require staking, while the bush varieties sprawl on the ground.

Tomatoes should be rotated, and should not be grown near maincrop potatoes, as they are easily infected with potato blight.

On the whole the same varieties can be grown inside and out, though tall varieties, because they make more productive use of the space, are normally used for the greenhouse crop, while bush varieties are generally only grown outdoors. Reliable tall varieties are generally only grown outdoors. Reliable tall varieties are 'Ailsa Craig', 'Alicante', 'Gardener's Delight' and 'Harbinger'. Reliable bush varieties are the F_1 hybrids 'Sleaford Abundance', 'Alfresco' and 'Pixie', which is a compact and heavy fruited variety.

OUTDOOR TOMATOES

Cultivation: If possible grow tomatoes against a south-facing wall or erect a windbreak or plastic film screen around them. They can also be grown outdoors in large pots or boxes (using soil-based John Innes No.3 compost or a peat-based potting compost), or in growing bags.

Prepare the ground beforehand by working in plenty of well-rotted manure or compost, so that the soil is well-drained but moisture-retentive. A base dressing of

Tall tomato plant varieties must be secured to stakes for support

a general fertilizer can be applied before planting.

Either raise plants yourself or buy some in, choosing stocky plants, preferably in individual pots.

If raising your own, sow in gentle heat indoors, in a seed compost, in early April. Prick out the seedlings when they have 3 leaves into 9cm (3½in) pots, using John Innes No. 2 potting compost or a peat-based compost. After hardening off, plant outdoors in late May/early June, after any risk of frost. Plants should be about 20cm (8in) high with the first flower truss showing. Protect them with cloches initially, if possible. Plant tall varieties about 38cm (15in) apart, and bush varieties about 45cm (1½ft) apart, though if planted a few inches closer they will usually give earlier, but slightly lower, yields.

Mulch plants with plastic to keep them clean, nip out the sideshoots of tall varieties, and 'stop' them, nipping off the growing point 2 leaves above a flowering truss, at end July/early August.

Tall varieties must be tied to 1.2m (4ft) stakes or horizontal wires attached to posts at either end of the row.

In well-prepared soil outdoor varieties generally need no further feeding. In dry weather water them about twice a week, once they have started flowering, at the rate of about 9lt/sq m (2gal/sq yd). Overwatering reduces the flavour. Tomatoes in pots or other containers will require more frequent waterng, and regular weekly feeding with a proprietary tomato fertilizer.
Pest and diseases: In wet seasons it may be necessary to spray against potato blight in July and August, using a copper-based fungicide.
Harvesting: Fruits normally start to ripen by the end of August. At the end of September hasten ripening by covering plants with cloches (cut tall varieties off their canes and lay them on the ground). Pull up remaining plants by their roots before

frost comes and hang them indoors, or in a greenhouse, to continue ripening.

GREENHOUSE TOMATOES
Cultivation: Tomatoes cannot be grown in the same greenhouse soil for more than 3 years as the soil becomes diseased. It then either has to be sterilized (which is difficult), or replaced. It is easier to grow tomatoes in pots, bags or boxes in fresh soil or potting compost, or to adopt a soil-less system such as ring culture.

Raise plants as for outdoor tomatoes, sowing in early/mid March and planting in mid/late April. Tie the plants to canes or wire supports, or twist them up strings hung from the roof. Once the first truss has set, feed weekly with a high potash tomato fertilizer. Remove sideshoots from the plants and stop them after 7–8 trusses. Remove yellowing leaves from the base of the plant, and keep the greenhouse well ventilated day and night, to reduce the risk of disease.
Pests and diseases: Uneven watering may cause blossom-end rot, which produces sunken patches on the fruits.
Harvesting: Indoor tomatoes can be picked from late July until October or November.

TURNIP
Provided the soil is reasonably fertile and there is plenty of moisture, turnips are among the fastest-maturing vegetables. They can be used fresh in spring and summer, or stored for winter use. When the plants are grown close together, leafy turnip tops can be used as greens.

The white-fleshed turnips are grown for summer use and should be pulled young and small, no more than 5cm (2in) across. Good varieties are 'Purple Top Milan' and 'Snowball'. Best for winter use are the yellow-fleshed varieties, such as 'Golden

Ball' and 'Manchester Market' ('Green Top Stone') which are hardier and slower-maturing.

Turnips are brassicas, so should be rotated accordingly (see pp. 112 and 114). They prefer ground that has been manured for a previous crop; if the soil is not very fertile, work in a general fertilizer before sowing.
Cultivation: For summer turnips make the first sowings under cloches in March, followed by sowings at monthly intervals until July, when the winter crop can be sown. The mid summer sowings can be made in light shade, as turnips dislike intense heat.

Sow the seed about 2cm (¾in) deep, the summer crop in rows 23cm (9in) apart, and thin to 10cm (4in) apart; the winter crop in rows 30cm (1ft) apart, and thin to 15cm (6in) apart. As turnips grow so fast, it is important to thin as soon as the seedlings touch one another.

White-fleshed turnips, pulled young and small

For turnip tops, sow winter varieties either in August or September, or summer varieties in early spring, as soon as the soil has warmed up. Either sow a small broadcast patch, or sow thinly in rows 15cm (6in) apart, leaving them unthinned.
Pests and diseases: Flea beetle attacks can be a problem at the seedling stage. On ground infested with clubroot, turnips may be affected.
Harvesting: Pull summer turnips from the end of May onwards. Lift winter turnips around Christmas and twist off the stems. Store them in a frost-free place, layered in boxes of moist peat or sand, or in clamps outdoors.

Turnip tops are cut 2.5cm (1in) above ground level when the plants are about 15cm (6in) high. The plants should re-sprout, so 2–3 cuts can be made.

THE GREENHOUSE

Although gardening under glass can be a pursuit in itself, in this short section we look at a greenhouse as a useful adjunct to the garden as a whole. Its main uses in this aspect are threefold: as a nursery for raising young flower and vegetable plants, to over-winter half-hardy plants, to extend the garden season of flowers, vegetables and fruit.

What sort of greenhouse?

Always buy the largest size that you can afford and have room for. Greenhouse gardening is apt to become compulsive and one always wishes a larger model had been chosen at the outset. The choice of size and design is now considerable and it is a matter of choosing what you fancy. It is worthwhile considering whether you choose a greenhouse with a timber or an aluminium alloy frame. Alloy is very durable, re-

quiring little or no maintenance, and the narrow glazing bars allow maximum light admission. However, metal is a better conductor of heat than wood and thus more heat is lost through an alloy than a timber structure. Aesthetically, red cedar wood, the best for greenhouses, fits in better to the garden scene and is almost as durable as alloy. Another point in favour of wood is the ease with which wire supports, benching and hanging baskets can be secured to it.

One further point to consider is ventilation. Almost without exception custom-built greenhouses have all too few ventilators. For reasons discussed under Conserving heat, a confined space surrounded by glass quickly builds up heat when the sun shines. Between late spring and mid autumn temperatures can rise to lethal limits without ventilation. Ridge and side ventilators are essential, and there should be at least one

or the other of each to every 2m (6½ft) of length. If it means buying extra optional ventilators then do so without hesitation. To use the greenhouse efficiently, make sure it has benching for both sides.

Siting

Although not obvious to the human eye, glass screens out a surprising amount of the sun's rays. For this and ancillary reasons the greenhouse should be sited in as sunny a position as possible. If the greenhouse is to be kept frost-free or warmer and contain growing plants in winter, then its position in relation to the sun is even more important. Bear in mind that the sun rises to only about 17° above the southern horizon in mid-winter and can easily be obscured by tall buildings and trees. For these reasons, align the long axis of your greenhouse east and west so that the long side faces

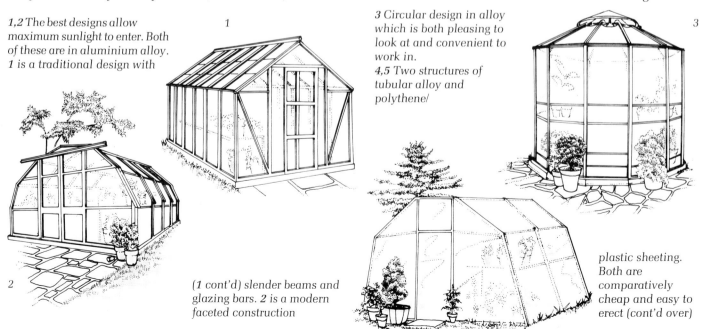

1,2 The best designs allow maximum sunlight to enter. Both of these are in aluminium alloy. 1 is a traditional design with

(1 cont'd) slender beams and glazing bars. 2 is a modern faceted construction

3 Circular design in alloy which is both pleasing to look at and convenient to work in.
4,5 Two structures of tubular alloy and polythene/

plastic sheeting. Both are comparatively cheap and easy to erect (cont'd over)

(4,5 cont'd) but are liable to wind damage and the sheeting has to be replaced every few years.

7 Small, wooden-framed lean-to design which takes up little room and reaps the benefit of extra heat from the house wall. 8 Dutch-light style in red cedar which is easily assembled, strong and windproof.

6 Traditional design in red cedar, boarded in the north side and at the east and west ends.

south. If possible, provide some shelter from cold east and north winds; for example, by utilizing hedges, open weave fences or the plastic mesh sold as a wind-break. From a convenience point of view choose a site as near to the house as possible. If you have a blank south-facing wall, seriously consider a lean-to greenhouse, ideally with a doorway directly into the home. Such a situation takes full advantage of the sun-warmed bricks of the house wall and, in winter, of the heat within the house. If artificial heating is contemplated, it can be easily taken from the house into the lean-to.

Heating
Artificial heat, although not essential, greatly increases the scope of a greenhouse. If half-hardy plants are to be over-wintered successfully, then just enough heat to keep out the frost is sufficient. If plants are to be grown during the cold months, eg salpiglossis in pots for a late spring display, or winter-hearting lettuce, a night minimum temperature of 7°C (45°F) must be provided. About 10°C (50°F) is a suitable night minimum in spring for young bedding plants (eg begonia, lobelia, antirrhinum) raised from seed in a heated case in late winter. These heating levels are not high and are easily provided by one of the readily available, fairly inexpensive thermostatically controlled electric fan heaters. If you make sure to go onto the low tariff night rate electricity supply, this is one of the best ways of heating a greenhouse.

Conserving heat
The sun's short-wave radiation passes easily through glass and warms all objects within the greenhouse. These objects re-radiate warmth as long-wave radiation which cannot pass through glass, hence the rapid build up of high heat in a closed greenhouse on a sunny day. This phenomenon is known as 'the greenhouse effect'. As soon as the sun sets or passes into shadow, heat is lost by conduction from framework and glass and the cracks around doors and vents. Artificially provided heat is lost in the same way. Heating costs can be reduced by using a heat conservation technique. Double-glazing with plastic sheeting so that there is a gap between it and the glass is fairly efficient, as is bubble glaze sheeting. Both reduce light intensity and are best not used on the south side.

Shading
During hot spells in summer even opening every ventilator and the door may not be enough to keep the temperature to manageable limits. When this happens, shading is the answer. The ideal is internal or external blinds, but they are expensive. The popular alternative is to use a proprietary shading compound which is painted or sprayed on the glass. Several are available; opt for one that rubs off easily when the weather dulls over and cools down.

Automation
For those who are away at work all day there are automatic vent and blinds operators. There are also various automatic watering systems, the easiest being sand trays kept wet by a refillable bottle or a header tank with a ballcock valve attached to the mains water supply.

Cultivation
The essential activities of propagation, potting, watering and feeding are dealt with in the introductions to House Plants (p.90), with further points under Garden Flowers (p.18).

Maintenance
Keep the greenhouse as clean and uncluttered as possible. Wash the glass at least once a year each autumn and if you live in a town, repeat at intervals in the winter. Smoke soon grimes up the glass and very seriously impairs light transmission. Spores of diseases and eggs of pests can lurk on wood and metal work so, ideally, empty the greenhouse once a year in late summer or early autumn and scrub the internal structure with a sterilizing agent (eg Jeyes Fluid), including benching. This will lessen the all too willing attentions of pests and diseases.

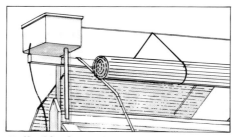

Roller blinds are the best type, either

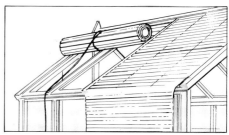

automated (left) or manual (right).

FRUIT

There is no reason why even the tiniest garden should not produce some sort of fruit for its owner. Most of the major crops are fairly adaptable in their demands, both for the available space and for the gardener's time. Some of the less usual fruits grow happily in deep shade, or on peaty soils, in very cold gardens, in pots on the patio or terrace, in sunrooms and greenhouses, in conservatories or even on a moderately sunny windowsill or protected balcony.

Climate
All gardeners, whether in Sussex, Yorkshire, or Ross and Cromarty should remember that local climate is far more important than mere latitude. For example, there are gardens in coastal parts of Scotland which will produce splendid crops of peaches, apricots and figs from wall-trained trees, yet a dozen miles inland even quince trees, reputed to be hardy, can be killed by the cold.

One of the best ways of finding out what will grow well in your area is to look at neighbouring gardens, to contact — or, better still, join — a local gardening society, ask at your local nursery or contact the nearest college of agriculture. You will discover which varieties and which crops do especially well in your area. It is best to seek local advice before ordering from a catalogue or buying from a garden centre. Supplement the information you get from books with other people's experience of actual conditions.

Whatever your location, however windy and cold, do not despair. There are excellent apple and pear varieties that will bear fruit in the coldest gardens; even wet mountain hillsides can provide strawberries and raspberries.

It is not possible to grow the major top fruits in a frost hollow. In such a garden, late spring frosts will ruin flowers and fruitlets and cold autumn nights will arrive far too early. In this situation, content yourself with growing late-flowering and early-ripening varieties of soft fruit only, and provide as much protection for it as you can.

The quality of the soil
Unless your soil is permanently waterlogged or completely dry, there will be some fruits that will grow for you. Having said this, most species are ideally suited by deep loamy soil with a pH of about 6.5. Dampish soils will produce excellent pears, plums, and raspberries. Dryish soils suit many apples, peaches, nectarines and figs. Acid peaty soils will produce blueberries and cranberries, but little else.

Fertilizers
Most of the soft fruits require a good diet. Apply garden compost, well-rotted manure or peat enriched with chemical fertilizer annually in winter. Strawberries, raspberries and redcurrants need extra potash. Apply 12g/m² (½oz/yd²) before planting out. Top fruits needing potash are apple and sweet cherry. Dress the soil in winter with potassium sulphate at 25g/m² (1oz/yd²).

If you cannot obtain manure, and do not have room to make a compost heap, feed the plants during the summer by watering them with suitable soluble fertilizers. Crops that need a diet rich in potash will like liquids of the type used for tomatoes. A general fertilizer will suit the rest.

Top fruits are worth cosseting for the first few years, while they are establishing themselves. Pears, plums, peaches and nectarines all benefit from good dressings of well-rotted manure or compost, while apples prefer potash.

Supporting trained fruits
Top fruit and soft fruit grown as cordons, fans or espaliers need some sort of system to support them, whether free-standing or against a wall. The framework should be set up before the fruit is planted to avoid disturbing the bush or tree. What you need is a system of horizontal wires set about 45cm (18in) apart. Use galvanized wire 2.5mm (⅒in) in diameter for permanence. Against a wall, attach them to tensioning bolts with vine eyes set every 2m (6½ft) along the length of the wires. In free-standing systems for fruit grown as screens or for espaliers in a fruit cage, the wires should be attached to strong timber posts. Use posts measuring 10 × 10cm (4 × 4in) and treat them with fungicide. The end posts will need extra support at the base. Again, space the posts about 3.4m (10ft) apart.

Planting top fruit
The amount of trouble you take over planting, the first piece of work that you will have to do for your fruit, will affect most of your subsequent tasks. It is important, especially for top fruit, that the plant gets the best possible start in life so that even if you eventually have no time to devote to it you will still have a tree that will try to go on being productive. Fruit that gets a bad start may take years to become established.

If you have ordered plants from a distant nursery, they will arrive some time during the late autumn, or in winter, and will be bare-rooted; that is, most of the soil will have been shaken from their roots. Although most nurseries send out well-packed healthy

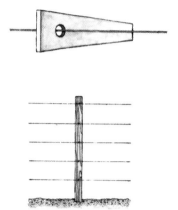

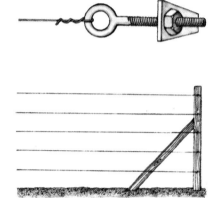

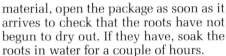

To support fruit, make a framework of horizontal wires threaded through vine eyes and attached to tensioning bolts .
In a free-standing support system, attach the wires to strong timber posts, with extra supports at the base of the end posts (*left*).

material, open the package as soon as it arrives to check that the roots have not begun to dry out. If they have, soak the roots in water for a couple of hours.

If you cannot plant immediately because the soil is frozen hard or sodden and too wet to work, the trees should be stored until planting is possible. Keep the plants in a shed, garage or cellar with the roots surrounded by moist peat. If the soil is fine for planting, but you do not have time to get the plants in the ground properly, simply dig a rough hole, put the roots in and cover them with enough soil to keep them firm. This process is known as 'heeling in'.

When weather conditions permit and you have enough time, dig a hole at the chosen site that will comfortably hold the roots when they are well spread out.

If possible, fork a bucketful or two of compost or well-rotted manure into the soil at the bottom of the hole. Failing these, use a good handful of bonemeal. Mix some bonemeal or compost into the excavated soil.

Staking: All top fruits, whether bush or tree, need support for the first year or two while the root system becomes strong enough to provide sufficient anchorage for the leafy top. It would be

heartbreaking to find new standards bent or snapped off at the graft, or bushes half rocked out of the ground by a summer gale because they have not been staked.

Once you have excavated the planting hole and worked in some manure, place the stake in position. Square or round stakes are equally good, but they must be strong enough to do the job. Poles 5cm (2in) in diameter or 5 × 5cm (2 × 2in) stakes will be sufficient for the average standard tree. The length of the support depends on the length of the plant's stem. The top of the stake, when driven into the base of the planting hole, should be just below the first branch of the standard. Position the stake on the prevailing windward side of the tree, so that the tree generally pulls on the stake. On bushes, the stake inevitably stands among the branches. Secure the base and/or strong central branch firmly to the stake.

Filling in: Stand the young plant in the hole to ensure that the size is right. Spread the roots out evenly. Neatly trim off any that are broken or damaged. Put a spadeful or two of excavated soil over the roots and shake the plant gently to settle the soil between the main roots.

To get the planting level right, find the graft, which is usually visible as an oblique swelling on the stem, and make sure that it is several inches above the soil level. Sometimes it is possible to see where the old soil level was when the plant was in the nursery bed, in which case simply plant to the same depth.

Shovel in some more soil and shake again. Firm down with the feet. Continue until the hole is filled, and the tree firmly planted.

Secure the tree to the stake. Strips of cloth make good ties, or stout twine threaded through a piece of hosepipe. Do not use nylon string or twine because it is so sharp that it will cut into the bark. A buffer of some sort between the tree and stake is useful.

Container-grown trees and bushes
These can be bought and planted at any time of year, using exactly the same method as for bare-rooted trees. Open up the lowest part of the root ball as much as you can before planting, paying attention to the coil of roots that often forms at the bottom of the bag or pot.

Once planted, if the weather is dry water the young tree or bush copiously over the whole root area. Keep a close watch on the plant in the following months, especially in hot weather. It will take at least a season before there are sufficient new roots to let the tree fend for itself.

Soft fruits
These are planted in the same way as top fruit. Bush soft fruits are small when

BELOW: *'Heel in' the fruit tree if you cannot plant it immediately.*

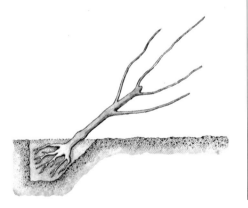

For permanent planting, position the stake before placing the tree in the ready-dug hole. Ensure that the roots are evenly spread (*left*). After filling in, secure the tree to the stake and, ideally, place a buffer between them to prevent damage to the bark (*above*).

FRUIT TREES: distances between plants

	APPLES		PEARS		PLUMS		CHERRIES	
	space between plants	rows	space between plants	rows	space between plants	rows	space between plants	rows
Centre leader bush	semi-dwarfing rootstock 4–6m / dwarfing rootstock 2–5m	4–6m / 3–6m	2–6m	4–6	3–6m	4–6m	sweet 5–8m / sour 4–6m	sweet 5–8m / sour 4–6m
Espalier	4–6m	2m	3–6m	2m				
Oblique cordon	1m	2m	1m	2m				
Fan	4–6m		4–6m		4–6m		sweet 5–8m	sour 4–6m
Standard	6–10m	6–10m	6–10m	6–10m	6–8m	6–8m	sweet 7–12in	

Distances between plants depend on the vigour of the variety: plants of a non-vigorous variety should be spaced according to the smaller of the recommended figures.

sold, and do not need staking. Strawberries are planted into a prepared bed (see page 161).

Pruning

Pruning ensures that the tree or bush is kept within bounds, furnishes a supply of fruiting wood, and allows light and air to reach the ripening fruit. The method of pruning varies from species to species, and depends also on the form of plant required.

Almost every tree and bush fruit that we are dealing with produces flowers along shoots that were formed the previous season (second-year wood). In some fruits (group 1) that second-year wood will not go on to produce flowers in the third year (eg morello cherries, peaches). In other cases (group 2), flower buds continue to form in subsequent years, often on short side shoots called 'spurs'. Most apples and pears, plums and sweet cherries fall into this group.

It is nevertheless useful to think in terms of the spur when treating the first group of fruit types, where pruning has to ensure a constant supply of new wood. In general, this replacement wood can be thought of as very long spurs. 'Long spur' fruit includes raspberries and blackberries, vines, peaches and nectarines.

Most pruning takes place in winter. Remember that fruit against a wall will start to grow as soon as the sunlight begins to gain strength. Get all pruning done before winter spraying starts, and well before there is the slightest sign of the buds expanding. Chemicals used at that time will harm green tissue.

Do not prune plums, damsons, greengages or cherries in winter, as this can allow the entry of silver leaf disease. Leave them to late July or August.

Fruit forms

It is very important to understand what the basic differences are between the various forms of fruit tree that are available (see illustrations on pp. 146–7).

Maiden: A single shoot, usually one year's growth after grafting. If you have sufficient self-confidence to go on to produce the other forms of tree from a maiden, and the time to wait an extra year or two for a crop, you can take advantage of the fact that maidens are cheap to buy and very easy to establish in the garden. Prune in winter.

Cordon: A cordon is simply a maiden with side growths pruned back to form spurs. Some soft fruits, particularly redcurrants and gooseberries, make good cordons, but these forms are most often used for the majority of apple and pear varieties, which easily form short spurs. They can be grown on wire frameworks, or against walls.

Fans: Trees of fan shape are always grown against a wall or supporting framework. The maiden is cut back to 20–30cm (8–12in), and the two uppermost shoots that then develop are allowed to grow. They are tied into wires or canes to keep them in one plane, and the next year are themselves cut back and allowed to sprout two or three new shoots. The resultant 'spokes' are kept in the same plane, and are also trained along canes to keep them neat and straight. Fans take time and care to produce, and are expensive to buy.

Fans are suitable for vigorous types of fruit, especially plums, peaches, nectarines, figs and morello cherries. However, apples and pears can make splendid-looking fans, and because the spurs are so short the structure shows up well.

Standards and half-standards: All side growths are pruned away and the leader allowed to grow to the required height — 2m (6½ft) and 1m (3¼ft) respectively. The growth point is then removed and th topmost three or four outward-facing branches that then develop are allowed to grow on.

Espalier: A well-trained and cared-for espalier looks marvellous in flower and fruit. They are more useful than fans, as they are easily trained to fill all available space. Each of the side branches can be extended as far as necessary.

The maiden is cut back to just above the height of the first wire, generally 45cm (18in) above ground level. Three new shoots are allowed to form; the uppermost is allowed to grow vertically; generally the other two are allowed to grow out at a wide angle, tied to canes to keep them straight, and are carefully lowered to the horizontal in autumn.

The following season, the vertical shoot is cut back to the level of the second wire, and so on for as many subsequent years as there are wires.

Bushes: These vary in shape, both according to the natural habit of the fruit variety concerned, but also to the needs of the gardener. Gooseberries and currants are most often grown in this way, but many of the top fruits are too. Bushes are useful because their size makes them easier to tend.

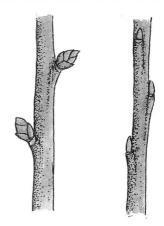

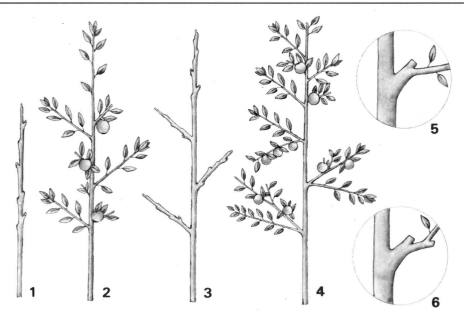

ABOVE: Fruit buds (*left*) and wood buds (*right*). Never reduce wood buds to less than 4–5 per stem.

ABOVE RIGHT:— *Replacement shoot fruits (Group 1):*

1 1st winter, fruit and growth buds along previous summer's shoot.

2 1st summer, prune shoots next to fruits to 2–3 leaves, allowing some shoots to grow for next year's fruit.

3 2nd winter, as 1st winter.

4 2nd summer, as 1st summer, but allow 5–6 leaves beyond last fruit on each fruit. Pinch out side growth to 2–3 leaves except for one near the base, which should be allowed to grow as replacement fruiting shoot.

5 2nd summer, after harvest, cut out shoot at junction with replacement.

6 3rd summer.

Most top fruit bushes are produced by shortening a maiden to about 60cm (2ft) and letting a number of side shoots grow which are in turn cut back annually by half for the first few years.

With short-spur fruits it is an easy matter to grow the main structure of the bush, and then encourage and prune spurs in exactly the same way as for an espalier or fan. For long-spur types, allow the bush to build up a structure, then remove fruited side shoots.

Soft fruit trees: These are naturally small and seldom outgrow their allotted space. Gooseberries, redcurrants and whitecurrants, which can be made to spur, are best treated in the same way as bush apples. When the main branches and the spurs become too congested, cut one or two branches out each year. Of the new, replacement shoots select the strongest and remove the others.

Blackcurrants should be cut to within 2.5–5cm (1–2in) of the ground just after planting. The prunings can be used as cuttings to raise new plants. No further pruning should be necessary until the bush is several years old when, after harvesting, you should cut out between one quarter and one third of the branches at near ground level. This will encourage plenty of new growth, while keeping the bush open enough to ripen both fruit and new wood.

Dwarfing stocks

Most top fruits are sold in a grafted form, since this method of propagation ensures constant characters for each variety. It is possible to grow some from cuttings, and the resultant plants are often exceptionally vigorous.

Grafting is an ancient art. Before the Romans practised it, it was known that the type of stock used affected the growth habit of the tree it supported. Over the ages, the selection of stocks became increasingly refined. Today, it is possible to buy most fruits on stocks that dwarf them to varying degrees.

When you buy a fruit tree, you are actually buying two plants, and you need to know what both of them are. If you have a small garden, and want bushes that remain in scale with it, check that the stocks will give you maximum dwarfing.

Most of the stocks, particularly for apples and pears, are known simply by code names. New sorts appear from time to time, so check with your supplier. Currently, M9 is the most dwarfing stock for apples, followed by M26; M7 and MM106 are semi-dwarfing. Pears are usually on Quince C (moderately dwarfing), or Quince A (semi-vigorous). Plums and their allies are usually on the semi-dwarfing St Julien A, though orchard trees may be on Myrobalan B. Sweet cherries are vigorous on Malling F12/1. The semi-dwarfing 'Colt' may sometimes be available, but is not always totally successful.

Pollination

Most fruits need pollination to take place before the crop can develop. The task is generally performed by bees, but for greenhouse crops you will need to do it by hand (see below). You will also need to do it for certain fruits, such as apricots and greengages, planted against walls.

Hand pollination is an annual operation; however, other aspects of pollination need to be considered when planting many outdoor fruits. In many cases it is sufficient if pollen from one flower, or from other flowers on the same plant, is transferred to the stigma. Fruit formation ensues. Such plants are called 'self-fertile', and in the garden a single plant will produce a crop.

Other fruits, called 'self-sterile', can only be pollinated by pollen from a plant of another variety. To ensure a crop, two trees of different varieties, but which flower at the same time, must be grown.

Apples, pears, plums and sweet cherries have varieties which flower at different times in the spring. If you plant an early and a late sort, cross-pollination may not result because the flowers of one have faded before those of the other have opened. Varieties of these crops have been split into groups, all members of which flower at the same time.

If possible, plant trees from the same group. The time of flowering is not related to ripening times, so you can still spread your crops over several weeks.

Tables of cross-pollinating varieties are given in the entries for the main top

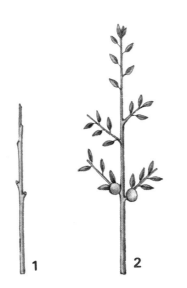
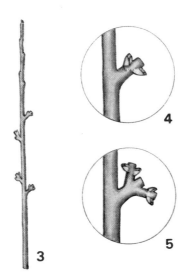
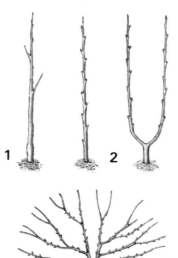
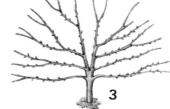
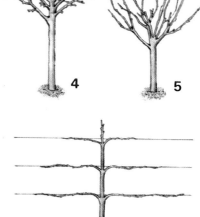
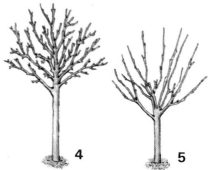
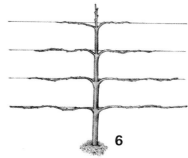

Spur-producing fruits (Group 2):
1 1st winter, growth buds only at the tip with fruit and growth buds mostly at the base of last summer's growth.
2 1st summer, prune side shoots so that 4–6 leaves remain.
3 2nd winter, prune side shoots to leave 2 buds, allowing the leading shoot to grow unless the space is filled; if so, treat the leading shot as a spur and cut back.
4 2nd summer, allow only one bud to produce a growth shoot.
5 3rd winter, after summer and winter pruning a small spur is gradually built which will need radical shortening after several more years.

fruits. The earliest and latest flowering groups have been omitted because they do not contain well known varieties. The list for each group is restricted to varieties which are easily obtainable, and have an excellent flavour.

The shelter and warmth of a wall or glass encourage fruit trees to flower early. Peaches, nectarines and plums grown against a wall may all be in flower long before there are any bees around to pollinate them. You will have to do it yourself, using an artist's camelhair paint-brush.

To see if the time is right, have a look at the anthers of the open flowers. It is easy to see if they have split open, revealing white or yellowish pollen. Dab the brush into each open flower you can find, transferring the pollen as you go. On a dry sunny day the brush should show the colour of the pollen.

Under glass, the same thing needs doing for peaches and nectarines. Strawberry plants being brought on early will need pollinating too, using the same method

The flower trusses of vines need tapping gently to shake the pollen on to the stigmas.

Harvesting

The time of ripening depends on the variety and season. If there is room for several varieties, choose some that ripen at different times, to ensure even supply.

Most fruits need to be picked as soon as they are ripe. Currants can be left on the bush for a week or two after they have reached their full colour, provided they are protected from the birds.

Test pears and apples for ripeness by lifting each fruit gently from the branch in the palm of your hand. If it separates easily, harvest time has arrived. Remove the fruits carefully, as bruised or damaged specimens cannot be stored. If possible, harvest them into shallow baskets or boxes.

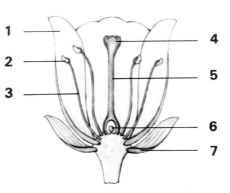

The parts of a flower: 1 petal or corolla. 2 anther and 3 filament, which form the stamen. 4 stamen. 5 style. 6 ovary. 7 sepals.

ABOVE: *Fruit forms – 1 maiden. 2 single and double cordons. 3 fan. 4 standard. 5 bush. 6 espalier.*

Storing fruit

A long-term storage place is necessary for winter varieties of apple and pear. It should be cool though frost-free, and humid. A cellar, shaded garage or shed or cool pantry are ideal. In old kitchen gardens, sheds on the north side of the north wall were often used for fruit storage. In small modern houses, a cupboard in a little-used unheated room may suffice. Lofts, and the cupboard under the stairs are usually so warm that the fruit will ripen too quickly.

Details on storing individual fruit species are given at the end of each entry.

Unfruitfulness

If a fruit bush or tree which has been planted within the last couple of years displays plenty of healthy growth but no flower buds, one or more of the following factors may be in operation.

Some young top fruits, especially if on vigorous stocks, may take several years to reach flowering size. Seedling trees, ungrafted, can take many years.

Some types of apple, some soft fruits and most figs, will produce only leaves if they are fed heavily with nitrogenous manure. Stop mulching. If you are growing apples as bushes or standards with bare ground beneath, try sowing grass. This will compete for the available nitrogen, and reduce the speed of growth of the bushes or trees. Where possible, dress the soil with a potassium-rich fertilizer in winter.

Check your pruning methods. Check also the variety of fruit you are growing. Some pears and apples are tip-bearers, with flower buds borne at the end of last season's growth. If your plants cannot now be identified by type, try not pruning for a year and see if the situation remedies itself. Some apple varieties fruit so heavily that they only manage a crop every second season. Again, wait a year and see what happens.

If the plant is growing well, there are plenty of flowers but no fruit follows it may be that the plants were in flower very early, before there were any bees to effect pollination; this is most common in wall fruit. Next year, try hand pollination.

A bad season, because of late frosts or a long wet spell at flowering time, may cause unfruitfulness. If it can be done easily, try protecting plants from late frosts with netting, sacking or plastic sheeting draped over them.

Alternatively, it may be that there is no variety nearby that is suitable for cross-pollination. It is important to check your variety's pollination requirements.

Renovating neglected fruit

If you have taken over a run-down garden, many of the fruit bushes and trees may have become unproductive.

If you are keen to keep some of the old soft fruit, try cutting blackcurrants to

within a few inches of the ground in winter, and selecting the strongest of the new shoots the following summer, discarding the rest. Tangled gooseberries and redcurrants can be heavily pruned, again in winter, so that only the best main branches are left. The final structure should be as open as possible so that new growth is not crowded.

Old top fruits are more of a problem. If you have neglected espaliers, fans or

cordons, try cutting back to the original form, even if this means removing large branches.

Less neglected wall fruits will probably only need their spurs thinning out. Do this in winter, cutting them back to within a few inches of the main structure.

On overgrown bushes or standards, it is fairly easy to thin out the branches to give a suitably open structure.

A maturing crop of Bramleys

A-Z

FRUIT

APPLE

The apple (*Malus domestica*) can form anything from a good sized tree to a single cordon. As well as exhibiting variations in flavour, apple varieties ripen over a wide season. The earliest is available in July while the last to ripen is ready the following May. If you have a small garden, or one in which there are many other fruits, it is probably best to plant late-season types, even if you have to wrap and store them.

Even if you only have room for cordons, plant as wide a range of apples as you can to give a number of different colours and tastes, rather than an enormous quantity of one sort. The other advantage of planting several varieties is that you will avoid pollination problems. Nevertheless, make sure that those you choose all belong to the same pollination group (see below).

Choosing varieties: Written descriptions of flavour and texture provide a basic guide. However, since different varieties do better in different parts of the country, the flavour varies too and it is best, if you can, to taste the ones that grow in your locality to find out what you like.

If you are going to grow your plants in a heavily pruned form, avoid 'tip bearing' varieties like 'Worcester Pearmain'. Though these will form fruit spurs, young plants most often bear flower buds at the ends of last year's growths. In general, tip-bearers are best left to gardeners who can let them grow as bushes or half standards.

Most apple varieties prefer to be cross-pollinated; for some it is essential. For various complicated biological reasons, and because of different flowering times, apples are split into seven groups of varieties, all of which can pollinate other members of the same group. If you want to grow an unusual variety, check its pollination requirements with your supplier. Popular varieties of good flavour in the three largest groups are shown in the table on p. 150.

Cultivation: The majority of apple varieties are remarkably easy to grow, being tolerant of a wide range of soils and climates. It is very easy to train apple trees into one of the artificial forms, and they can be used to make screens, low hedges, tunnels, arbours, as well as cordons

A good example of the impressive structure formed by a well-trained espalier

Group 2

Egremont Russet	Oct–Dec
Ribston Pippin	Nov–Jan
St Edmund's	
Pippin	Sept–Oct
George Neal	Aug–Oct

Group 3

Cox's Orange	
Pippin	Oct–Dec
Discovery	Sept
Epicure	Aug–Sept
Katja	Sept–Oct
Kidd's	
Orange Red	Nov–Feb
Sunset	Nov–Dec
Worcester	
Pearmain	Sept–Oct
Blenheim	
Orange	Nov–Jan
Bramley's	
Seedling	Nov–Mar

Group 4

Ashmead's	
Kernel	Dec–Mar
Ellison's Orange	Sept–Oct
Orleans Reinette	Dec–Feb
Tydemann's Late	
Orange	Dec–Apr
Annie Elizabeth	Dec–Mar
Golden Noble	Sept–Jan
Lane's Prince	
Albert	Jan–Mar

'Discovery' apples ready to harvest

and espaliers. For heavily pruned sorts, ensure that the trees are grafted on only a moderately dwarfing stock. For free standing bushes in a small garden, the stock should be the most dwarfing stock of all.

Spacing is important, for there's no point in wasting space, nor in trying to cram too many trees into too small an area. Single cordons are best planted 60cm–1m (2–3ft) apart. Espaliers need a minimum of 4m (12ft), but will appreciate more if you have room. So that you don't waste valuable wall space while the espaliers are maturing, put redcurrants or gooseberries between the apples, and gradually grub them out as the espaliers expand. Bush trees need at least 2m (6ft) spacings if on dwarfing stock. In a proper orchard, standard trees need planting at least 6.6m (20ft)

apart. The ground beneath wall fruit can also be planted up. Bulbs are a good idea because they are below ground level when you need to spray the trees with tar oil.

The most important pruning takes place in winter, preferably in December or early January. This enables winter spraying to take place safely before the buds begin to expand.

For details of winter and summer pruning, see p. 145.
Pests and diseases: The most troublesome pests are codling moth and apple sawfly, while the most common diseases are canker and scab.
Harvesting: Ripe apples will easily lift away from the branch. Early ripening sorts need to be eaten at once, otherwise they turn soft and mealy. Harvest such varieties a short time before they ripen, and keep them for several days.

Apples for winter should be left on the branch as long as possible, though not into the season of hard frosts. Pick them carefully, and place them with equal care into the basket or pail. Do not throw them in, or rot will set in where the fruit has been bruised and will spread fast.

In the kitchen, wipe them over gently, wrap them in newspaper or proprietary fruit papers and pack them into boxes. It is also possible to keep the apples in polythene bags with breathing holes punched into them. Allow 8–10 apples to a bag, and place them loosely and in a single layer in boxes.

Apples must be stored somewhere cool and not too dry. A garage or well-shaded garden shed is excellent. If you have a modern house, do not use the loft for storing apples: it is almost certainly too warm.

Over the subsequent weeks, check the fruit regularly for ripening. If more ripen than you can eat, remember that even wrinkled fruit cooks perfectly well.

BLACKBERRY

A familiar native, the blackberry (*Rubus fruticosus*), is to be found in almost every hedgerow in Britain, but its fruits are of variable quality. For large, juicy fruits of good flavour go for one of the garden varieties without thorns. Recommended are 'Merton Thornless', 'Oregon Thornless' and 'Thornfree'.

Cultivation: The best way of growing blackberries in quantity is on a wire framework of exactly the same sort as is used for espalier top fruit. The frame can be freestanding or attached to a wall, but in either case it needs to be sufficiently large to accommodate 2 years' canes.

One wire supports canes from the right and left of each crown. If one plant only is required, it can be grown like a rambler rose up a start post 2.2m (7ft) tall.

Since the amount of fruit you get depends on the length of the canes grown the previous season, an annual mulch of manure is very beneficial.

If by chance you need more plants, or want to replace the ones you have, new ones are easily produced. Simply let a cane or two grow so that its tip touches the soil and in early September keep it in place with a stone or a wire peg. It will soon take root. The following spring detach the new plant.
Pests and diseases: Diseases are rare and the worst pests

A blackberry bush hung with ripening fruit

strong new growth. Immediately after planting, cut back the stems to leave 5cm (2in) of growth to encourage strong, new basal shoots. The prunings can be used as cuttings to raise new plants. Next season, cut out weak growths, which are unlikely to fruit, and give the plants a mulching.

When the bushes are mature, take out whole branches to let light and air into the centre of the bush. If you do not prune in this way the bush will become overgrown and unproductive.

Where the bush is grown against a wall, tie in shoots to wires to make a fan. Mulch the root area to encourage growth. When the plant is mature, remove a spoke or two every year to ensure you get new shoots.

The bushes should be planted 2m (6½ft) apart. This looks over-generous with new plants, or even semi-mature ones, but closer spacing makes harvesting impossible when bushes splay outwards loaded with fruit.

Pests and diseases: Big bud can be a nuisance in some gardens. Aphids, though, can be the worst pest.

Harvesting: It is easy to tell from the taste when blackcurrants are ready, but this can be a week or two after the berries have turned black. After full ripening, the berries can be left on the branches for a week or two without deteriorating too much if there is no time to harvest them.

If you can harvest the berries in peak condition but want to store them for a while, pick the whole bunch by the stalk. Ideally the berries should be picked as soon as they are ripe and cooked soon afterwards.

are, not surprisingly, birds. Raspberry beetle grubs can occasionally be a nuisance.

Harvesting: Fruit for eating fresh or for wine-making needs to be as sweet as possible, so leave it on the plant for as long as you can. Fruit for jams, jellies and pies is better if picked a little earlier just as the berries turn black.

BLACKCURRANT

Like the redcurrant, the blackcurrant (*Ribes nigrum*) is native to the woodlands of northern Europe and Asia,

and a comparatively recent addition to the kitchen garden.

The bushes have a slightly different mode of growth to red and white currants, since they are less ready to spur, and do best in bush form in the fruit cage. It is possible to train them as fans against a wall, in which position they will fruit well, even when north-facing. Because this gives a correspondingly later crop, it was an early method of extending the season.

There are a number of varieties available, none of which differ greatly from the wild plant. 'Baldwin' and

'Ben Lomond' are excellent for flavour. 'Wellington XXX' is a commonly seen midseason plant and 'Amos Black' is very late. Yield is sometimes improved by planting several varieties to ensure cross-pollination.

Cultivation: Blackcurrants do well in most soils, providing they are not waterlogged or bone dry. They will give fruit in cold gardens, and will also tolerate shade quite well in warmer ones.

Since fruiting is best on second-year wood, but less good on anything older, the gardener needs to ensure a continual production of

BLUEBERRY

Long popular in the United States, blueberries are building up a following in this

Ripe blackcurrants

area supports good ericas and rhododendrons, which belong to the same family as the blueberry, it is suitable for this crop. Blueberries need moist sandy or peaty soil with a pH between 4.3 and 4.8.

In suitable areas, high-bush plants are spaced with their centres 1.2m (4ft) apart. On acid sandy soils, give an annual mulch of compost or rotted manure at a barrow-load for 3sq m (4sq yd). On peaty soil, an annual dressing of general fertilizer at 50g/sq m (2oz/sq yd) will keep the plants cropping well.

Since blueberry bushes bear fruit on last season's wood, prune high-bush sorts lightly in the first few years, only taking out the weakest shoots. Later on, take out a few of the main branches each year, cutting them out at ground level to encourage strong new growth at the base. Each main shoot should only last 5–6 years before it is pruned out.

Blueberries are easy to propagate by taking cuttings in very early spring before the buds begin to expand. The cuttings should be about 20cm (8in) long. Rub out any flower buds. Insert the cuttings into sandy, moist soil in frames. Move the rooted plants to their final positions the following autumn.

Pests and diseases: Birds adore the berries.

Harvesting: Depending on the variety grown, fruit ripens from mid-July onwards, when the full 'blue' colour has developed.

CHERRY

Sweet cherries are derived from the gean or wild cherry (*Prunus avium*) and the morello from the sour cherry (*P. cerasus*). Duke cherries, which are worth growing if you can find them, are hybrids between these two. In small gardens the morello and duke types are much the most useful as they are self-fertile. Because they will also fruit nicely in shade, they can be grown against north-facing walls. As they are less vigorous than the sweet types, they can be trained as fans.

Sweet cherries can be trained as fans but only on the largest walls. You may do better to grow them as bushes in a fruit cage; eventually they will need heavy pruning, but you will have had several years of risk-free cropping by then. Cherries also grow quite nicely in pots. Providing the plants have had an abbreviated winter, they can be brought into warmth in January, and forced. By this means grand garden owners had cherries well ahead of the normal season. If growing sweet cherries, you'll need two varieties which must be hand pollinated with a tuft of fur or a camel hair brush. Try 'Early Rivers' with 'Bigarreau de Schrecken' or 'Merton Heart'; 'Merton Bigarreau' with 'Kent Bigarreau' or 'Napoleon

country in areas with cool moist summers, and acid soils. High-bush (*Vaccinium corymbosum*) cultivars are the ones most often seen here; they are branching deciduous shrubs 1.5m (5ft) or more high, with urn-shaped flowers, and neat foliage that turns vivid red in autumn. The fruit is a delicious round and black berry, heavily waxy-white bloomed like a grape, and in some varieties up to 2cm (¾in) in diameter. They are borne in sprays of 8–10.

Of the great number of varieties available in the United States, only a few are offered here. These include 'Early Blue', 'Grover', 'Jersey' and 'Pemberton'. You will need to buy two sorts to ensure cross-pollination and a good yield.

Cultivation: If the soil in your

Blueberries can succeed well and are becoming increasingly popular

Bigarreau'. Bigarreau denotes that the cherry has slightly crisp flesh. There are other delicious cherries to be had, many of which will happily accept pollen from the morello.

Cultivation: Cherries do well on a variety of soils, as long as they are well fed. Apply mulch of rotted manure or compost at least each other year, plus a light dressing of a potash-rich fertilizer.

If planting free-standing trees, bear in mind the difficulties of protecting the ripening fruit from birds. You are bound to lose the fruit on the upper branches, but it is possible to enclose the lower ones in large tubes of netting and thus manage to keep some of your crop. Otherwise, it might be worth trying some of the model hawks available.

If you want to try cherries against a wall, sweet varieties like south, west or east aspects. Once the basic branch structure has been

Ripe cherries ready to be picked

built up, prune lateral shoots in summer to six leaves; prune again in early autumn to three buds. Do not prune in winter.

The best way to treat morellos is to cut out a certain amount of fruited wood each year, and so encourage the production of new wood, while still keeping the tree within the bounds of the wall. Cherries can be grown as bushes in the fruit cage using the same methods.

Pests and diseases: Keep a constant check for the black, cherry aphids. Silver leaf disease can be a problem. Bullfinches can take the flower buds, and other species will completely clear the trees of ripe fruit. Wall fruit is most easily protected, but take care to do it thoroughly. Birds find cherries very attractive and will find the tiniest chink that will let them into the fruit.

Harvesting: Once the colour has developed to its maximum, keep tasting for the sort of sweetness you like. The stalks of sweet cherries

come away from the branch very easily. Sour cherries require more care; pulling too hard can remove leaves, stem and all. Use small sharp scissors to cut the stalks. When harvested, eat the cherries at once; alternatively they may be bottled, soaked in brandy, or made into cherry wine.

DAMSON

Botanically, damsons are cultivars of *Prunus domestica insititia*, a sub-species of the common plum. Although variable in vigour, they form small trees usually under 6m (20ft) in height. Their flowers, which are small and white, are borne on naked twigs in early spring. The fruits are small, blackish purple outside, amber yellow within. The flesh is disappointing eaten raw, but a delectable and unique taste develops as soon as it is cooked.

The damson will crop well in good conditions

The trees are happy in most soils and in the least sheltered of situations, but they prefer the eastern counties of Britain with cold winters and, it is to be hoped, hot dry summers. Damsons produce prodigious crops when well suited to the growing conditions.

Some varieties are self-fertile; others cross easily with other damsons or true plums. They are easily trained against west- or east-facing walls, either as fans or espaliers, though plums or greengages better deserve the space. On a wall, damsons may need hand pollinating.

'Farleigh Damson' has fruit of excellent flavour, but needs pollinating by another variety. Use 'Oulin's Gage' or even the plum 'Kirke's'. 'Merryweather' will self-pollinate, but its flavour is inferior.

'Brown Turkey' fig

Cultivation: Although damsons can be grown in unpromising conditions, they will benefit from good soil and are best treated as plums qv.
Pests and diseases: As for plums qv.
Harvesting: Pick the fruit when it softens. As damsons are less sweet than most plums, birds and wasps are less of a problem. Picked fruit will store in a cool place for a week or two.

FIG
The fig (*Ficus carica*) is a deciduous tree with bold handsome foliage; its unique fruit – green, purple or brown skinned – has flesh in various shades of dusky pink.

In warm parts of the country, a good single crop of figs can be had from free-standing plants. Elsewhere, the trees need the protection of a south-facing wall. For these there is always plenty of competition, but a dish of properly ripened figs is a strong inducement to find a space.

Under glass, even without much heat, most varieties of fig can be persuaded to give two crops, the first developing from young fruit buds that have withstood the winter, the second from fruit buds on the earliest part of the new growth. A much wider range of cultivars can be grown as well, many with flavours far superior to the commoner kinds.

Outdoors, most figs, which are native to hot, dry Mediterranean countries, adapt to our climate by producing masses of foliage and few mature fruits. Most need to be planted in situations where there is a very restricted root run. Sunken brick boxes containing about 1m^3 (35ft^3) of soil are the usual arrangements. The box has no bottom, but the lowest 22–30cm (9–12in) is filled with coarse rubble or gravel which slows down the roots from exploring outside.

Figs also fruit well in large pots or tubs, though they need to stand somewhere sheltered. Large plants are easily toppled by a sudden summer gale.

The most frequently seen variety is 'Brown Turkey', unusual in that it does not need to have its roots cramped and can be planted in open ground. The fruit is not large or in the first rank for flavour. 'White Marseilles' is delicious and reliable, if you restrict its roots. It does well in pots.
Cultivation: Against a wall, or under glass, figs are best trained as fans. When the fan is full-grown, some of the major spokes need to be removed every few years to ensure new growth, and so fruit, at the centre. Alternatively, cuttings will root very easily, so overgrown and unproductive trees are quite easily replaced.

Do not leave figs grown outdoors to fend for themselves in winter. New wood may be killed by the cold, and you will lose the chance of fruit in the following summer. Provide some protection; the usual method with a fan is to untie the spokes, bunch them together, and cover them in a straw coat. Alternatively cover with plastic sheeting.
Pests and diseases: Under glass, red spider can be a nuisance. Outdoors, birds are the main problem.
Harvesting: When the fruit ripens, the skin near the fruit's opening begins to split, revealing the juicy flesh. By that stage, the fig should come away from the branch easily.

Some people are slightly allergic to the skin of the fig. It is perfectly easy to remove this, starting at the split.

GOOSEBERRY
The gooseberry (*Ribes uva-crispa*) has long been a popular garden plant. Its fruit is immensely variable – early or late, smooth or hairy, sweet or sour, soft or crisp (some sorts were used as salads in Elizabethan England) – and it comes in all sorts of colours including green, yellow, red and white. They all make delicious desserts, jams, jellies and wines, and the sweet sorts are lovely eaten straight from the garden. Since dessert fruits do not travel well, they are less often seen at the greengrocer.

The bushes make good hedges as most plants are quite spiny. They are easily trained against walls, where they are happy to face in any direction. All kinds are easily trained as cordons or fans. Even neglected plants fruit quite well, though they

Ripe gooseberries take on a translucent quality

eventually become badly tangled and need savage thinning out every couple of years.

Recommended cultivars are: 'Careless' (green to whitish), 'Lord Derby' (red) and 'Leveller' (yellow). 'Lancashire Lad' is resistant to mildew.

Cultivation: Gooseberries are fairly undemanding; they do well in most soils, but prefer well-drained loam. An annual or biennial mulch of manure or compost is helpful, and keeps down weeds. Potash deficiency can show up as scorched leaf margins; use a potash-rich fertilizer, or apply a light dressing of sulphate of potash. About 28g (1oz) will suit a well-grown bush.

Clear out weak and twiggy growth that will not bear much fruit.

As the structure of the bush develops, encourage formation of fruiting spurs by cutting back laterals to 7.5cm (3in). In summer, shorten laterals so that they have 5 leaves left.

Gooseberries make good single, double or triple cordons. Allow the leader or leaders to grow unchecked until they are as tall as you need. Winter-prune laterals to 3 buds, and in summer prune to 5 leaves.

If new bushes are required, in autumn take cuttings of the summer's growth about 30cm (12 inches) long. Remove all but the top 4 buds and insert so that about 15–18cm (6–7in) is below ground. Set them in sandy soil in a partially shaded position. Transplant to permanent site one year later.

Gooseberries will fruit quite well with no attention at all, though you will get a much higher yield if you find time to prune. Cut back the main growth shoots of young bushes by half each winter to encourage strong new growth. Varieties with a drooping habit of growth should be cut back to an upward-facing bud.

Pests and diseases: Birds are the worst menace; bullfinches peck out young buds in early spring and several species attack swelling fruits later in the season.

Gooseberry sawfly and magpie moth caterpillars can be a nuisance. In some seasons aphids can also be a problem. Watch out also for gooseberry mildew.

Harvesting: Once the berries have swollen to a reasonable size they can be picked for jams, jellies, and sauces. They do not have to be harvested all at once. Those left on the bushes will ripen until they split.

Undamaged berries can be kept for a short time in the refrigerator.

GRAPE VINE

The grape vine (*Vitis vinifera*) is not at all difficult to grow, but requires fairly constant work from mid-spring to autumn to ensure a good crop. Even a small vine can supply a large quantity of fruit.

In favoured parts of the southern counties, vines can be grown as free-standing plants in vineyards, but most dessert grapes do best against a south-facing wall. In such a situation grapes will fruit well quite far north and even the warmer parts of Scotland can produce good fruit in a warm season.

Many amateurs will achieve the best results in a

ABOVE: *Training a newly planted vine (**left**). Young grape fruitlets must be thinned out (**right**).* LEFT: *Grapes ripening on a mature vine*

greenhouse or conservatory, whether there is room for one large pot, yielding perhaps a dozen good bunches, or for a full-sized vine yielding hundreds. A slightly heated greenhouse would permit some of the choicer late-ripening grapes to be grown, particularly the various muscats, whose fine flavour repays the cost of heating in spring and autumn.

The choice of varieties now available is increasing, reflecting a renewed interest in the grape vine. Many are most suited to the wine producer, but good dessert varieties include 'Siegerrebe', and the various 'Chasselas' and 'Strawberry' types for walls outdoors; 'Black Hamburgh', 'Forster's Seedling' and 'Buckland Sweetwater' are for cold greenhouses, 'Frontignan' is good for pots, and the marvellous 'Muscat of Alexandria' for slightly heated greenhouses.

Vines are ornamental in their own right. The leaves are handsome, the plants graceful, and the clusters of berries spectacular. For even more visual effect, choose from the varieties with particularly decorative leaves. The one called 'Purpurea' has deep purplish foliage which looks handsome when grown near some of the more refined and pale-coloured clematis, and the leaves of 'Brandt' go a magnificent scarlet in autumn to set off the berries.

Cultivation: Vines are vigorous plants which must be pruned frequently and ruthlessly to avoid a picturesque but barren tangle.

Vines grown in pots can be treated in the same way as raspberries, with two canes allowed, one from last year to fruit, one of this year to grow. The old cane will attempt to grow too, but stop it by pinching out the main growing tip and all the side shoots 4–6 leaves after the flower truss if there is one, 2 if not. Allow only 1 shoot, the lowest, to grow and make a new cane. In late autumn cut the fruited shoot back to 2 buds (easily visible), above the junction with next year's fruit cane. If both buds want to grow next spring, rub out the topmost one.

Grown against a wall, or in the greenhouse, a simple way to train a plant is to cut back the newly planted vine to 3–4 buds if you have glass to ground level, higher if not. Let 2 shoots develop, and train them horizontally along wires to right and left. Next year, allow buds to develop every 30 cm (12in) and train them vertically. You should now have a fork-shaped plant, with as many tines as you have room for. Thereafter, treat each cane as you would a potted plant.

Take great care not to let vast amounts of foliage develop. Ripening grapes need sun and warmth for flavour, and the free movement of air is important, as the bunches of fruits are less likely to rot. Thin the leaves out if they become too dense.

The flowers will be opening by early June. Outdoors, pollination is no problem. Indoors, the clusters need tapping gently with a cane to shake pollen on to the stigmas.

When the young fruitlets begin to form, the bunches must be thinned out by about half to leave the remainder room to develop. Equip yourself with a pair of scissors with long narrow blades. Surgical scissors are suitable in the absence of proper vine scissors. Snip away at each bunch to clear the fruitlets away from the centre. In general, you can cut out whole bunchlets. Pay special attention to the top or 'shoulder' of each bunch.

Continue nipping out unwanted vegetative growth and when the berries are one third their full size, have another look over each bunch. Once again, they will be congested. Using a twig, small spatula or an eraser-tipped pencil, lift up each branch of the bunch and snip out yet more fruit. Experience will tell you how much to cut out, but once more about half the fruitlets should go. The aim is to get a well-filled bunch, but one in which each berry has room to swell, and in which air can freely circulate. Without this drastic thinning, the berries will be small and cramped.

In winter, prune back 'spurs' on espalier-trained vines to 1–2 buds. On vines trained raspberry-fashion, cut out the old canes and untie the newly grown ones so that they hang from the main trunk. This looks untidy, but makes sure that the buds break evenly along the cane and have equal vigour.

When the bunches are ripening under glass, keep the greenhouse vents open as much as possible when the weather is warm.

Pests and diseases: Under glass scale insect, mealy bug, red spider and whitefly can all be a nuisance. Outdoors, wasps, birds and mildew can spoil the crop.

Harvesting: Grapes will not be ripe until a week or more after the full colour has developed.

Under glass, the fruit can be left on the vine more or less until it is needed. The last bunches should still be good well into November if they were properly thinned, and if the greenhouse has been kept dry. Keep examining the bunches for split or mildewed fruit, and cut them out as soon as you see them, otherwise the rot will quickly spread. 'Black Hamburgh' hangs especially well.

GREENGAGE
See under Plum

LOGANBERRY, TAYBERRY AND BOYSENBERRY

A number of species in the genus *Rubus*, both American and European, can be crossed with each other. The hybrids are all fairly modern, the loganberry (*Rubus x loganobaccus*) having arisen around 1880 in the USA. They are crosses between the raspberry and an American blackberry. The tayberry is a recent Scottish hybrid, which is very mild in taste and quite similar in shape to the loganberry.

The hybrid berries all crop exceptionally well, which is the main reason for their success. Some loganberry stocks no longer crop well, however, and you will need to buy 'LY59' or 'LY54' to get a good yield. The thornless hybrids are useful.

The fresh berries are colourful, sweet, and abundant. They can be made into very good jams and jellies.

Cultivation: As might be

Good-sized nectarines ripening under glass

Even a modest sized peach tree will yield a worthwhile crop

expected, the culture of these hybrids resembles that of both parents. Since the canes are generally 2–2.4m (6–8ft) long, they can be trained up or along wires depending on the amount of space available.

Pests and diseases: The same as for raspberry and blackberry (qv).

Harvesting: Pick the fruit when the full colour has formed. Ripe berries are easily crushed, so go carefully.

NECTARINE
See next entry

PEACH

It is difficult to know why so few people grow their own peaches. In most of the southern counties, peaches crop heavily as free-standing trees, and they are fairly easy to manage against a wall, in a pot or under glass. The peach (*Prunus persica*) is a small deciduous tree with attractive pink flowers before the leaves in spring. The colourful fruits have a densely, finely downy skin. The nectarine is a mutation of the peach with glossy, hairless fruits of an arguably richer flavour.

Cultivation: Peaches thrive in any well-drained soil. In general, it is best not to feed them too heavily, or the foliage becomes too luxuriant, making pruning and training harder, and keeping sunlight from the fruit.

On walls, they are usually treated as fans, using the 'long spur' system (see pp. 145 and 147). Under glass, either grow them as bushes in large pots, using high-yielding varieties on dwarfing rootstock, or plant them out in cold greenhouse borders.

Peaches were traditionally grown in south-facing lean-to greenhouses, with

the trees trained up the back wall. In modern free-standing greenhouses, it is possible to train the trees up the inside of the glass, attaching the branches to wire stretched along the main struts of the greenhouse. The main disadvantage is that the spurs and their replacements grow upwards and touch the glass. As a result, the leaves are scorched by hot sun.

If the greenhouse is large enough, it is simplest to plant the trees in the centre. The main pruning, to keep them within bounds and allow you room to move, takes place in summer.

Peaches do not need winter heat. Heat is only necessary in early spring if you want to force an early crop and that is only useful if you want to sell the produce. Peaches and nectarines grown in unheated greenhouses bear fruit just as the price of imported peaches begins to drop.

Under glass, the flowers need hand-pollination. The trees are self-fertile. For tall plants in which the uppermost flowers are difficult to reach, try attaching the handle of the paintbrush to the end of a bamboo cane.

Do not let plants dry out in

the early stages of fruit formation otherwise the fruits open at the base and begin to rot. It is particularly important to keep potted specimens well watered.

Prune young side shoots – which are not needed to extend the tree or for replacement 'spurs' – to 4 leaves. It is essential to thin out young fruitlets. It is tempting not to do this, but the tree will only reward your negligence with small fruits of poor flavour, if any.

Peach varieties are available with different periods of ripening, flesh and skin colour and flavour. In general, the white-fleshed sorts have the best flavour. 'Peregrine' is a good one, and often seen. 'Rochester', later-ripening, is red-skinned but not of quite as good flavour. Recommended nectarines are 'Early Rivers' and 'Lord Napier'. Always go for named cultivars; seedlings do not come exactly true to type.

Pests and diseases: The main scourge of outdoor peaches is peach leaf curl disease. Birds, of course, attack the ripening fruit. Under glass, red spider can be troublesome.

Harvesting: Peaches are best

picked in the morning. If anything more than the lightest tug is needed, leave the fruit on the branch. It is not ripe. Better still, let the peach fall off. Rig up netting beneath the tree to stop the fruit bruising itself on the ground or, under glass, pile crumbled newspaper beneath the branches.

Peaches only last at their peak for a day or two at the most. They can be kept longer in the refrigerator.

PEAR

The common pear (*Pyrus communis*) is basically a large deciduous tree with a profusion of white flowers in spring and leaves which can colour brightly in autumn. It has a long history in cultivation, about 40 cultivars being known in Roman times. Nowadays, pears are commonly grafted on to one of the quince stocks. This keeps them to a smaller size.

The fruit itself can be tricky to manage. Unlike apples, pears remain in eatable condition for a very short time. Unripe pears are too hard to eat, though they may be poached, preferably in red wine, but over-ripe ones are only fit for the compost heap.

That there are a large number of varieties with a corresponding range of flavours is not surprising in such an ancient and important crop. Good ones are listed below in their pollination groups.

Cultivation: Pears on pear stocks will grow on a wide range of soils, even on those that would support no other fruit. On quince stocks, they need fertile garden soil, with plenty of moisture and rich in nitrogen. Such trees need feeding every year with a good mulch of manure or compost.

Since pears are quite as tractable as apples, they can be trained and pruned in exactly the same way. Ensure that wall fruits never lack moisture, for the ground

Conference pears are self-fertile and will produce fruit from a single tree

at the base of old walls can be very free draining.

Many dessert pears ripen late in the season, so gardeners in cold counties should plant slightly less choice, early-maturing sorts. Do not despise old varieties with small fruits. 'Jargonelle' is old (pre-1600) but the fruits are delicious, and it does well in cold, even shady, conditions. The cooking pears, too, make excellent winter eating, baked or stewed.

Pollination needs to be considered. Some varieties are fairly self-fertile, and so a single tree can be planted. 'Conference' is the usual one suggested, but there are others. Check with your supplier. In general, it is much better to plant 2 trees of different varieties. As with apples, the crop is split into

---

Group 1 – self-fertile
The following cultivars will set a crop of fruit if only a single tree is planted.
Double Williams
Fertility Improved
Glou Morceau
Gorham
Laxton's Superb

Group 2
Louise Bonne of
Jersey   Oct–Nov
Packham's Triumph Nov

Group 3
Beurré Hardy   Oct
Beurré Superfin   Oct
Conference   Oct
*Jargonelle   Aug
Joséphine de
Malines   Dec–Jan
*William's Bon
Chrétien   Sept
        *=suitable for
        a north wall

Group 4
Doyenné de Comice Nov
Onward   Sept–Oct
Catillac (cooking) until Apr
Pitmaston Duchess
(cooking)   Oct until Feb

several pollination groups. Widely available varieties are listed here in pollination groups (see table left):
Although pears produce flowers in substantial bunches, it is best not to let them fruit in the same manner. Where possible, thin each cluster to one or two fruits. If you do not thin them out you will have large quantities of small fruits. Unlike peaches and nectarines, however, the flavour will not be impaired.
Pests and diseases: The worst disease is scab; 'Catillac', 'Hessle' and 'Dr Jules Guyot' are never infected. Peach midge can be a nuisance in some gardens. Birds are the worst pest.
Harvesting: When pears ripen depends on variety, locality, season and location in the garden, so experience is the surest guide. In gen-

eral, pick fruit just before final ripening. Handle the fruit carefully, for although the flesh will still be hard, bruises at this stage may cause uneven ripening.

Store the picked fruit somewhere cool, keeping ones you want to eat soon somewhere warmer. Later-ripening varieties will take anything up to several months to become ripe. Since they need frequent checking, it is unwise to wrap and box them. Test them both by smell, and by gently pressing the fruit. You will soon become good at detecting fruit at the peak for eating. Unless you have somewhere cool to store the fruit, you may find that an entire crop has ripened more or less simultaneously. This is one reason why, if you have several varieties, they

should be chosen with a spread of ripening times.

Cooking pears never soften. Most varieties can be used throughout the winter.

PLUM

The plum (*Prunus domestica*) is easy to grow in all but the coldest wettest parts of the country, and does exceptionally well against walls if you can give it one of sufficient height. It is attractive when in flower, and looks magnificent when the branches are loaded with fruit.

If you are prepared to plant something other than the reliable 'Victoria', there are some delicious alternatives. One of the reasons why so many people plant 'Victoria' is that because it is self-fertile, only one tree is needed. There are other self fertile varieties worth considering, particularly 'Czar' and 'Warwickshire Drooper'. The dessert plum, 'Kirke's', is self-sterile, and needs something to fertilize it.

'Denniston's Superb' is the hardiest and best cropper, having also the advantage of self-fertility. 'Early Transparent' is the most delicious, and trains well as a fan. The small yellow-green 'Greengage', which is halfway between a plum and a bullace, and rich-flavoured is sometimes available but a rather unreliable cropper.
Cultivation: Plums are happy in most locations. Areas subject to late frosts are not suitable, however, as flower and fruitlets can be damaged. Wall fruits are usually safe from frosts. Indeed, in the north of England and in Scotland the choicer varieties must have the shelter of a wall. If they are grafted on the dwarfing stock St Julian A, plums can fairly easily be trained as fans. Check which stock has been used with your supplier. Allow at least 4.5m (15ft) of wall for a fan, and as much between plants if you are putting in dwarf bushes. It is preferable to buy

'Malling Admiral'. If you like unusual-looking fruit, try growing some of the yellow fruited sorts. They have also a subtly different flavour.

Autumn-fruiting varieties extend the season in favoured districts. The flavour is slightly inferior to the summer-fruiting varieties.

Cultivation: The rootstock throws up shoots from below ground. They last two years; in the first they make growth, in the second they bear fruit. New roots or canes are planted 45cm (18in) apart, with about 2m (6ft) between the rows if you have more than one. New canes are tied to a wire or string framework, either free-standing or against a wall. The simplest way of keeping the canes upright is to insert a 2.1m (7ft) bamboo cane every 2m (6½ft) or so with horizontal strings 1m (3¼ft) above ground level and, when the new growth needs more support, at 2m (6½ft) above that again.

If the canes outgrow the wires or strings, simply cut them off, or tie them into the topmost support. Do not let them grow through the fruit cage roof.

Pull out new shoots that interfere with the pathway between the rows of canes. As soon as fruiting has finished, cut out spent canes to give plenty of room and light to the new ones.

The autumn fruiting sorts are treated differently. They fruit on canes grown the same season. Fruiting stops in late autumn and the canes are cut down to within a couple of centimetres of the ground in February. The rootstocks tend to produce very large numbers of new shoots each spring, so pull out all thin, weak ones and any others not required.

maiden plants and do the initial pruning yourself. Remember to prune only between June and August, otherwise your plants may contract silver leaf disease.

Plums need plenty of nourishment, especially when they are young. Mulch annually with compost or rotted manure.

In cold springs, fruits against a south wall may flower before the bees are around. Use a small soft-haired paintbrush to assist pollination. If you have planted varieties that need cross-pollination, pick a bunch of flowers from one plant and brush it against the flowers of the other (and vice versa).

Plums may crop very heavily. The fruits can be thinned, which will give you a smaller number of larger fruits. It may be necessary to ensure that the branches do not break when fully laden by tying them to canes or poles as supports.

Pests and diseases: Aphids and birds are the commonest pests.

ABOVE: The 'Czar' plum is a self-fertile cooking variety.
BELOW RIGHT: Raspberries

Harvesting: Plums may soften rather before they are sweet enough to eat. If you cannot keep the pests away, harvest the fruits as they soften, and store them on a shelf in the kitchen, pantry or garage. You will lose a little of the flavour as the fruit subsequently ripens, which may take several days, or even a week. After ripening, the fruit will last on the shelf for about a fortnight.

RASPBERRY

Several kinds of raspberries are native to the northern hemisphere but only one is commonly cultivated in the British Isles – *Rubus idaeus*. This is native to Asia and Europe, including Britain, mainly in light woodland.

Well-grown rows, neatly tied and weighed down with lovely soft red fruit, look wonderful in the kitchen garden. Good dessert varieties are 'Glen Clova', 'Malling Jewel' and the late ripening

All raspberries appreciate an annual mulch of compost, manure, or peat and artificial fertilizer. In either case, keep the plants well watered, especially as the fruit is swelling.

Pests and diseases: Aphids and raspberry beetles can be a major nuisance.

Virus diseases, transmitted by both aphids and eelworm, are common and ineradicable.

Raspberries are so attractive to birds that you will be very lucky if you can harvest a respectable crop on canes grown outside a fruit cage.

Harvesting: Pick the fruit when it is fully coloured and use as soon as possible.

REDCURRANT AND WHITECURRANT

The redcurrant (*Ribes sylvestre*, syn. *R. rubrum*) is

A bunch of ripe redcurrants

native to North West Europe, and does not seem to have been cultivated until the sixteenth century. By nature a woodland plant, it is not surprising that it will grow and fruit well in light shade. Whitecurrant is a mutant form with amber-yellow fruits entirely lacking red pigment. Recommended red cultivars are: 'Earliest of Fourlands' and 'Laxton's No 1' (early), Red Lake (mid season), 'Wilson's Longbunch' (late). 'White Dutch' is a good mid season whitecurrant.

Cultivation: Young plants to be grown as bushes are set 2m (6¼ft) apart. Single cordons should be 60cm–1m (2–3¼ft) apart, doubles and triples 1.2–1.5m (4–5ft) apart. Neither sort is fussy about soil type, but they like regular annual mulches of compost or manure.

Pruning is not difficult. Against a wall, especially a stone one, you will find that the plants have a natural inclination to keep to the surface. This helps if you do not have much time for pruning. They are easily made into fans and cordons. Select the main growth shoots, and induce spurs by summer pruning the lateral shoots back to 5 leaves; winter prune back to 2 buds. Reduce the leaders or main branches on a bush by about half of the season's growth each autumn, or back to a bud or two if the plant has filled the available space.

The plants like a potash-rich diet. Add a small handful of sulphate of potash for each square yard of soil.

Pests and diseases: Birds and aphids are the main troubles.

Harvesting: Can take place as soon as the strings of berries have full colour. Whitecurrants become amber and translucent; keep tasting to check for ripeness. The berries will hang in good condition for several weeks.

RHUBARB

The familiar long-lived denizen of neglected gardens and allotments, the rhubarb (*Rheum rhabarbarum* syn. *R. rhaponticum*) is a handsome and generous provider of the earliest fresh desserts of the year.

Rhubarb seeds prolifically, and there are many varieties in cultivation. There is not an enormous difference between them, but 'Champagne' and 'Early Albert' are good. Virus-free stocks have been produced but are not easily obtained.

Cultivation: Rhubarb grows in most types of soil, and in spite of neglect. However, it is best in a humus-rich, moist soil, with plenty of feeding. If you have a compost heap, plant rhubarb nearby and you will get giant plants.

When it is doing well, rhubarb will flower. The spikes are very striking, but it is best to break them off at ground level. Plant new crowns in autumn 1m (3¼ft)

apart. Do not harvest any stems the following season, and only a few the next. This allows the crown to build up its vigour. Three or four plants are enough for most families. The first few spring croppings are particularly delicious and very welcome at a time when other fruit in the garden is not productive.

Rhubarb can be forced if you want something fresh once the last of the apples and pears have been used up by March. Put a black plastic bucket over a vigorous crown, and pile manure round the outside to warm the interior. Alternatively, dig the crown up, prop it up with soil or moist peat in the bottom of a plastic sack, and take it indoors. Store somewhere with slight warmth with the bag closed. After a few weeks there will be some nice blanched shoots.

After forcing, the crowns need a rest. Feed them up with mulches of compost or rotted manure, or water them fortnightly with liquid fertilizer. Take no more stalks for the year. If you need the space, discard them and plant new crowns next season.

Pests and diseases: Generally trouble-free, but sometimes crown rot and swift moth caterpillars are a nuisance.

Harvesting: Let the young leaf stalks reach a reasonable length before you pick them. It is always recommended that leaf stalks should be pulled off rather than cut, but cutting does not seem to damage the plants. Do not eat any of the green leafy part; it is poisonous.

STRAWBERRY

Strawberries are easily grown and speedily produce a crop. They are also easily propagated and maintained.

The large sorts now so widely grown are almost all hybrids (*Fragaria x ananassa*) between three American species. They started appearing in the mid-1700s, and are still the consuming passion

Standard strawberries

of plant breeders. New varieties are bred for colour, size, marketability, season of fruiting and disease resistance. Do not be persuaded to buy the latest variety by enthusiastic publicity. Buy or beg a few plants of as many varieties as you can, and see which you like best. There are great variations in flavour. Use only obviously healthy plants, the leaves of which are unblemished and well-coloured. Recommended cultivars are: 'Gorella' (early) 'Senga Sengana' (mid season), 'Elsanta' (late). For perpetual fruiting, try 'Ostara' or 'Rabunda'.

Cultivation: Having settled on the variety or varieties you want, find out if virus-tested stocks are available. Rooted runners can be planted in the garden at any time of year. Runners planted by July, however, can be cropped the following summer; those planted later than August should be given a year to build up a strong crown. To do this, remove most of the flowering shoots as soon as they appear.

Modern strawberries should be planted 38cm (15in) apart, in rows 75cm (2½ft) apart, to give plenty of space for tending and spreading out the developing sprays of fruit.

Ideally all runners should

Planting strawberries: LEFT: *correct positioning, with the crown level with the soil.* CENTRE: *incorrect – the crown is too high.* RIGHT: *incorrect – the crown is too low.*
FAR RIGHT: *Superfluous strawberry runners should be removed*

be removed during the growing season, unless you want to increase the number of plants. This leaves the strawberries in neat rows, and certainly makes life easier. In many gardens, however, the strawberry patch is allowed to become a jungle of new plants. If the ground was in good shape when the bed was formed, such tangles can be extremely fruitful for the next two seasons or so. After that, disease troubles generally build up, especially if the dead leaves are not removed each winter, and the plants become starved. You should then root as many runners as you need to restart the bed. Clear out the old plants at the end of the second or third crop. Manure the ground, add a handful of potash for each square m/yd of ground, and replant.

If you have time to keep the strawberries in neat rows, lightly mulch between the rows in early spring, using compost or rotted manure. Use about a spadeful for each crown, spreading carefully to avoid burying the leaves and growth points.

Replace the old plants with young ones every 3–4 years.

Plants grown in rows can have their trusses of fruit placed on straw or even special fibre mats to keep them clean and less susceptible to disease: worth doing if you want top quality fruit.

There are early, mid- and late-maturing strawberries. It is possible to speed up the production of any of them by using cloches. Glass ones give the earliest crop of all, but plastic ones, even if just of polythene sheeting, can be quite effective. Put the cloches in place as the days begin to lengthen. Once the flowers are open allow plenty of air to circulate, especially on warm days. The flowers need full pollination if the fruit is to develop evenly, and if the cloches are closed the insects will not be able to get in. Later on, as the fruit swells, keep the cloches ventilated to prevent grey mould.

In the greenhouse, simply plant strawberries in open beds, or pot up vigorous plants in autumn.

A large pot of strawberries

can look attractive on a patio. Strawberry barrels or custom-made containers allow a small crop to grow when there is no room in the garden.

In order to have strawberries over a long period, you can grow perpetual fruiting types which produce a light crop throughout summer and early autumn.

Pests and diseases: Aphids and slugs are primary pests, grey mould (botrytis) and virus the main diseases.

Harvesting: The large fruit that ripens first is known as the 'king' and should be picked as soon as it turns a good red colour. The other berries ripen quickly thereafter so check the bed every day. Ripe fruit will store for several days if chilled.

ALPINE STRAWBERRIES

Alpine strawberries have developed from the common European wild strawberry. The small fruits are slightly fiddly to pick, but the flavour is marvellous.

The plants are usually runnerless, and are propagated by seed, or by teasing apart mature plants. To grow from seed, simply scrape some seeds from a ripe fruit and sow them at once in soil-based compost in a 10cm (4in) pot. Seed will germinate in two weeks or so. If you have sown seed in July or August, the seedlings will be big enough to prick out directly into the garden next spring. Space them 25–30cm (10–12in) apart, with 45cm (18ins) between the rows. The plants should be in fruit by early July. If you sow in spring, you should have some fruit by the autumn. Protect the ripening fruit from birds with flapping plastic strips.

Several varieties are available. 'Baron Solemacher' is recommended; 'Reines des Vallées' is superb. Particularly delicious are the white-fruited ones.

For harvesting and pests and diseases, see preceding entry.

CULINARY HERBS

The use of plants to cure diseases and disorders of the body and to flavour food began in the ancient world; certainly they were valued by the Greeks and Romans. Culinary herbs seem to have reached a peak of popularity in Elizabethan times, but thereafter steadily declined until this century. At the present time they are again popular and very much 'the in-thing' in the modern kitchen. No doubt the current interest in foreign foods, most of which demand herbs, has been a primary factor, but reaction to the many artificial flavourings has also helped.

Since Roman times and probably before, herbs have been grown in special beds and borders. This reached its greatest development in the Elizabethan period when specially designed and often intricately architected gardens were laid out, each bed edged with dwarf, clipped hedges of box, rosemary or lavender. Herb gardens are again popular though usually only on a small scale and without the clipped edging. Nicely done, they can be a decorative feature in their own right. The best basic design to work upon is a paved area near the house with small formal or informal beds let into it. This allows easy and dryshod access for the cook and the not inconsiderable visual attractions of the herbs themselves to be admired from a house window.

Soil and site

As a surprisingly large percentage of the popular herbs come from southern Europe or the Mediterranean region, they need a sunny site sheltered from cold winds; the south or west side of the house, a wall or thick hedge are ideal. With the exception of mint, angelica and parsley, which thrive best in a moderately moist soil, all the other herbs listed here need a well-drained rooting medium which is not rich. Too rich a soil produces sappy growth of poor flavour and keeping quality. Where soils are heavy and liable to hang wet in winter or after heavy rain, create raised beds 10–15cm (4–6in) high filled with a sandy medium. Alternatively, grow the herbs in pots or larger containers. A collection of herbs in a large container can make a pleasing, decorative and useful feature for the sunny corner of a patio. Herbs take well to pot culture and can be grown on window ledges both outside and in. Plant or pot purchased perennial herbs in spring, using techniques described under Garden Flowers, p. 18 and House Plants, p. 90.

Propagation

Herbs are easily raised from seed and division in spring, softwood cuttings in early summer, or semi-hardwood cuttings in late summer or early autumn. See under Garden Flowers: Annuals, p. 16 and Propagation, pp. 19–20.

Harvesting and drying

Herbs grown for their young stems and foliage must be harvested when young before flowering, eg angelica, borage, chives, fennel, parsley. All are best used fresh, but the last three can be dried. A few herbs are grown for their seeds, eg dill and fennel. For these, the seed crop must be yellowing and starting to turn brown. Lift or cut the plants at ground level, tie in small bundles and hang head-downwards in a warm, dry place until the seeds fall easily when touched. Strip the seed and store in sealed opaque jars in a cool dry place. Bulbous herbs such as garlic are lifted when the leaves yellow, dried in the sun or in any dry place, then cleaned and hung up for use. The remaining herbs described below, though best used fresh, can be dried for winter use. Just as the plants come into flower, gather healthy sprays and space them out in trays kept in a warm airy place. An airing cupboard or the warming drawer of a cooker are suitable provided there is adequate ventilation. A microwave oven completes the process in a few minutes. Do not mix herbs, otherwise the aromas will mingle. Turn the herbs once a day until they feel brittle to the touch. They should then be crumbled and stored in opaque jars, ideally in a cool, dark place.

Freezing

Tender-leaved herbs such as parsley, mint, chervil and chives retain more flavour if frozen. Blanch small sprays by dipping them in boiling water. Cool, drain, and then place small amounts in polythene bags and put them in the home freezer.

The following culinary herbs are the best known and most useful:

ANGELICA
Angelica archangelica

A robust, erect biennial or short-lived perennial which, if allowed to flower, reaches 2m (6½ft) or more in height. It has handsome leaves divided into several leaflets and tiny greenish flowers in terminal, rayed clusters. Only young leaf and flower stalks are used for candying and adding to stewed apples or marmalade. Propagate by seed.

BASIL
Ocimum basilicum

This half-hardy annual, also known as sweet basil, can make a bushy, erect plant to 60cm (2ft) or more in height,

Chives, coriander and basil planted with lavender and screened at the back by Hemerocallis and Phormium tenax.

with small, oblong leaves in pairs. The tiny tubular flowers are white. The cloves scented leaves must be used when young. Propagate by seed.

BAY
Laurus nobilis
Also known as sweet bay, this is the tree of heroes, the leaves used to wreathe famous people in Grecian times. Although an almost hardy evergreen tree it stands clipping well and can be easily rooted from cuttings so it is not necessary to provide a lot of room for its growth. The aromatic leaves are best used when newly matured. Propagate by semi-hardwood cuttings.

BORAGE
Borago officinalis
A decorative hardy annual up to 60cm (2ft) tall, but often less. It has large, rough oval leaves smelling of cucumber and sprays of delightful sky blue starry flowers which can be candied and used to decorate cakes. Propagate by seed.

CARAWAY
Carum carvi
This hardy annual forms slim stems 60cm (2ft) or more in height, clad with ferny leaves and topped by flat heads of tiny white flowers. Its seeds are a favourite cake flavouring, but also try the young leaves chopped in soups and salads. Propagate by seed.

CHERVIL
Anthriscus cerefolium
Similar in overall appearance to caraway this biennial attains about 45cm (1½ft) and is grown for its parsley-flavoured leaves. Propagate by seed.

CHIVES
Allium schoenoprasum
This densely tufted perennial has grassy, hollow leaves to 25cm (10in) long with a delicate onion flavour. If allowed to develop, 2.5cm (1in) wide globular heads of small rose-purple flowers top the foliage. Ideally, pinch out the flower spikes when small to promote more leaves, and use young leaves in preference to mature ones. Propagate by seed or division.

DILL
Peucedanum graveolens
Much like fennel but with a single stem to 90cm (3ft) in height and of annual duration only, this herb is grown for its aniseed-flavoured leaves and seeds. Propagate by seeds.

FENNEL
Foeniculum vulgare
Naturalized around the coasts of England and Wales where it looks truly native, fennel is a graceful clump-forming perennial. Its dark, almost blue-green, sweetly aromatic leaves are cut into numerous filaments and make a distinctive fish sauce. The flowering stems are best removed when young, unless seed is required. Allowed to grow, they rise 1.5–2.5m (5–8ft) tall and produce flattened heads of tiny yellowish flowers. Propagate by seed or division.

GARLIC
Allium sativum
The familiar white bulb of this plant is composed of several narrow bulblets known as cloves. The narrow leaves grow to 45cm (1½ft) tall. Sometimes, rounded heads of tiny white, purple-tinged flowers are produced on stems above the leaves. Propagate by cloves.

HYSSOP
Hyssopus officinalis
This hardy perennial grows up to 45cm (1½ft) in height. Technically it is a low shrub but needs annual pruning to keep it low and compact. The narrow aromatic leaves are in opposite pairs, and small tubular blue, pink

or white flowers form showy erect spikes. Both leaves and flowers can be used to flavour stews and salads. Propagate by seed or semi-hardwood cuttings.

LOVAGE
Levisticum officinale
In leaf, this clump-forming perennial resembles celery. Allowed to grow, it sends up stems to 2.5m (8ft) tall which branch and bear yellowish flowers in umbels. Both seeds and leaves are used, the latter being nicest when blanched as for celery and used in salads. Propagate by seed.

LEMON BALM
Melissa officinalis
Sometimes simply known as balm, this is a widely clump-forming hardy perennial with pairs of corrugated lemon-scented oval leaves and clusters of small, tubular, white flowers which form leafy spikes. The leaves can be used fresh or dried. Propagate by division or seed.

MARIGOLD
Calendula officinalis
As a herb this is best known as pot marigold to distinguish it from tagetes. See Garden Flowers section, p. 27, for description. The petals make a colourful garnish to a salad. Propagate by seed.

MARJORAM
Origanum majorana
Of the four different sorts of marjoram, this is the one commonly used in Britain. Usually listed as sweet or knotted marjoram, it is a shrubby-based half-hardy perennial grown as an annual from seed. It has slender stems about 45cm (1½ft) tall with pairs of elliptic leaves and loose clusters of small, hop-like (knotted) flower spikes bearing minute white or pinkish flowers. Its leaves are mainly used in meat dishes. Propagate by seed under glass.

MINT
Mentha
There are several different kinds of mint, all hardy perennials 60–90cm (2–3ft) tall and which can be invasive. They have opposite pairs of simple leaves and tiny, tubular, mauve flowers in terminal, often branched spikes. Common spearmint (*M. spicata*) is the form most usually grown, with smooth, bright green lance-shaped leaves. Apple mint

(*M. suaveolens* syn. *M. rotundifolia*) has broadly oblong to rounded, white hairy leaves. Better known is its hybrid with *M. spicata*, called Bowles mint (*M. × villosa*). This is larger leaved and the best for mint sauce. Peppermint (*M. × piperita*) yields the world's supply of peppermint oil. It is similar to spearmint (one of its parents) but is easily distinguished by its smell. Propagate by division.

NASTURTIUM
Tropaeolum majus
Better known in the flower garden (see Garden Flowers section, p. 49), this plant yields seeds which are a substitute for true capers. The edible flowers and leaves can garnish salads. Propagate by seed.

PARSLEY
Petroselinum crispum
This very familiar hardy biennial, which can also be grown as an annual, forms a tufted rosette of finely cut leaves which are flat in the original species but in the best known cultivars are 'crested' or mossy. If allowed to bloom it produces an erect branched stem to 45cm (1½ft) or more tall with tiny yellowish flowers in umbels. Propagate by seed.

ROSEMARY
Rosmarinus officinalis
A bushy evergreen shrub (see p. 84) to 1.5m (5ft) or more tall, this herb is better known as an ornamental with its dark, almost needle-like leaves and lavender, sage-like flowers. The leaves go well with meat dishes. Propagate by hardwood or semi-hardwood cuttings.

RUE
Ruta graveolens
This evergreen shrub to 60cm (2ft) or more tall is primarily grown for its dissected blue-grey leaves and open clusters of yellow flowers with cupped petals. The very pungently smelling foliage can be used to flavour egg and fish dishes, but must be used sparingly. Propagate by semi-hardwood cuttings or seed.

SAGE
Salvia officinalis
Like mint and parsley this is a very popular herb in Britain. It is an evergreen shrub to about 60cm (2ft) tall with finely wrinkled grey-green leaves and

spikes of quite large, tubular, two-lipped blue-purple flowers. There are purple and variegated leaved cultivars for the flower garden. Propagate by hardwood, or semi-hardwood cuttings or seeds.

SALAD BURNET
Sanguisorba minor syn. *Poterium sanguisorba*
A clump-forming hardy perennial, attaining 60cm (2ft) or more in bloom. The long pinnate leaves are composed of 9–21 oval leaflets and have an almost fern-like quality. The oval greenish flower-heads are not showy but have a flower-arranging potential. The flowering stems are, however, best removed when young to promote more young leaves, which are used in salads and sauces. Propagate by division or seed.

SAVORY
Satureja
There are two kinds of savory, summer and winter. The latter (*Satureja montana*) is a hardy, wiry shrublet 15–30cm (6–12in) tall with small narrow leaves and short spikes of small, pale purple flowers. Summer savory (*S. hortensis*) is a slender, erect hardy annual with similar but longer leaves and white to pale purple flowers. The leaves of both are used in fish, egg and salad dishes. Propagate by seed or semi-hardwood cuttings.

TARRAGON
Artemisia dracunculus
This not quite fully hardy perennial forms wide clumps of erect stems to about 60cm (2ft) in height. The narrowly lance-shaped leaves are a greyish-green and an essential constituent of *fines herbes*. Small, greenish, bobble-like flower-heads may appear in good seasons.

THYME
Thymus
Several sorts of thyme have herbal uses, but only two are popular in Britain: common thyme (*Thymus vulgaris*) and lemon thyme (*T. × citriodorus*) are both hardy, wiry, spreading evergreen shrublets to 20cm (8in) or more in height with tiny leaves and small pale purple to whitish flowers. The leaves of common thyme are grey-green and finely hairy and aromatic; those of lemon thyme are smooth bright green and smell of lemons. Both are used in *bouquet garni*.

CONTROLLING PESTS AND DISEASES

The charts which follow cover all the pests and diseases mentioned in the various sections of this book. Although preventive measures are preferable, there are many chemicals for controlling pests. Read the labels carefully to see what is appropriate. Chemicals extracted from plants, such as derris and pyrethrum, are safest to use in the garden. These and other contact sprays such as malathion are sprayed directly onto the insects to kill them. Systemic insecticides such as dimethoate are absorbed into the plant, killing insects that subsequently feed on them. They cannot be washed off by rain and they do not harm ladybirds, bees or butterflies. Do not use them on edible plants unless the details specify that it is safe to do so.

Diseases spread rapidly in favourable conditions and are much harder to control, once established, than pest attacks, so any spraying either has to be done in anticipation of attacks, or as soon as the first symptoms are noticed. Even more than with pests, prevention is better than cure. Healthily grown plants, rotation, garden hygiene, and burning all diseased material are of paramount importance.

If you decide to use one of the recommended pesticides or fungicides, remember that some of them are highly poisonous and have unpleasant odours which linger in the confines of a greenhouse. Before purchasing, read the makers' instructions carefully. When making up to use, follow the instructions to the letter. Too great a concentration could damage the plant, one too weak probably will not kill the pest or disease. Wash out the sprayer immediately the job is finished and never leave empty containers lying around once the fungicide or insecticide has been used up.

Greenfly on a rose shoot

PESTS	DESCRIPTION	CONTROL
Aphid (greenfly, blackfly)	The colour may vary, from green to black, but all are 1–5mm long, soft-bodied, and with relatively long legs. They do not always have wings, in which case the plump body is conspicuous.	There are many greenfly killers; malathion is popular, pirimicarb and permethrin are also good. Try dimethoate if you want a systemic insecticide.
Big bud mite	Only likely to affect blackcurrants. The buds become swollen – hence the common name. A tiny mite is responsible. Also known as blackcurrant gall mite.	Chemical control is difficult. Pick off affected buds. Regular spraying with benomyl (actually a fungicide) seems to give some control.
Birds	Certain birds, notably bullfinch, pigeon, house sparrow, starling, blackbird, blue tit, jay, eat fruits and seeds and damage flowers, young leaves and buds.	Hanging strips of glittering foil or erecting scarecrows can be successful. Fruit must be netted and spring flowers and newly sown seeds strung with black cotton (not nylon thread which can trap the legs of a bird).
Bryobia mite	Rather like a larger version of the red spider mite of greenhouse plants, this attacks the leaves of primroses and other primulas, various alpine plants plus gooseberry, apple, pear and ivy, causing bronze-to-brown mottling, then shrivelling.	Spray with malathion as soon as the symptoms are seen and repeat once or twice later at weekly intervals.

Cabbage root fly	Although mainly a pest of cabbages, cauliflowers, and Brussels sprouts, cabbage root fly also attack wallflowers. The plants wilt and become stunted. If lifted, the small maggots will be seen eating the roots.	Not much can be done once the plants have been attacked. As a precaution dust the soil with bromophos or diazinon when transplanting or thinning.
Capsid bug	You are most likely to see the symptoms before you see the pest. It leaves small ragged holes in the leaves, and flowers and leaves become deformed. The insects are up to 6mm long, but very active and are likely to drop to the ground when you look for them. The colour is usually green, but may be yellowish or brown.	A systemic insecticide such as dimethoate is particularly useful. For a non-systemic, try fenitrothion or malathion.
Caterpillars	Too well known and too diverse to warrant description. The appearance obviously depends on the species, but it makes little difference to control.	Bioresmethrin, malathion and trichlorphon will achieve control. Derris — as a spray or dust — is also effective. You can try gamma-HCH.
Chafers	These are the grubs of various beetles which feed on roots and underground stems. Affected plants wilt and may die if too many roots are severed. The most conspicuous is the 4cm (1½in) long, C-shaped dirty white grub of the cockchafer or May bug.	If these chafers are known to be present, treat the soil with HCH, bromophos or diazinon prior to planting.
Codling moth	A pest of apples. You are unlikely to notice the moths, but you will see the maggots inside the apples.	Spray with permethrin or fenitrothion just after the petals have dropped, and again three weeks later.
Cutworms	Caterpillars of certain moths, eg yellow underwing, heart and dart, etc, live under the soil eating roots and stems at ground level or just below. These are yellowish, brownish or greenish fat caterpillars which roll up when discovered. Swift moth caterpillars are a dirty white and often wriggle when touched; they tend to live deeper in the soil. Affected plants wilt or grow very poorly and may die.	Keep the ground clear of weeds and if these pests are known to occur treat the soil with HCH, bromophos or diazinon prior to planting.
Earthworms	These familiar soil creatures are useful rather than harmful, but certain kinds make casts on the surface which can damage the edges of mower blades and look unsightly.	Use a solution of potassium permanganate or derris dust well watered in. This treatment brings the worms to the surface which are then promptly swept off and disposed of. If a killer is required use chlordane.
Earwig	Earwigs are usually about 2.5cm (1in) long, brown in colour, and with 'pincers' at the end of the body. Suspect them if plants, such as dahlias (but also many others), have ragged holes in the leaves or petals.	Spray or dust with gamma-HCH, or use carbaryl dust. Traps should not be dismissed. An upturned flower pot on a cane, filled with straw, will attract them. You will have to empty the trap regularly and kill the earwigs.
Eelworm	Eelworms are microscopic — less than 2mm, mostly smaller. There are many kinds, and symptoms vary. The ones mentioned in this book are mainly bulb and stem eelworms, affecting plants such as hyacinths and narcissi. On these plants the neck of the bulb usually feels soft and if the bulb is cut across there will be dark rings of dead tissue. Growth is usually malformed or stunted.	There is no effective cure available to amateurs. Lift and burn affected plants, and do not replant the same kind of plants in that piece of ground.
Flea beetle	Flea beetles make small, usually round, holes in the leaves of seedlings, and occasionally older plants. The beetles are about 3mm long, and tend to jump.	Dust with derris or gamma-HCH.
Froghopper	It is not the froghopper insect that you are likely to notice first, but the frothy 'cuckoo spit' that appears on plants from May onwards. It protects pale coloured nymphs inside. The mature insects are up to 6mm long, and jump when disturbed.	Malathion should give control. You may need to use a forceful spray to remove the protective froth.
Leaf miner	The caterpillars of certain tiny moths and grubs of flies tunnel between the upper and lower leaf skins, creating pale sinuous tracks or brownish blotches, both of which are unsightly. Among plants commonly affected are chrysanthemum, lilac, laburnum and holly.	Remove and destroy infected leaves if there is only a small infestation. Alternatively, spray with HCH or trichlorphon.
Leatherjackets	These greyish maggots of the cranefly are about 2.5cm (1in) long, and are found feeding on the roots of plants, which may turn yellow and wilt, and even die.	Work bromophos or diazinon into the soil around susceptible plants.

Blackfly

Capsid bug

Caterpillar

Codling moth damage

Mealybugs on Chrysanthemum

CONTROLLING PESTS AND DISEASES

Mealybugs	Many plants under glass may be infected with one of various species of mealybug. They are like large fat greenflies with short legs, and are completely covered with white waxy filaments like wool. They suck sap and weaken plants. See also Root mealybugs.	Brush with spray strength solution of nicotine or malathion, or use methylated spirit.
Narcissus fly	The bulbs produce yellowish, distorted leaves, and usually fail to flower. The maggot will be found inside the rotting tissue of the bulb.	It is best to lift and burn infected bulbs.
Raspberry beetle	The grubs of this tiny beetle feed in blackberries, raspberries and loganberries, reducing their palatability.	Spray with fenitrothion immediately the last petals fall to ensure clean fruit.
Red spider mites	Several sorts of minute mites (known as 'red spider') attack a wide range of plants under glass and fruit trees outside. In the summer they may be either yellowish or greenish with or without red spots or entirely brownish-red. In autumn some sorts turn bright red. All suck sap and cause a yellowish mottling, followed by yellowing, browning and premature leaf fall. Established infestations are covered with a very fine webbing.	Spray with derris, dicofol, malathion, dimethoate, formothion, diazinon or pirimiphos-methyl and repeat at weekly intervals until infestation is eliminated. Red spider can become resistant to insecticides and more than one type may have to be tried. To discourage breeding, spray daily with water.
Root mealybugs	Very much like the common stem mealybugs but living on roots, especially of succulents (including cacti) and other pot plants under glass. Plants fail to thrive, may wilt or yellow prematurely.	Soak the rootball with a spray solution of malathion, nicotine or dimethoate.
Sawflies	These are the caterpillar-like grubs of a fly-like insect related to bees and wasps. Those on gooseberry and solomons-seal are the most conspicuous. The commonest sawfly on rose causes the leaflets to roll tightly, while apple sawfly feeds within developing apples and is often mistaken for codling moth.	Spray the conspicuous grubs with HCH, derris, malathion or trichlonphon. Leaf-rolling sawfly responds to dimethoate or formothion. Apple sawfly must be sprayed the moment the petals fall with HCH, dimethoate or malathion.
Scale insects	Various species of scale insects can infect a wide range of plants under glass and outside. The common brown scale insect occurs on shrub stems in sheltered sites and in greenhouses. It looks like a minute glossy brown tortoise and sucks sap, weakening the plant. This is one of the hard scales. Soft scales are oval and much flatter and soft to the touch. They are more likely to be on leaves or non-woody plants.	The tiny young scales are mobile and known as crawlers. They are easily killed. Late spring to early summer is their period of main activity on outside plants. Spray with malathion, diazinon or nicotine. Under glass, crawlers may be active at any time, so try a systemic insecticide such as dimethoate or formothion, bearing in mind that some plants can be damaged by them.
Slugs and snails	Too well known to need description. There are several kinds of both slugs and snails to be found in the garden. All respond to the same treatment.	Slug pellets based on metaldehyde or methiocarb will protect plants reasonably well.
Thrips	These tiny insects are cylindrical in shape and usually under 3mm (⅛in) in length. They have narrow, fringed wings and certain species swarm in summer when they are known as thunderflies. Not all species are pests, but those which are suck sap and cause pale mottling or silvering of leaves and flowers, which can also be crippled and die prematurely. Among garden plants likely to be attacked by various thrip species are onion, pea, gladiolus, rose, carnation and privet. Onion and privet thrip also attack a wide range of plants, particularly those under glass.	As soon as an attack is recognized, spray promptly with HCH, malathion, nicotine, etc, and be prepared to repeat the treatment 2–3 weeks later.
Whitefly	Small, white flies like minute moths. Not normally a problem outdoors, but may attack the plants that you take indoors or into the greenhouse for the winter.	A systemic insecticide such as dimethoate is effective. You can spray with non-persistent insecticides such as malathion, bioresmethrin, or pyrethrum, but be prepared to repeat at intervals.
Wireworms	These are the grubs of various species of click beetles. The commonest sort is cylindrical with a tough yellow skin. It feeds on roots including those of carrot, beetroot and potato tubers.	If wireworms are known to be in the soil apply HCH, bromophos, or diazinon prior to sowing or planting.

Red spider mites on Tradescantia

Root mealybugs on Dracaena

Scale insects on Stephanotis

DISEASE	DESCRIPTION	CONTROL
Black spot	This very familiar fungal disease, which mainly affects hybrid roses, shows as dark brown to black blotches on the leaves. Further symptoms are premature leaf fall and weakening of the whole bush.	Spray with captan, benomyl or thiophanate-methyl when the leaves expand in spring. Repeat at 2-week intervals. Rake up and burn infected leaves in autumn as the fungus overwinters in this way. Where this disease is common, consider planting only disease-resistant cultivars. Check the catalogues of rose specialists for varieties. The following are resistant in varying degrees: *Large-flowered Bush (Hybrid Tea)* – 'Alec's Red', 'Blessings', 'Colour Wonder', 'Kings Ransom', 'My Choice', 'Peace', 'Rose Guajard', 'Super Star', 'Troika'. *Cluster-flowered Bush (Floribunda)* – 'Allgold', 'Arthur Bell', 'City of Leeds', 'Moon Maiden', 'Orange Silk', 'Queen Elizabeth', 'Sea Pearl', 'Southampton'.
Blight of tomato and potato	One of the best known of all plant diseases, potato blight caused the Irish potato famine of the 1840s. Brownish black blotches appear towards the leaf tip then spread rapidly in damp weather leading to collapse and rapid rotting. Tomatoes are also susceptible to blight and show the same symptoms.	Immediately blight is recognized, spray or dust with zineb or maneb. If your area is attacked regularly, apply a preventative using the same substances, starting in early July and continuing at 10-day intervals.
Botrytis (grey mould)	As the common name suggests, the main symptom of this disease is a grey mould – usually on dead flowers or on fruit, but it can occur on leaves or stems. A cloud of dust-like spores may be released when the affected part is moved.	Remove any infected parts and destroy them. Then spray with benomyl or thiophanate-methyl, repeating at intervals if necessary.
Canker	Mainly on apples and some pears. Branchlets show sunken and cracked dead areas and some die-back occurs.	Cut out infected part, back to healthy wood. Check soil drainage (canker worst in wet soils). Spray young trees with benomyl at leaf-fall.
Club-root	Although a problem of brassicas – such as cabbages and cauliflowers – it will also affect ornamentals such as wallflowers and stocks. Growth is poor and stunted, and the roots are enlarged, often with unsightly swellings.	Use root dips based on calomel or use thiophanate-methyl when transplanting. For ornamental crops it is best to grow something different if you know the land is infected with club-root.
Damping off	This is a disease (which can be caused by several fungi) of seedlings. The seedlings collapse where they have rotted at soil level.	Use sterilized compost as a preventative measure whenever possible. Spray with thiram at weekly intervals.
Dollar spot, fusarium patch, red thread, ophiobolus patch	These are all fungal infections of lawn grass. Dollar spot causes 5–7.5cm (2–3in) wide brown patches, and fusarium patch larger areas up to 30cm (1ft) across. Red thread causes even larger patches with the addition of red fungal threads. All are most common on fine lawn grasses especially fescues. Ophiobulus patch creates bronzed or bleached areas of grass which die and leave bare, slightly depressed areas.	Immediately after mowing, apply benomyl or thiophanate methyl. Improve aeration and fertility of the soil by feeding with general or special lawn fertilizer but avoid those with high nitrogen in autumn which will create soft, disease-prone leaves.
Dry rot	Dry rot can affect a number of plants with bulbs or corms, but gladioli are particularly vulnerable. The leaves turn brown and die; the corms show a number of small sunken lesions, or larger blackish areas.	Do not plant corms known to be infected; avoid replanting on infected ground. As a precaution soak the corms in a solution of benomyl or thiophanate-methyl for about half an hour before planting. (This is primarily a treatment for gladiolus corms, but it can be used for other cormous and bulbous plants.)
Fairy rings	Various soil-living fungi grow in a more or less circular fashion year by year. Liberation of nitrogenous substances as a result of a breakdown of organic matter by fungal threads causes the grass to grow extra vigorously and a richer green.	Very difficult to eradicate though certain rather poisonous mercurial compounds may be successful. Alternatively, dig out the turf for 60cm (2ft) beyond the ring, fork the soil and soak with a 1 in 50 solution of 40 per cent formalin. Cover with plastic sheeting for 2 weeks, and 3–4 weeks later fill in with soil and re-seed or turf over.
Fireblight	Flowering shoots die, leaves look scorched and do not fall. All members of the rose family are at risk.	Cut out and burn diseased wood to a point 60cm (2ft) beyond visibly infected tissue. Notify local branch of Ministry of Agriculture.
Leaf spot	There are several leaf spots. They may vary from small, fairly regularly shaped spots to larger, irregular blotches. The colours vary from brown to black.	Spraying with benomyl or Bordeaux mixture is likely to achieve some control, but remove badly affected leaves, and be prepared to repeat the treatment.

Whitefly on Saintpaulia

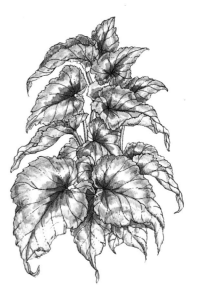

Botrytis on Begonia rex

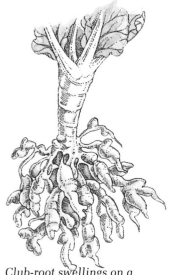

Club-root swellings on a cabbage plant

Mildew, downy	The plant becomes covered with a whitish or somewhat purplish growth. Easy to confuse with powdery mildew. If you wipe the growth off with a finger, downy mildew tends to leave the plant beneath rather yellow.	Mancozeb should give some control. Not easily controlled.
Mildew, powdery	The plants – particularly leaves and shoot tips – become covered with a white, powdery-looking growth. Infected parts may become distorted.	Try thiophanate-methyl, benomyl, or dichlofluanid. Be prepared to spray once a fortnight to achieve control. If this does not work, it may be downy mildew – in which case try mancozeb.
Peach leaf curl	This is a distinctive disease; affected plants produce distorted leaves with ugly reddish blisters.	Collect and burn infected leaves, as soon as you notice them. Spray with Bordeaux mixture after the leaves fall and again as the buds swell in late February or early March.
Rust	There are numerous rust diseases, but most produce brown or orange spots or pustules on the leaves.	Mancozeb should achieve some control, but you may have to persist with the treatment. Where rust-resistant varieties are available – as with antirrhinums – choose these if you have had trouble in previous years.
Scab	Scab is common on apples. Greenish-brown blotches appear on the leaves; cracked, corky spots on the fruit.	Thiophanate-methyl or benomyl sprayed fortnightly from bud-burst onwards should achieve control.
Silver leaf	Leaves at first silvered (not white), then brown and shrivelled. Shoots die. Plums, cherry, rarely apricots, currants and apples and many other trees and shrubs can be attacked.	Cut out dead shoots or branches to 15cm (6in) behind infection. Paint wound with fungicidal paint. Wash pruning tools after use. Do not prune very susceptible crops in winter.
Soft rot	Affects many different plants, including vegetables such as turnips and parsnips. Bulbs can become soft and slimy, with a bad smell.	There is little to be done about this disease except to destroy infected plants, and to make sure you plant a similar crop on different ground next time.
Tomato blight	Brown blotches appear on the leaves, dark brown streaks on the stems. Fruit tends to rot. See Blight.	Spray with mancozeb as a precaution in damp seasons, once the first fruit has set. Repeat at 10-day intervals.
Tulip fire	Leaves and shoots are distorted, and often withered. Flower buds usually fail to open.	Lift and destroy infected plants immediately. Do not plant suspect bulbs, and do not replant more tulips on infected land. If neighbouring tulip bulbs seem unaffected, soak them in a benomyl solution for half an hour before replanting, as a precaution.
Virus	There are many different viruses, and the symptoms vary with the disease and the plant. Suspect any plants that have distorted or stunted growth, or yellowish, mottled leaves that you canot put down to another problem.	Virus diseases cannot be cured, and leaving the plants risks spreading the infection. Lift and burn any suspect plant.
Wilt	As the name suggests, the most common sign of wilt (there are several kinds) is wilting leaves on the plant – though they may recover at night. If the stem is cut through some distance above ground level it will be discoloured internally.	Try drenching the soil with benomyl or thiophanate-methyl (made up as for a spray), and repeat the treatment. If this fails, uproot and burn the plant.

Powdery mildew

Downy mildew

Peach leaf curl

Scab on a ripe apple

INDEX

ACKNOWLEDGEMENTS
The Publishers thank the following for their kind permission to reproduce
photographs in this book:
A–Z Botanical 122; Pat Brindley 21; Bob Challiner 18; R.J. Corbin 14;
Brian Furner 87, 149; David Hoy 15; Harry Smith Horticultural
Photographic Collection 14 left, 57, 124, 151, 156.

The following photographs were taken specially for Octopus Picture
Library:
Michael Boys 143, 154 above, 155, 163, 164; Melvin Grey 89; Jerry Harpur
1 (half-title), 2–3 (title), 9, 13, 17, 134 below, 148, 150, 152 above, 153
above, 154 below, 158, 159 below, 161; Neill Holmes, 19, 61, 115–121,
123, 125–134 above, 135–139, 152 below, 153 below, 157, 159 above;
Margaret McLean 5; Roger Philips 93–110; George Wright 20, 55, 60, 160.

The Publishers thank the following for allowing their gardens to be
photographed:
Mr & Mrs Martin Furniss, Cobblers, Crowborough, East Sussex 1 (half-
title), 17; Mrs Aileen Mitchell, Dogginghurst, Essex 13; Mr Mark Rumary,
Magnolia House, Saxmundham, Suffolk 9, 87; Mrs Helen Schofield, Liss,
Hampshire 53; Mr & Mrs J. Wright, Yew Tree Cottage, Liss, Hampshire 83.